Working with Computers:

Theory versus Outcome

Computers and People Series

Edited by

B. R. GAINES

The series is concerned with all aspects of man–computer relationships, including interaction, interfacing modelling and artificial intelligence. Books are interdisciplinary, communicating results derived in one area of study to workers in another. Applied, experimental, theoretical and tutorial studies are included.

Working with Computers:
Theory versus Outcome

Edited by

GERRIT C. VAN DER VEER
Department of Mathematics and Computer Science,
Free University, Amsterdam, The Netherlands.

THOMAS R. G. GREEN
MRC Applied Psychology Unit, Chaucer Road, Cambridge, UK.
(currently Rank Xerox Ltd, Regent Street, Cambridge, UK.)

JEAN-MICHEL HOC
Université de Paris 8, UFR de Psychologie, Equipe "Psychologie
Cognitive du Traitement de l'Information Symbolique",
93526 St Denis, France.

DIANNE M. MURRAY
Division of Information Technology and Computing,
National Physical Laboratory, Teddington, Middlesex, UK.

1988

ACADEMIC PRESS

Harcourt Brace Jovanovich, Publishers
London   San Diego   New York   Berkeley
Boston   Sydney   Tokyo   Toronto

ACADEMIC PRESS LTD.
24/28 Oval Road,
London NW1 7DX

United States Edition published by
ACADEMIC PRESS INC.
San Diego, California 92101–4311

British Library Cataloguing in Publication Data

Working with computers: Theory versus Outcome.
1. Computer systems. Design. Human factors
I. Veer, G. C. van der (Gerrit C.)
004.2'1'019

ISBN 0-12-711705-9

Printed in Great Britain by St Edmundsbury Press Ltd,
Bury St Edmunds, Suffolk

CONTENTS

SECTION 1
MODELS AND THEORIES IN COGNITIVE ERGONOMICS

SECTION 2
EMPIRICAL EVIDENCE IN COGNITIVE ERGONOMICS

CONTRIBUTORS

BARNARD, P.J. MRC Applied Psychology Unit, 15 Chaucer Road, Cambridge CB2 2EF, U.K.

BEISHUIZEN, J.J. Free University, Department of Psychology, Cognitive Psychology Division, De Boelelaan 1115, 1081 HV Amsterdam, Netherlands.

CURTIS, B. Microelectronics and Computer Technology Corporation (MCC), PO box 200195, Austin, Texas 78720, USA.

DAVIES, R. MRC/ESRC Social and Applied Psychology Unit, University of Sheffield, Sheffield S10 2TN, U.K.

GREEN, T.R.G. MRC Applied Psychology Unit, 15 Chaucer Road, Cambridge CB2 2EF, U.K.
current address: Rank Xerox Ltd, Cambridge EuroPARC, 61 Regent Street, Cambidge CB2 1AB, England.

HOC, J.-M. Université de Paris 8, UFR de Psychologie, Equipe "Psychologie Cognitive du Traitement de l'Information Symbolique", 2 Rue de la Liberte, 93526 St Denis, Cedex 21, France.

LANZARA, G.F. University of Bari, Italy.
current address: Department of Urban Studies and Planning, M.I.T. Cambridge, Mass. 02139, U.S.A.

MACLEAN, A. Xerox EuroPARC, Ravenscroft House, 61 Regent Street, Cambridge, U.K.

MATHIASSEN, L. University of Aarhus, Denmark.
current address: Computer Science Department, Institute of Electronic Systems, University Centre of Aalborg, Strandvejen 19, DK 9000 Aalborg, Denmark.

MURRAY, D. Division of Information Technology and Computing, National Physical Laboratory, Teddington, Middlesex TW11 0LW, U.K.

PAYNE, S.J. Depts. of Psychology and Computing, University of Lancaster, Lancaster LA1 4YT. U.K.

POTTS, C. Dept. Computing, Imperial College of Science and Technology, London, U.K.
current address: Microelectronics and Computer Technology Corporation (MCC), PO Box 200195, Austin, Texas 78759, U.S.A.

SCHIELE F. MRC Applied Psychology Unit, Cambridge CB2 2EF, U.K. Current address: Arbeitswissenschaftliches Forschungsinstitut GmbH Bayreuther Strasse 3, 1000 Berlin 30, Germany.

TAUBER, M.J. Department of Computer Science, University of Pittsburgh, USA. Current address: Universität of Paderborn, FB 17 Waerburgerstrasse 100, D-4790 Paderborn, Germany.

TRAUNMÜLLER, R. Johannes Kepler Universität Linz, Institut für Informatik, 1-4040 Linz-Auhof, Austria.

Van der VEER, G.C. Free University, Department of Mathematics and Computer Science, De Boelelaan 1081, 1081 HV Amsterdam, Netherlands

WILSON, M.D. Building R1, Informatics Division, SERC, Rutherford Appleton Laboratory, Clifton, Didcot, Oxon OX11 0PX, U.K.

PREFACE

Everyone knows that computers and information technology are becoming part of the fabric of daily life in many countries, and that many different interface styles and new designs are constantly being tried out. However, perhaps relatively few people realise how difficult it is to decide which designs are good designs and to decide why they work when there are so many different criteria upon which to base a judgement.

Computing systems are a great force for change and can have a significant impact in encouraging free or repressed societies, in bringing fulfilment and happiness, or unemployment and misery; in making production more efficient and work tasks enjoyable, or in helping to make leisure more absorbing and creative. Computer software itself and the human-computer interface can be assessed and evaluated as being efficient, or cheap, or fun, or robust, or hard to learn, or easy to live with, or functional, or usable, and so on over a large and constantly changing set of criteria.

No one book can tackle the universe, and no one book can sensibly claim to examine all the aspects of computing and informatics. This book is about the usability of computers in work environments. But, just what is it that determines usability? One aspect is hardware - for instance, today's systems with high-resolution graphics offer all sorts of advantages over earlier text-display-only models - but that is not our focus. This book addresses problems to do with the design of the information system rather than the usability of the hardware.

Here is a historical parallel. We can imagine that in the fifteenth century many merchants were considering whether to switch from using roman numerals to using arabic ones. The new numerals used the same hardware (pen and paper) but they used a different representation for information; a different software, so to speak. Once the new system had been mastered it was much faster for practical book-keeping. Merchants would have had to ask themselves whether the benefits were worth the effort of understanding new ideas, learning new methods for doing arithmetic, and perhaps having difficulties with suppliers or customers who did not understand the new system.

Computer users today are faced with similar questions. Many different kinds of research and much practical experience will be needed to guide us during the next decades of invention. Central to this research are the two issues which we emphasize here: developments in theoretical approaches, and the relevance of such theoretical approaches to real-life issues and situations. Most of the theory has been drawn from task analysis and cognitive ergonomics; in the jargon of research, these papers study the relationship between the task domain, the conceptual structure of the information system, and the cognitive psychology of the user.

To extend the historical parallel, we can imagine scientists in the fifteenth century asking themselves just why arabic numerals were better than roman ones. They would look for an answer partly in terms of what tasks the arabic numerals were good for (e.g., easier to read, although harder to carve), partly in terms of the functioning of the human perceptual and cognitive systems, and partly in terms of exactly what features of arabic numerals made those tasks easier. Today, we ask ourselves the same questions, but we have much a vaster array of information systems to study.

Preparing a book with such an international authorship, and with editors in three countries, has proved to be much harder than we all expected. We owe thanks to our friends, helpers, assistants, and partners, and we especially want to record our thanks to the staff of Academic Press, notably Rosie Altoft, for forebearance and prompt help, and - above all - to Elly Lammers, of Amsterdam, who was responsible for the markup, formatting, and printing of the camera-ready copy. The size of this task can only be appreciated by those who have tried to do it.

Finally, we would like to dedicate this book to our various children, who, for better or worse, will inherit the information systems we leave behind: to Owen and Martin, Frits and Els, to Lauren and Katharine Vivienne, and to Tristan and Tanguy.

Thomas Green
Gerrit van der Veer
Dianne Murray
Jean-Michel Hoc

INTRODUCTION

This book is about the role of theory in the study of Human-Computer Interaction and about how well some of the existing theories face up to being applied to the problems encountered in real life.

To many people it will seem odd to have a "theory" in this area. It is clear that we need to improve the relationship between computers and people, since progress in computer-related technology is overwhelming, but why is a "theory" needed at all? What would it look like? After all, psychology and ergonomics are about people, computer science is about computers - what else do we need?

Why theory is important

The combination of psychology, ergonomics, and computer technology has generated an area of inter-disciplinary knowledge known as "Human-Computer Interaction" (HCI). There are HCI guidelines to assist designers, who no longer have to rely on guesswork or personal experience and expertise to decide between possibilities. HCI standards are developing to help evaluators decide whether a particular design is good enough. There is a strong belief in the power of progress, especially technological progress, to remove all difficulties in using computers. There is not, however, very much theory.

There is much to be said for the point of view that theory is not required, but that what is needed is merely a body of experience and practical conventions. It is true, for example, that the difficulties of using computers are being greatly reduced. The old command-language systems have given way to mouse-and-pointer systems, and we can soon expect to see an even wider spread of direct manipulation systems. The editors firmly believe that while guidelines and standards and belief in progress are all very well, they are not enough.

Take guidelines, for instance. These are a codification of current good practice, and as such, do not cope well with future possibilities. For a particular technology and a particular context of use, they can be very effective: "Use no more than 3 colours in a VDU display" may perhaps be an excellent guideline for a programmer designing the interface to a simple educational program. A specific guideline like that, however, only works for a technology where the only available colours are the eight coarse colours obtained by switching red, blue, and green on or off. That technology is already becoming obsolete. On many of today's systems, the designer could, if it seemed desirable, shade the text display gradually from red in one corner to blue in the opposite corner. How would the guideline help to decide whether that was desirable or not?

To decide on what to do with the new possibilities offered by advances in technology, the designer needs a deeper understanding. He or she needs to understand why the guideline is effective in today's technology. This means understanding, first, what the user is trying to do - the task; and second, how the system's features help the user achieve that task - the *underlying psychology* of Human-Computer Interaction. The designer can then suggest how the features of a proposed new system, employing improved technology, will assist the user with the task. If the purpose of using colour is to indicate highlighting (bold face, underlining, etc.) or error messages, as is sometimes the case, then it is not immediately obvious that improved colour presentation would materially assist the user, compared to improved presentation of monochrome text; whereas if user's task is to locate material about a given topic, and the purpose of colour is to indicate topic areas in the text, it may conceivably be useful to use continuous variations in colour to represent the various degrees of approximation to the target topic. Whether that would be useful would depend on such factors as how people search documents, and how relationships between topics are mentally represented (as continuous variations or as discrete quantities). Both those are questions of what has become called *cognitive ergonomics*.

One purpose of a theory, therefore, is to support a guideline and to extend it to new purposes, new technology, and new contexts; in short, to make it "future-proof".

Another purpose is to explain ideas that are otherwise purely intuitive, and especially to make them rigorous enough to be useful. A familiar example is the exhortation to "be consistent" in designing user interfaces. This exhortation is only useful if we know what kinds of consistency are helpful. Would it help to make all commands start with the same letter? Assuredly not, it would be dreadful. But it would be a form of consistency. As it happens, one of the chapters in this book deals with a theory which attempts to describe what types of consistency are genuinely useful to users.

A third use for theory is to cope with the larger issues of how a particular system will affect interpersonal relationships. What will the teacher do with an educational computer system? That depends both on the features of the system, and on the style of teaching adopted by that teacher in that school.

The same is true of other types of work organization; and one of the chapters in this book discusses this very topic.

In short, there is a need for well-grounded generalisations - theories - about how people interact with complex artefacts in general and computer technology in particular. These theories must describe the knowledge people bring to bear, and how people view the tasks they want the artefact to perform. They must describe the ways in which people interact with other people, so that in due course we can understand how these systems will change the interactions. They must describe how people interpret what they see or hear when they look at the computer system. And all these descriptions must be at a fundamental level, because that is how we can make them "future-proof". Generalisations that simply reflect the current state of technology will be made obsolete overnight.

Why is there so little theory?

Although there may be a need for theories, there is a definite lack of examples. Deep theorising has been less fashionable than studying surface features of systems. To understand the reason for this lack of theory one must take a historical perspective, and look back to early days when research on HCI did not exist. What bliss it must have been for programmers, analysts, and designers: they could fearlessly create whatever took their fancy. If one wanted to design a programming language, one could produce Fortran, Snobol, or APL. If one needed an editor, one could come up with TECO or the Unix *ed* editor. And so on. The criteria were efficiency and power. All these creations were hard to use, but what of that? Using computers was a craft, mastered by long hours of concentration. You expected it to be hard, and you expected to make mistakes. Your mistakes were your own fault and no-one else's. In return you could accomplish feats that were near-magical, because all these creations, when you got things right, were wonderfully powerful.

The study of human factors and of HCI, when it began, paid most attention to the surface level because remarkable improvements could be demonstrated by quite simple techniques. Word processors today are usually much less powerful than TECO was, but at least they can be mastered much faster. In general, little attention was given to deeper questions because it was widely felt that sufficient could be accomplished by cleaning up the surface details. We suspect that industrial design, however, often found it difficult to use HCI research findings. The findings were hard to locate, being reported in obscure conference proceedings in highly technical form, and they were so concerned with detailed features of design that, even when some research relevant to a design problem was located, it was hard to apply those findings to the current problem.

As a result, guidelines and standards were developed. By codifying some of the research findings and presenting a distillation, gathered into a single volume, they could be made available to designers, consumers, and evaluators of technology. Even then, however, HCI research had less impact than might have been expected. Nor have efforts to bring HCI into the design procedure itself been very successful. The present pattern seems frequently to be that a design is created following the traditional criteria of efficiency and power, and it is then evaluated by HCI specialists. At that point, there may be little room for any serious change in the design; only surface details can be altered, and so only surface details are evaluated.

In short, HCI research has not led to much development of theoretical ideas for the following reasons. First, much could be achieved by a hard look at surface detail. Secondly, by the time HCI specialists got to see a design, only surface details could be changed anyway. And thirdly, a sociological reason: to work from HCI theory rather than from precept has never been the practice in design. Changing the way designers work requires changing their reward structure very substantially, which is extremely difficult; it also requires changing the resources available to them and changing their training. The current practice, therefore, is likely to change only slowly, though some indications of what should change are given in some of the chapters in this book.

What is an HCI theory?

An effective theory must, we believe, look deeper than the surface of the artefact or the technology with which it deals. Guidelines and standards are essentially normative analyses, based in many cases on computer science concepts, and with very little reference either to the task domain or to the psychology of human performance.

Fortunately, for some years the development of cognitive science has encouraged computer science, psychology, and other theoretical and empirical sciences to construct models of an adequate degree of complexity. These models have been applied to HCI by a number of researchers and have shown considerable promise, since they are based not just on the design of the artefact but also on the psychology of the user.

A "model", in this context, can be regarded as a simplified account of a mechanism or an algorithm which displays similar behaviour to that of the user, or which contains similar structure to that which theory says the user possesses. For instance, if theory says human long-term memory is probably structured in certain ways, then a model can be constructed which represents a simplified fragment of long-term memory. The model could be constructed as a paper-and-pencil model or as a computer program. It does not matter which. What does matter is that the model, by being simplified, can achieve a rigorous statement, even though it can probably not account for all the phenomena to which the parent theory might be applied.

Modelling techniques drawn from computer science have already provided non-psychological, but rigorous and fairly complete descriptions of devices and interfaces. These descriptions cover both the lexical and syntactic levels of the interface, which are the levels at which individual commands are organized, and also cover the semantic level, which includes the underlying "logical operations" and operations. (The distinction between these two is not always easy to draw in a particular case, but examples should make it clear. At the semantic level, one graphics package might support lines and simple curves as its logical objects, while another supported "pencils", "brushes", and "spray-cans". At the lower level, one might be based on mouse operations while the other used command lines and cursor keys.)

The first component of a psychologically-based model, however, is the individual user. Rather simplistically, we could consider that the individual user brings knowledge, perception, and action. Cognitive psychology has had some success in modelling the performance of individual actions and groups of actions, from speech production to skilled typing, although these models have not been widely used in HCI as yet. Modelling some of the user's knowledge seems harder, but still tractable, using techniques drawn from Artificial Intelligence. However, modelling *enough* knowledge seems to be quite another question! Finally, modelling the user's perception of the artefact is very poorly represented at present.

The second component of a psychology-based model should be the larger system of which the user and the device are both part. The user brings a particular view of the task and of the organisation, and the way in which a device is perceived depends very much on what role it can successfully play in that view. The same word-processor might be seen as a threat or a blessing. Modelling views of organisations is a difficult business, but among the chapters in this book are two which make a start.

Theory versus outcome

HCI theories can be evaluated in several ways. In conventional psychology, the usual method of test is *competitive experimentation*, where two or more theories are used to predict the outcome of a controlled study. Research in HCI has also sometimes used the type of study where a single theory or model is used to predict performance and the measure reported is *predictive success*, usually measured by the percentage of variance accounted for by the theory's predictions. Although this book is intended to evaluate some existing theoretical developments, it contains little that could be described under either of those headings.

We believe that theoretical developments at present are at a stage where one of the first tests that should be applied is that of *explanatory adequacy*. Does a given theory describe enough of the everyday phenomena revealed by common sense and simple observation? If it does not, then it is already not interesting. Conversely, if a theoretical development succeeds in describing a phenomenon that was perfectly well-known but which has so far eluded any degree of theoretical description, then that in itself is interesting.

The chapters in this book, especially in section 1, are mostly concerned with issues of explanatory adequacy. To what degree can the theories and models that we present be regarded as adequate? This question brings up one of the noticeable differences between theories, which are usually informal, and models, which are typically more rigorous but more restricted. It is not uncommon for a theory to achieve a higher degree of explanatory adequacy than any associated model. A rigorous model is an attempt to devise a mechanism that will capture some of a theory: it is a piece of ingenuity, showing what can be achieved, it should be judged as much on what it manages to capture as on what it leaves out. This is particularly true of the more formal models, several of which are presented in this book.

Even if a theory is a success in terms of explanatory adequacy, however, that only means that it succeeds in describing or predicting a reasonable range of phenomena. We must still ask whether it is *relevant*. Does the theory leave out the important phenomena? Does it tell us how to manipulate matters in the way that we would like, as applied scientists - does it provide leverage, as Bill Curtis asks in his chapter? A useful HCI theory will have high predictive power in an area that brings high returns. The chapters in section 2 are mostly concerned with issues of relevance, in a particular area, the production of software. By confronting theoretical developments with real-life issues, they force us to consider whether today's theoretical work is on the right lines. For this reason, they describe observational studies in the field rather than laboratory studies in controlled settings.

To complete the pattern, we need to consider the *scope* of theories. Far more work has been put into research on the cognitive side of performance than into the relationship mentioned above, between the user, the device, and the organisational system. Section 3 treats the problems of individual users responding to their own perceptions and their own needs, and attempts to show what is needed in the development of future theories. At present, theories appear to be developing separately and in isolation for these different areas - one theory to describe the user's cognition, another to describe individual differences in cognition, still another to describe relationships at the organisational level. One development that is badly needed is to create unified theories. In their chapter on modelling techniques, Wilson et al. assess the shortcomings of present techniques and point out how little work has been done on treating cognitive strategies or individual differences. Even less work has been done on unified theories that can extend to the organisational level as well as to the modelling of cognition. We think the most important message of this book is that theories *are* needed in HCI; but they *must* have adequate explanatory power, they must be relevant to real problems, and their scope must be wider than those of the present theories.

SECTION 1

MODELS AND THEORIES IN COGNITIVE ERGONOMICS

The unifying theme of the chapters in this section is that of analysis of the various forms of '*model*' and modelling theory in HCI and user interface design as discussed in the Introduction. Tauber details the variety of mental models and presents formalised descriptions of such models within a more general theory of the representation of conceptual structures. The need for predictive formalised descriptions of task models for evaluative and design purposes is addressed in the chapter by Green, Schiele and Payne and a critique of task analysis methodologies (used to highlight relationships between the performance of user tasks and specified systems) is presented in the chapter by Wilson, Barnard, Green and Maclean. All employ examples in the Task Action Grammar formalism, extended and reformulated to illustrate in real applications how cognitive ergonomics can assist in the design of HCI interfaces, and providing an example of one form of working with computers.

Chapter 1 is a formal description of 'internal' task models ('*how to do it*' knowledge) to provide predictive performative measures of the interaction between a user and some device. A description and comparison of existing formal representations is accomplished within the overall structure of the performance and competence models which have been used in the past. The authors present a detailed analysis of one commercial application using TAG after setting the scene vis-a-vis user's knowledge, specification of how to use the '*grammar*' or language which describes permissible operations and description of the task structure as seen by the user.

Chapter 2 is a presentation of the task analysis methodologies which can highlight relations between user performance in knowledge-based HCI tasks and interactive systems. This contribution is a major review and critique of techniques and classifies knowledge-type; user-centered task dynamics; use, and cognitive limitations. Within one of the four headings in the categorisation of techniques, similar ground to that of the previous contribution is covered from a different and contrasting perspective. The paper as a whole provides a general critical overview of these theory-based aspects of HCI in order to provide the designer with the deeper understanding identified as necessary in our Introduction.

In the final chapter in this section, Tauber presents a exposition of the difficult area of mental modelling. He describes a large number of models within the framework of a general model theory which could derive a unifying description. The theme of the two previous chapters and the ethos of this book are continued by a cognitive ergonomic description of a real-world application presenting another viewpoint on TAG (the reformulation ETAG - Extended Task Action Grammar) as a '*mental grammar*' with which to view HCI.

FORMALISABLE MODELS OF USER KNOWLEDGE IN HUMAN-COMPUTER INTERACTION

Thomas R. G. GREEN*, Franz SCHIELE*[+], Stephen J. PAYNE**

*MRC Applied Psychology Unit,
Cambridge CB2 2EF, U.K.

[+] current address: Arbeitswissenschaftliches Forschungsinstitut GmbH
1000 Berlin 30, Germany

**Depts. of Psychology and Computing
University of Lancaster, U.K.

1 INTRODUCTION

1.1 Aims

The virtues and vices of formalisms are well known. On the one hand, they are precise, and by their precision they reveal slipshod thinking or unwarranted assumptions; on the other hand, when the material to be formalised fails to conform to the expected structure, formal systems encourage ingenuity in squeezing difficult material into shape rather than rethinking the system and developing a better approach. At its worst, a formal system is unable to generate testable predictions and its adherents split the finer points of pedantry into smaller and still smaller hairs. But at its best, it enables meaningful predictions to be made in the real world.

In this chapter we are concerned with formalisms for expressing the knowledge required to use applications programs, such as text editors, spreadsheets, and interactive graphics programs. We are particularly concerned with representing expert knowledge of *how to use* the applications program, and with using that representation to obtain predictions of difficulties in learning and performance. Since it is knowledge about the program, rather its application domain, that concerns us here, the tasks we shall study are tasks of program usage, such as 'how to edit a formula in this spreadsheet'. They will not be tasks in which knowledge of the application domain is paramount, such as how to perform revenue forecasting. In the terms of Moran (1983) we shall be studying 'internal' tasks rather than 'external' ones.

3

In the present state of theory such representations must be limited and incomplete, but it is our belief that even limited representations are useful. They increase the precision of our descriptions, and hence they may reveal important similarities and differences between one applications program and another that might otherwise go overlooked; just as the adoption of concise descriptions of syntax, such as Backus-Naur Form, helped to reveal similarities and differences between programming languages.

Our first aim, therefore, is to compare a number of these formalisms and to exhibit their strengths and weaknesses. Our second aim is to present rather more fully a particular formalism with which we have been associated, the Task-Action Grammar. This formalism was first developed (Payne, 1985) using interesting, but very limited, examples. Here we shall present for the first time in print an analysis of a commercial application using this method.

It is important to establish that the aim of the formalisms in this chapter is not to describe the program interface itself. Several formalisms for that purpose already exist (Chi, 1985, presents a helpful comparison of various methods, including 'behavioural' algebra, event algebra, set theoretic approaches). Because they incorporate no psychological structure, however, these formalisms do not lead to predictions of difficulty in learning or use.

The only way to construct a formalism that will lead to psychological predictions is, of course, to build it around a psychological model. There are many available models in psychology that can be or have been applied to human-computer interaction. For instance, analyses of the cognitive processes involved in the use of metaphor and analogy have been taken as a model of how users make use of existing, pre-computer knowledge to help them (or, as it may be, hinder them) when they come to use computers for a task they previously performed manually (Carroll and Mack, 1985). Not all cognitive models lead to formalisable statements, however, and the metaphor work is an example. It has been sufficiently seminal to have influenced the designers of the Xerox Star and its descendants, such as the Apple Macintosh, in their use of the 'desk-top metaphor', but it has not so far proved possible to formalise it.

Formalisability, and the power to generate predictions, are not one and the same. The metaphor model has been used predictively even though it is informal. Conversely it is not clear how to derive predictions from some formalisms. We shall focus on formalisable models, but we do not wish to imply that other approaches are worthless.

1.2 Overview: Types of Model

In this chapter we present a number of approaches to modelling the interaction between a user and a device. The first, the Keystroke Level Model (Card et al., 1983) is conceptually very simple. It uses simple numerical approximations to predict times taken for particular tasks. These predictions have the distinction of being genuinely quantitative, unlike most psychological predictions.

The next two models (Card et al.'s GOMS, and the production system model proposed by Kieras and Polson, 1985) are 'process' models. Process models attempt to supply a simple model of the mental processes involved in using an interface, including remembering items, starting a new subgoal, etc. They yield predictions which are less quantitative in nature, based perhaps on how many items must be simultaneously retained in working memory or on other measures.

At heart these are all *performance* models; they make statements about the time or effort required to perform a typical operation. From the second two models it is also possible to derive a statement of what it is that the experienced user knows about the interface and how that knowledge is organised. The subsequent models concentrate primarily on that aspect, and so they model not performance but *competence* - what the user knows how to do.

The distinction between competence and performance first arose in the field of linguistics, where competence has typically been modelled by generative grammars. Ideally these grammars would generate all and only the sentences of a given language, and they describe what the experienced language-user knows about the structure of that language. Not surprisingly this approach has been exported to our domain, where Reisner (1981) seems to have been the first to describe the user's knowledge in terms of the grammar of an 'interaction language'. Her work forms our fourth model. Just as the performance models contain implied statements about competence, so the competence models can contain implied statements about performance. For instance, Reisner predicts that users will find difficulty with 'sentences' (operations) which can only be generated from the grammar by a large number of steps. Turning such predictions into quantitative form is not easy, though.

Process models and grammatical models are alike in that they postulate a mechanism (whereas the Keystroke Level Model only offers descriptive generalisations). Process models make their mechanism explicit, while grammatical models leave it implicit in the structure of the grammar. All the models described so far, of both process and grammatical types, appear to postulate mechanisms which are very similar in certain important ways. Our fifth model, the two-level Set Grammar model of Green and Payne (1984), uses a more powerful grammatical structure. This model predicts that users know more about the interface language than is contained in the previous models, which we believe are epistemologically inadequate. In particular, this model predicts that users can perceive and make use of distributional properties of the system, such as internal consistencies in the interaction language, or family resemblances between syntactic rules, which are not catered for in the simpler models.

However, the Set Grammar model captures purely syntactic consistencies; it does nothing about the deeper level of consistency which says that similar tasks should be performed in similar ways. Our final model, Task-Action Grammar (Payne, 1984; Payne and Green, 1986) is another competence model built round a grammar, but in this case a grammar in which the 'sentences' describing the user's actions are derived from postulated semantic features of the task. Such a model obviously requires analysis of the user's perception of the structure of interface tasks. Our presentation of this model includes an application to a commercially available spreadsheet package, to show how the formalism reveals the structure of the interface language in a reasonably compact form.

(Incidentally, all such task-oriented models run into problems about the nature of a 'task'. No doubt large tasks are decomposed into smaller tasks and then into smaller still. The process must stop somewhere, with tasks that are indivisible and atomic. What is an atomic task? The models we shall describe make different claims: the process models refer to 'unit tasks', for which the user knows an immediate method of solution, and the task-action grammar refers to 'simple tasks' which contain no control structure. We shall not be able to discuss this issue in depth.)

Essentially, process models describe both "what the user knows" and "how the user uses that knowledge". Competence models describe only "what the user knows", and leave a hole for an account of "how the user uses that knowledge". Our final section outlines a possible mechanism for the use of such knowledge, in which we describe how the user might possibly decompose larger tasks into an interrelated series of smaller tasks; then use the task-action grammar to translate those tasks into descriptions of actions; and finally turn the descriptions of actions into executed actions. This account, unlike the earlier process models, leaves room for describing some of the patterns of action slips that characterise even the performance of expert users. It also leaves room for attaching a task planner as part of the theoretical structure.

2 PERFORMANCE MODELS

2.1 Time Predictions and the Keystroke Level Model

When trying to model the difficulty of using an interface, the simplest beginning is to count the number of actions the user needs to make to perform some standard tasks. If all actions take approximately the same time, and if we can ignore thinking time, this will give a prediction of the relative time required.

The Keystroke Level Model is a more sophisticated version of that approach. Its authors, Card, Moran and Newell (1983), chose to predict performance times of expert users performing familiar tasks - "routine cognitive skills" - who would need little thinking time and whose action times would be less variable than those of novices. Their model builds on the engineering psychology of the fifties, notably Fitts' Law of hand motion, to predict speed of errorless performance. In this model, the user's task is subdivided into "unit tasks", which are near or at the level of single commands to the interface. Time to execute is estimated from the sum of the "acquisition time" for a unit task, which they compute at 1.8 seconds in their work on text editing, and a modified sum of the times required for mental operations and keystrokes. They clock the mental operations of their model at about 1.4 seconds, while the keystroke times are an average depending on the physical layout of the device in use, as Fitts' Law predicts, and the typing speed of the user.

To form the modified sum of mental and keystroking times, they assume that one mental time unit (M) is required for each choice of command (but not for the command arguments); that when an operator following an M is "fully anticipated" in the operator immediately preceding the M, no M is needed; that no M is needed for redundant terminators; etc.

This approach has many limitations. It cannot cope with errors, let alone predict them; it cannot easily represent different methods for performing the same task, even though experts often select from a wide repertoire; it is insensitive to many of the niceties of physical layout; it has little to say about interfaces outside the "glass teletype" style; and it can make no predictions about difficulty of using the interface, of generalising to or from other interfaces, etc. The limitations of the model are, however, deliberate choices made by its authors to obtain a very high degree of predictiveness.

2.2 Process Model 1: GOMS

The Goals, Operators, Methods and Selection model, or GOMS, developed by Card, Moran and Newell (1983), is a higher level version of the same authors' Keystroke Level Model described above, meeting some of the limitations of the simpler model. Following in the footsteps of Newell and Simon's approach to problem solving (1972), GOMS describes the operation of an interface in terms of a "state space". The user's goal is to achieve a particular state; each available operator takes the user to the same state or a new state, in which different operators will be available.

Fundamental to the GOMS model is the notion of a "unit task", a subtask which can be performed by the user within his or her performance limitations. We shall describe in more detail below the characteristic properties of unit tasks and their relation to the difficult question of task analysis; typical examples, however, might be deleting a line, or changing a word.

A typical GOMS *goal* might be EDIT-MANUSCRIPT. This might create a subgoal, EDIT-UNIT-TASK, which is to be repeated until no more unit tasks remain to be performed. This in turn might create new subgoals. *Operators* are "elementary perceptual, motor, or cognitive acts" which change the task environment or the user's mental state, e.g. GET-NEXT-TASK, or DELETE-WORD. Methods define procedures for accomplishing goals, in terms of operators or subgoals. *Methods* usually require conditional tests on the contents of the user's working memory (as simulated in the model) and the state of the environment. Finally, when more than one method is available to accomplish the goal, the *selection* rules resolve the conflict; for instance, for the goal LOCATE-LINE there may be two methods, repeated cursor movements or else a quick string search, and a selection rule is required saying (perhaps) "use cursor movements for 4 lines or fewer". Figure 1 shows an example of the GOMS structure for EDIT-MANUSCRIPT, taken from Card et al. (1983, p. 142).

```
GOAL:EDIT-MANUSCRIPT
. GOALS:EDIT-UNIT-TASK          repeat until no more unit tasks
. . GOAL:ACQUIRE-UNIT-TASK
. . . GET-NEXT-PAGE             if at end of manuscript page
. . . GET-NEXT-TASK
. . GOAL:EXECUTE-UNIT-TASK
. . . GOAL:LOCATE-LINE
. . . . [select: USE-QS-METHOD
             USE-LF-METHOD]
. . . GOAL:MODIFY-TEXT
. . . . [select: USE-S-COMMAND
             USE-M-COMMAND]
. . . . VERIFY-EDIT.
```

Figure 1.   Fragment of a GOMS model for text editing

In the experiment from which the example is taken (op. cit. Experiment 5A), the selection rules were derived individually for each user. A typical example of a selection method, given for subject 22 (p. 153), is:

Rule 1: Use the QS-METHOD unless another rule applies.
Rule 2: If less than 5 lines are to be covered, use the LF-METHOD.

Time estimates were made for each operator and for each subject, and the experiments compared both the sequence of operators executed and also the total time taken. GOMS produced good fits to the data, although only a small number of subjects were tested - and although, with individual time estimates and selection rule derivations, there was a certain amount of 'tuning' possible, by choosing selection rules to fit individuals.

GOMS, unlike the Keystroke Level Model, has some capacity to deal with errors, but is at its best with error-free performance. Extensive applications have been made to certain types of text-editing, usually with good results. It is evidently possible to use GOMS to predict user performance at the time level, at least for some classes of interface design. However, there remain many cognitive aspects that have not been brought into account, and the next sections will reveal some of them.

GOMS describes individual differences by the selection rule device. Selection rules are modelled separately for each user and they are entirely pragmatic, capable of no coordination between themselves, nor of incorporation into a higher level planning component. This difficulty results from the authors' aim to produce a *performance* model, not a *competence* model. If we are content to model competence then pragmatic, user-specific devices can be safely omitted.

GOMS has some difficulty in defining the important concept of the 'unit task' in a satisfactory way. This concept is fundamental to the operation of GOMS:

> "In each of the cases of unit-task behavior studied, there has been a structured cycle of repeated actions. The user first acquires a task and a method for doing it (reads or decides what to do and how to do it) and then executes the method." (p. 386)

The authors continue:

> "The most important point to understand about the unit task is that *the unit task is fundamentally a control construct, not a task construct.*"

Different modifications to a manuscript present distinct tasks to the user; but if two modifications are nearby, the user may decide to organise the editing around that fact, and deal with both at once, as a single unit task. The limits on the construction of unit tasks lie in the user's performance limitations, and the authors analyse some example tasks to reveal possible limitations.

Their observation is undoubtedly correct and shrewd. There are two problems. The first is, we do not yet know enough to be able to make generalisable statements about the construction of unit tasks in a wide range of situations. The second is that the authors do not go into how users perform the planning operations necessary to combine two or more *task* constructs, such as two distinct editing tasks, into a single *control* construct. The organisation of knowledge in the GOMS model does not lend itself to application of conventional planning techniques in any obvious way.

2.3 Process Model 2: Kieras and Polson

Kieras and Polson (1985; Polson and Kieras, 1985) have developed a two-component model based on the GOMS mechanism, much of which they have succeeded in simulating. One component is a production system model for what they call the user's *how-to-do-it* knowledge; the other component is a representation of the device itself.

Their papers have devoted much attention to the task of operating the IBM Displaywriter. Their model for the expert's knowledge of how to delete a word uses production rules (Figure 2) to model the different "methods" (in the GOMS sense) for deleting characters, words, and arbitrary strings, each method being based on the description given in the IBM Displaywriter documentation. (One of the interesting features of this example, as the authors point out, is that the method given for word deletion is "buggy": it relies on the presence of a space following the word to be deleted). The style rules for their system follow Card et al. in assuming that the task of editing a manuscript is decomposed into a sequence of unit tasks, each of which is an independent activity and has two stages: 'acquiring' the unit task, and performing the necessary actions. A top level, not shown here, starts and stops the process.

Selection and control rules for deletion methods

```
(SELECT-CHARACTER-DELETION
IF (AND       (TEST-GOAL perform unit task)
              (TEST-MSS function is delete)
              (TEST-MSS entity is character)
              (NOT (TEST-GOAL delecte character))
              (NOT (TEST-NOTE executing character deletion)) )
THEN (        (ADD-GOAL delete character)
              (ADD-NOTE executing character deletion)
              (LOOK-MSS task is at %UT-HP %UT-VP)) )

(CHARACTER-DELETION-DONE
IF (AND       (TEST-GOAL perform unit task)
              (TEST-NOTE executing character deletion)
              (NOT (TEST-GOAL delete character)) )
THEN (        (DELETE-NOTE executing character deletion)
              (DELETE-GOAL perform unit task)) )

(SELECT-WORD-DELETION
IF (AND       (TEST-GOAL perform unit task)
              (TEST-MSS function is delete)
              (TEST-MSS entity is word)
              (NOT (TEST-GOAL delete word))
              (NOT (TEST-NOTE executing word deletion)) )
THEN (        (ADD-GOAL delete word)
              (ADD-NOTE executing word deletion)
              (LOOK-MSS task is at %UT-HP %UT-VP)) )

(WORD-DELETION-DONE
IF (AND       (TEST-GOAL perform unit task)
              (TEST-NOTE executing word deletion)
              (NOT (TEST-GOAL delete word)) )
THEN (        (DELETE-NOTE executing word deletion)
              (DELETE-GOAL perform unit task)) )
```

```
(SELECT-STRING-DELETION
IF (AND       (TEST-GOAL perform unit task)
              (TEST-MSS function is delete)
              (TEST-MSS entity is string)
              (NOT (TEST-GOAL delete string))
              (NOT (TEST-NOTE executing string deletion)) )
THEN (        (ADD-GOAL delete string)
              (LOOK-MSS task is at %UT-HP %UT-VP)
              (ADD-NOTE executing string deletion)) )

(STRING-DELETION-DONE
IF (AND       (TEST-GOAL perform unit task)
              (TEST-NOTE executing string deletion)
              (NOT (TEST-GOAL delete string)) )
THEN (        (DELETE-NOTE executing string deletion)
              (DELETE-GOAL perform unit task)) )
```

Method for deleting a single character

```
(PDELC1
IF (AND       (TEST-GOAL delete character)
              (NOT (TEST-GOAL move cursor to %UT-HP %UT-VP))
              (NOT (TEST-CURSOR %UT-HP %UT-VP)) )
THEN (        (ADD-GOAL move cursor to %UT-HP %UT-VP)) )

(PDELC2
IF (AND       (TEST-GOAL delete character)
              (TEST-CURSOR %UT-HP %UT-VP))
THEN (        (DO-KEYSTROKE DEL)
              (DO-KEYSTROKE ENTER)
              (WAIT)
              (DELETE-GOAL delete character)
              (UNBIND %UT-HP %UT-VP)) )
```

Method to delete a single word

```
(PDELW1
IF (AND       (TEST-GOAL delete word)
              (NOT (TEST-GOAL move cursor to %UT-HP %UT-VP))
              (NOT (TEST-CURSOR %UT-HP %UT-VP)) )
THEN (        (ADD-GOAL move cursor to %UT-HP %UT-VP)) )

(PDELW2
IF (AND       (TEST-GOAL delete word)
              (TEST-CURSOR %UT-HP %UT-VP))
THEN (        (DO-KEYSTROKE DEL)
              (DO-KEYSTROKE SPACE)
              (DO-KEYSTROKE ENTER)
              (WAIT)
              (DELETE-GOAL delete word)
              (UNBIND %UT-HP %UT-VP )) )
```

Figure 2.   Process model for deletion methods on IBM Displaywriter. From Kieras and Polson (1985). Only the methods for deleting words and characters are shown here.

Production rules can be rewritten in many different forms, thereby affecting the apparent complexity in terms of number of rules, number of times each one is used, etc. The expert-level model of Figure 2 seems to be designed to be as compact as possible within a given vocabulary of primitive actions and a given production-system architecture. The same authors have developed a novice-level model; the productions of this model are constrained by style rules developed by Kieras and Bovair (1983), which assume that novices explicitly test all goals that are in working memory, explicitly attend to feedback information and verify each step they take, and execute only one control action in each production.

The representation of generalisation is through the 'common elements' theory of transfer:

"If a similar production is learned during the acquisition of another method, it is assumed that this production will be incorporated into the representation of a new method at no cost in time to learn. Thus, the time to learn a given method is a function of the number of 'new' productions, that is, the number of productions unique to the new method."

(Polson and Kieras, 1985, p. 209). This point is not pursued in sufficient detail to be entirely certain what the power of the proposed mechanism might be.

The performance demands of the user model can also be assessed by counting the depth of the goal stack generated during operation. For instance, "the general delete [of arbitrary strings] has a goal structure that is three levels deep, while the specialised functions are two levels deep" (Kieras and Polson, 1985). They predict from this difference (1) that the general method will be harder because it places increased demands on working memory, and (2) that it will be harder to automate into skilled cognitive performance (following the ideas of ACT, Anderson 1982).

Empirical results appear to support their predictions. In the first of two experiments reported by Polson and Kieras (1985) they found that learning time for the IBM Displaywriter depended on the order of training on selected editing tasks (insert, delete, etc) in a way that agreed reasonably well with the predictions from the 'common elements' theory of transfer. In the second experiment they obtained a good fit between observed execution time for different editing methods, and a prediction derived from the number of productions firing in a simulation run and the number of items entered into working memory. It must be pointed out that the authors had available a number of different predictors, and chose to present the results from the best predictor. Also, among the editing tasks compared, the most difficult one (transposition of material) was likely to be predicted as more difficult than the easiest one (simple deletion) by any reasonable predictor at all, so that the agreement between observation and prediction is not as striking as it appears at first sight. Nevertheless these are promising results.

To illustrate the device component of their model, Kieras and Polson (1985) also present a description of the Displaywriter editor itself, using a different notation, the Generalised Transition Network. The notation resembles that of a conventional transition network with the addition of subnets which can be nested under conditions, actions, or state nodes; in particular, they suggest that subnets nested under state nodes can be used to represent the modes of a system, such as "REVISE" mode on the Displaywriter. By combining the hierarchical component of this notation with the goal structure obtained from the production system representation, they obtain suggestions about 'mismatches' between the two structures and how to cure them. In particular, they postulate that where they find it convenient to introduce 'subroutine calls' (or 'push arcs', in the vocabulary of transition networks), these should correspond to creations of new subgoals in their model of the user, and vice-versa.

The generalised transition network is certainly a more successful description language than a conventional transition network would have been. However, decisions about where to include nesting of components appear to be essentially arbitrary. This means that the conclusions reached on the basis of the mismatch between the goal structure and the device hierarchy, although intuitively plausible, have no firm foundation; different decisions about how to represent the device structure would have led to different conclusions. Moreover, the conclusions are also vulnerable to decisions to use a more powerful notation than generalised transition networks. A strong contender in the same spirit would appear to be the 'statechart', a notation devised by Harel (in press) which also includes nested components but which allows many other interesting features as well, including methods to indicate the mode of a system which do *not* rely on nested properties (see above). The decision to use Harel's notation would therefore seemingly alter the predictions obtained. Finally, it is not made clear why the user's creation of new goals needs to correspond to push arcs in the device representation, and we find ourselves puzzled by it.

All in all, then, although Kieras and Polson have introduced a potentially important idea here, the formal relationship between a representation of the device and a representation of the user's model, each in its appropriate description language, we feel that it needs more working out.

3 COMPETENCE MODELS

As we noted in the Introduction, the developments of linguistics have led to attempts to use linguistic techniques in this area. This seems a highly promising approach. The formal apparatus of linguistics has been refined by application to many different types of phenomena at many levels - from phonetics at one end to pragmatics at the other. Many issues about the status of evidence, the goals of linguistic theory, and the ontological status of linguistic objects, although not perhaps finally settled, are at least clearer than their counterparts in our area. As it turns out, the ideas imported from linguistics have mostly concerned the speaker's knowledge of syntax, and in particular the attempt to formalise that knowledge as a 'generative grammar' - that is, a finite structure that is capable of generating all and only the sentences of some target language.

This emphasis on syntax has led to a corresponding weakness in describing the semantics; but we shall say more of that below.

3.1 Competence Model 1: Reisner's "Psychological BNF"

The definitions of programming languages have frequently been formalised, often in Backus-Naur Form (BNF), a linguistic structure which provides generative, context-free, phrase structure grammars.
Here is a sample:

> \<statement\> ::= \<for-loop\> | \<conditional\> |
>   \<simple-statement\>
> \<conditional\> ::= if \<boolean expression\> then \<statement\>
>   else \<statement\>
> etc.

This is to be read as "the syntactic class 'statement' is defined as a 'for-loop' OR a 'conditional' OR a 'simple-statement'. A 'conditional' is defined as the terminal symbol *if*, followed by a 'boolean expression', followed by *then* ... etc."

Reisner (1977), looking for techniques to predict the usability of interface languages, extended BNF to the formalisation of command languages. By analogy, the grammar represents the whole language and specific sentences now represent specific sequences of actions. She hoped to use a BNF grammar as a predictor of the psychological complexity of the language:

> "A natural index of the complexity (of a statement) might be the number of rewrite rules ... used to describe it. ... By this we mean to suggest that a BNF description of a language, usually intended to describe the set of valid statements, may have psychological validity,"

and she goes on to propose an experimental search for "a single, consistent, psychological BNF".

While accepting her desire to find a psychological index of complexity, Green (1980) heavily criticised Reisner's proposal to take BNF as a model. As a counter argument, Green presented two Algol 60 statements which were (intuitively) very similar, and showed that the BNF descriptions of them were very different. The statements in question were conditionals, in one of which a technical problem known as the "dangling else" was avoided by a method that is quite elaborate to describe in BNF, but which is quite easy to conceptualise: "If you've written *if ... then for ... do* and now you want to put an else-branch on the end, you must go back and put *begin-end* round the for-statement". This corresponds to an *exception rule* - a far more powerful feature than BNF contains. Green's conclusion (p. 293) was that "a psychological index of complexity would be a fine thing, but it cannot be arrived at from BNF. What we need to know is what the grammar might look like in the head".

However, Reisner's next paper (1981) appeared to show that Green's criticisms were misplaced, since she had remodelled an interface in accordance with principles derived from her BNF work and had successfully demonstrated that the new version was easier to use than the old. Her method was to create a BNF grammar of the 'action language' of the original interface, a graphics package called ROBART 1, and seek for knotty areas. There were several knotty areas, because ROBART 1 designers had minimised the number of actions needed by the user, even when the result was increased grammatical complexity. For instance, to select a shape in ROBART 1 the user turned on a "shape switch" and then pressed "GO", but to select text no selection action was required. A BNF-style description would therefore need two rules, one for text, one for all other shapes. Reisner's remodelled version, ROBART 2, treated text uniformly with all other shapes, so that users needed one rule instead of two. Observation showed that users made fewer mistakes at this point in their work when using ROBART 2, as predicted.

Closer examination indicates that Green's strictures on BNF are still valid. In the example given, the ROBART 1 action language would look something like this in BNF:

<select circle> ::= <select circle switch>   <press GO button>
<select line> ::= <select line switch>   <press GO button>
<select square> ::= <select square switch>   <press GO button>
<select text> ::= NULL

It is clear that 'select text' has a different *shape* from the other rules, but changing the rule to have the same shape,

<select text> ::= <select text switch>   <press GO button>,

does not change the actual *number* of rules - which, as we saw above, is the principal metric of complexity employed by Reisner.

Reisner was evidently conscious of this difficulty, and she writes in her 1981 paper that the need is to reduce "the number of forms of rules ... Better notational schemes need to be found or devised which reveal both the structure and the legal strings." (p. 237). We shall show below how one can indeed describe the "forms" of rules, more powerfully than BNF.

But there is a different type of shortcoming in the approach as described so far: it describes the *device*, rather than the user. Subsequent work by Reisner (1984) attempted to incorporate into her scheme some of the thinking behind Card et al.'s time-predictive Keystroke Level Model described above. The concept of "task acquisition" in that model was expanded into a new class of actions in Reisner's new model, the "information seeking actions" which refer to "what a user has to do to get the information he needs", as opposed to the physical input actions already modelled in her earlier papers. (See Tauber, this volume, for an example.)

Unfortunately the class of "information seeking" actions is evidently very large and diverse, and we would be prepared to hazard the guess that drawing predictions from this model would be correspondingly hard. That apart, the new version of Reisner's model has some interesting features. It models the interaction process, not the interface alone, as her earlier work did; it is oriented towards the user's tasks; it recognises that the user must frequently solve problems, find information, and choose between methods, none of which activities were represented in the Keystroke Level Model; it recognises that different users will have different knowledge bases, and Reisner suggests ways in which the difference between a novice and an expert might be modelled; it has the potential to predict times; and it provides a different way to model the same problems of inconsistency as

Reisner's earlier work. Nevertheless, in our opinion it still fails to capture the notions of *consistency, generalisation* and *analogy* which form such an important part of interface knowledge.

3.2 Competence Model 2: Set Grammar

Intuitive assessments of languages frequently invoke such phrases as "consistent" or "orthogonal" syntax, meaning that many of the syntax rules bear a family resemblance to each other. This point has been made succinctly by Ichbaiah, chief designer of the programming language Ada, replying to criticisms that Ada might be conceptually too big for programmers to learn and understand:

> "The human mind has an incredible ability to understand structures. Provided it understands the major lines of a structure, it will make inferences and immediately see the consequences. When you judge something, the complexity is not in the details but in whether or not it is easy to infer details from the major structural lines. From this point of view I consider Ada to be very simple." (Ichbaiah, 1984, p. 993)

Although Ichbaiah was speaking as a computer scientist with an armchair view of cognitive processes, his argument is fully in line with the emphasis that cognitive psychology today places on the distributional properties of a set.

> "People learn structures, not isolated pairings (fallacy of composition). An interface system must be a coherent structure ... The orientation of modern cognitive learning theory emphasizes that people do learn structures and not isolated pairs. The learning of any paired associate reciprocally affects the learning of all other paired associates." (Carroll and Thomas, 1980)

A "consistent" language will be easy to learn. It will also be easy to relearn after prolonged disuse. Why? Because if you know a little of it, you can regenerate the remainder.

Reisner's work, cited above, gave empirical support to the notion of consistency, but her BNF formalism ran aground because what she wanted was to measure the number of different *forms* of rules, not the total number of different rules. BNF cannot do that; but the two-level grammars that we shall now introduce, can do that.

The two-level grammar devised by van Wijngaarden (1966; Pagan, 1981) offers a means of formalising grammars in which meta-rules - i.e., rules to generate rules - were used as a means of exhibiting structures such as sequence that were common to many rules. If all the rules of a language have a family resemblance, then a W-grammar for the language will have relatively few meta-rules; conversely, an inconsistent language will need more meta-rules.

Payne and Green (1983) present a modified form of W-grammar, the set-grammar, which replaced van Wijngaarden's "meta-notions" with the simpler device of *set of grammatical objects*; this reduces the power of the grammar in ways which seem - intuitively - realistic. They also introduced "selection rules", which governed the allowed combinations of choices from sets; these simply express the "uniform replacement" constraint, free replacement, or a third type, the "linked set", which will not be described here. A number of experiments were reinterpreted in set grammar terms, including the ROBART work by Reisner cited above. This turns out to work very simply. A set grammar (in a simplified notation) for the fragment of ROBART 1 given in BNF above would look like this:

< select SHAPE > :: = < select SHAPE switch >
    < press GO button >
< select text > :: = NULL
SHAPE is one of {circle, line, square}

In ROBART 2, 'text' is made to behave like the other members of the SHAPE set, so only one rule is needed:

< select SHAPE > :: = < select SHAPE switch >
    < press GO button >
SHAPE is one of {circle, line, square, text}

This, then, achieves Reisner's aim of counting "the number of *forms* of rules".

The claims have been put to empirical test. Green and Payne (1984) describe an experiment in which the command set of a commercially available text editor was shown to contain two different forms of organisation, leading to conflicts in the cases where both applied; three modified forms, without conflict, were all shown to be easier to learn than the original. Payne (1984) briefly describes a study in which two artificial languages were compared, called languages G and B. The set-grammar of G contained fewer rules than the set-grammar of B; but the BNF grammar of G contained *more* rules than that of B - so if BNF is really the "language in the head", language B would be easier to learn, while if set-grammar is the language in the head, language G would be easier to learn. The results clearly favoured language G.

Although few in number, these results undoubtedly support the premise that the human parsing mechanism has more power than a BNF mechanism, at least in the context of artificial languages. Moreover, concurrent developments in grammatical circles have shown that substantial fragments of English can be described by grammatical devices based on the meta-rule (Gazdar et al., 1985). Parsimony suggests that we should assume that the grammatical procedures used in learning artificial languages can draw upon the same computational resources as the procedures used in natural language, although obviously not upon the same huge amount of practice.

Despite this support, the two-level set grammar does not go far enough. Payne and Green (1983) list four postulates of set grammar, and the weakness is evident in the fourth: "Elements within sets are both syntactically *and semantically* similar". This model successfully captures some of the types of syntactic family resemblances that humans can perceive, and it captures more of them than BNF; to that degree it meets its aim of describing "consistency". But it contains no mechanism for describing other types of family resemblance, and it cannot capture the notion of "semantic similarity" - even though that notion is one of its postulates.

4 TASK-ACTION GRAMMAR

4.1 Requirements for a Model

It would not be unreasonable to suggest that some attempts at modelling the user of a device have attempted to model the entire relevant psychology at one swoop. To remind ourselves, in this chapter we are concentrating on models of the user's knowledge. (Other types of model are reviewed in the chapter by Wilson in this volume.) We have singled out the distinction between performance and competence models as the most relevant dimension to discuss in this chapter, because the way that knowledge is modelled is very different; in the performance models, the representation of knowledge is distributed through the model, entwined with other aspects of the psychology.

Another important distinction, however, is between models which only describe the device language as seen by the user (e.g. the early version of Reisner's BNF model), and those which describe knowledge of how to use the language. A convincing model should give some account of the task structure as seen by the user. GOMS, although a performance model, meets this requirement by describing "Methods" available to the user and selection rules for choosing between alternative methods. The Set Grammar model fails to describe task structure in any way at all.

The model we shall now describe, Task-Action Grammar (Payne, 1984, 1985; Payne and Green, 1986) sets out explicitly to describe the mapping between the user's task structure and the action sequences that accomplish those tasks. The underlying philosophy resembles that of Set Grammar, in that the user's knowledge is represented as a grammar and a highly consistent system will be representable by fewer rules than an arbitrary system. In this case, however, the rules of the grammar no longer describe the surface syntax, but aspects of the mapping between task structure and action structure.

4.2 Introduction to TAG

TAG starts with a specification of a task, such as "move cursor up", and generates the required action sequence. Since TAG is a competence model, the knowledge component is to be divorced from the process component. TAG only models the knowledge component, represented by a grammar; it makes no attempt to model the "grammar-runner", the process of using that knowledge. The grammar rules must therefore operate solely from knowledge of the task structure and its relationship to the action language - unlike process models, which rely on observing the current state of the device and modifying their course of action according to the circumstances.

TAG therefore defines the rewriting of what Payne and Green, (1986), call "simple tasks". These simple tasks do not include any tasks that require monitoring of plan progress; they are the largest units that the user can handle without having to enter a problem-solving mode. Higher levels of planning needing coordination between task sequences are best modelled, we believe, by a separate planning component. Figure 3 illustrates a possible overall architecture of the user, showing where TAG fits into the whole. To accomplish a goal, the user may make a plan, which will require him or her to perform one or more simple tasks; these simple tasks are then rewritten as action sequences (or, more correctly, perhaps, as sequences of action *specifications*, as we argue below).

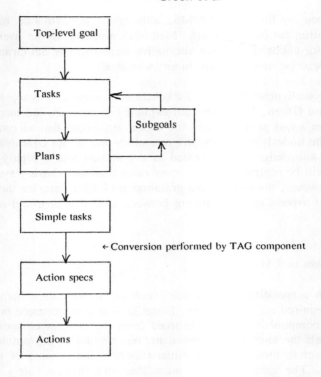

Figure 3.   A simple schematic overall architecture of goal-oriented
                  computer usage

In brief, a Task-Action Grammar rewrites "simple tasks" into action sequences. "Simple" tasks are those which can be accomplished with no problem-solving component or control structure; they may be at a very low level, for novices, or may be composed into larger groupings with experience.

The strict constraints on simple tasks dictate that they are heavily affected by the device itself. Rather than representing the task structure of the application domain, which will almost certainly deal in entities such as words and paragraphs or their equivalents in other domains, simple tasks are determined primarily by the characteristics of the device itself. If the device has no direct way of handling paragraphs, the user may still form a simple task at the paragraph level - but only if the execution of that task requires no problem-solving and no control actions. TAG describes *internal*, not *external*, tasks.

Psychologically, a simple task can be regarded as a concept. TAG follows Tversky (1977) and Rosenberg (1983) in the use of feature sets as models of concepts. Feature sets allow a theory of similarity computations, based on shared features, and they also allow an intensional semantics, based on the relationship of one simple task to all others. An example of a feature is "direction of movement": this feature can have the value "forwards", "backwards", etc. Where the only possible values are presence or absence, they can be represented by " + " and "-". (The value of a feature is sometimes referred to in the literature as a "component", and this view of semantics as "componential semantics".)

A TAG description of a device interface requires a dictionary of simple tasks, and a set of rewriting rules to map tasks into actions. Each entry in the dictionary of simple tasks associates a concept name, such as "move up", with a set of feature-values, such as [Movement = +, Direction = up], and these are used to guide the derivation of a "sentence" or action-sequence from the rules. It is normally convenient to precede the task dictionary and rewriting rules with an explicit statement of the feature names and their permissible values, if the grammar is of any appreciable size.

A rule that rewrites a symbol marked with features may be regarded as a *rule-schema* summarising all possible ways to replace the features with their range of values. Features, unlike symbols, must be replaced identically throughout the rule. Thus the rule

move [Direction] := letter [Direction] + RETURN

can be regarded as a summary form of the rules

move [Direction = up] := letter [Direction = up] + RETURN
move [Direction = down] := letter [Direction = down] + RETURN
move [Direction = left] := letter [Direction = left] + RETURN
move [Direction = right] := letter [Direction = right] + RETURN

(assuming that the feature "Direction" has the possible values shown).

Since the purpose of a TAG is to convert a task, defined by a set of feature values, into the appropriate actions, the TAG grammar's first rules redefine the start symbol "Task" in various ways marked by various features. Each task in the task dictionary will have a set of features that corresponds to one of the rules that rewrites the start symbol. In an interface language with a high degree of internal consistency all the tasks will be rewritten into sequences that have strong family resemblances, and so several tasks can be expressed by one rule, using the power of the semantic features to bring the tasks together as a single schema; conversely, an arbitrary and inconsistent interface language will need a different derivation for each task.

The psychological theory behind TAG states that humans can perceive and utilise just those types of consistency that can be modelled by the TAG language. The force of this assertion (which is really quite fierce) will become more apparent as we give examples.

4.3 A Fragment of EMACS

We now present two illustrative examples of TAG models for miniature systems. The first comes from an EMACS-like text editor command set, in which the commands are

ctrl-C:	move cursor one character forward
meta-C:	move cursor one character backward
ctrl-W:	move cursor one word forward
meta-W:	move cursor one word backward

List of commands

move cursor one character forward	ctrl-C
move cursor one character backward	meta-C
move cursor one word forward	ctrl-W
move cursor one word backward	meta-W

List of features	**Possible Values**
Direction	forward, backward
Unit	character, word

TAG definition

Dictionary of simple tasks

move cursor one character forward
{Direction=forward, Unit = char}
move cursor one character backward
{Direction=backward, Unit = char}
move cursor one word forward
{Direction=forward, Unit = word}
move cursor one word backward
{Direction=backward, Unit = word}

Rule Schemas

Task [Direction, Unit] → symbol [Direction] + letter [Unit]
symbol [Direction = forward]→ "ctrl"
symbol [Direction = backward]→ "meta"
letter [Unit = word]→ "W"
letter [Unit = character]→ "C"

Figure 4.   TAG description of a fragment of an EMACS-like editor

The TAG definition is as shown in Figure 4. To illustrate the operation of this, suppose the user desires to move the cursor one character forward. This is, as it happens, a concept for which there is a simple task in the dictionary. The simple task is marked with the feature-values Direction = forward, Unit = char. Consult the rule schemas to find a start symbol ("Task") whose features can include those of the simple task. (In this example there is only one start symbol.) Replace the features by their values, throughout the rule:

Task [Direction = forward, Unit = char] :=
    symbol [Direction = forward] + letter [Unit = char]

Now rewrite the new non-terminals in the same way, giving the result "ctrl" + "C".

When a feature mentioned in a rule can take any of its possible values, we shall in future not mention it explicitly. The abbreviated form of the previous rule becomes

Task := symbol + letter

4.4 The IBM Displaywriter

This example is presented to enable comparison between a production-system model of interface knowledge and the much more compact TAG description of the same material. We shall use the Kieras and Polson example, shown above in Figure 2, for this purpose. The TAG version is shown in Figure 5. Two versions are presented. In (a), the rule schemas are based on the productions used by Kieras and Polson, which in turn are based on the IBM training manual. In this version, string deletion is treated as an arbitrary and inconsistent part of the task repertoire. As they point out, it is possible to organise the user's knowledge differently, by using "delete string" as the fundamental command. Version (b) shows that TAG can represent this version equally easily. Our suggestion is that this version should be easier to learn, since fewer simple task rules are required.

List of features   Possible Values

Size   character, word, string

TAG definition

Dictionary of simple tasks

delete word   {Size = word}
delete character   {Size = character}
delete string   {Size = string}

(A) Rule Schemas, Version 1: string deletion treated as a special case

Task [Size = character OR word] → mark-first-point + indicate +
              "ENTER"
Task [Size = string] → mark-first-point + mark-last-point +
              "ENTER"
mark-first-point → locate-cursor-at-start + "DEL"
mark-last-point → locate-cursor || type (last character of string)
indicate [Size = character] → (empty)
indicate [Size = word] → "SPACE"

(B) Rule Schemas, Version 2: all forms of deletion treated uniformly

Task [Size = ANY] → mark-first-point + mark-last-point +
              "ENTER"
mark-first-point → locate-cursor-at-start + "DEL"
mark-last-point → locate-cursor || type (last character of string)

Figure 5.   TAG description of selected operations on IBM Display-
             writer. Two versions are shown, corresponding to the
             two possibilities described in the text and identified by
             Kieras and Polson (1985). Version 1 treats string deletion
             as a special case; version 2 makes string deletion the fun-
             damental operation. Compare with Figure 2 (which only
             describes word and character deletion).

4.5 Towards a Life Size TAG Application

Using the notation developed in the previous sections we shall now use
TAG to describe a fragment of the interface of a genuine commercial application program, the Multiplan spreadsheet produced by MicroSoft for the
Apple Macintosh. Spreadsheets breathe intelligence into arithmetic. The
user sees a piece of 'squared paper' on which sums may be performed.
Each cell has coordinate references, absolute or relative (and it can also be
given its own name, if desired). Inside each cell one may put (a) a number,
(b) a string of text, or (c) a formula deriving a number from other cells
whose value is a number or another formula. The effect might be this:

apples	60
pears	25
melons	140
TOTAL	225

The words are text strings and play no part in the arithmetic computations. The numbers entered beside the fruits are pure numbers, we can suppose; but the "total" cell contains a formula, something on the lines of $A[1]+A[2]+A[3]$. The intelligent part is that when the price of a fruit changes, the user can change the appropriate cell, and the value of the total changes automatically. For large linked computations the spreadsheet is invaluable.

On the Macintosh, it is customary to use the mouse to point to locations whenever possible. Multiplan is no exception. To enter a number, a word, or a formula, the user points to the desired location, indicates, and types. Changing and removing entries is similar. Multiplan also permits a variety of commands, which are rather different in that they systematically change the indicated entries, for instance by right justifying them or by copying one column to another column.

The appendix shows an analysis of the tasks of adding and removing material from the spreadsheet. The semantics are straightforward: to add material, users can write an entry into an empty cell (simple task 1 in the dictionary), insert additional material into a cell (3), insert cells taken from somewhere else in the spreadsheet (8), or insert new rows or columns (9). In some of these cases, the clipboard can or must be used as a temporary storage buffer, from which material can be fetched to be added to the spreadsheet. Similar possibilities exist for removing the material. The user can delete parts of a cell-entry (5), erase cell-ranges (6), or not just erase the entries but delete the cells themselves (7). A third set of tasks that replaces material shows up in simple task (2) which over-writes a whole cell-entry, and in simple task (4) which overwrites parts of a cell-entry.

The dictionary of simple tasks describes these possibilities in terms of semantic components, based on the five features listed. The task-level rules show the breakdown of simple tasks into sub-tasks (each of which builds on sub-task rules) and primitives. The sub-task rules prescribe the expansion of sub-tasks into primitives.

Creating the sub-task rules presents a few problems, in that it is not always apparent what will give the simplest overall representation. In Multiplan, it turns out that some of the tasks require two selection operations, while others only require one. Since all the tasks requiring two selection operations involve some local changes to a cell-entry we have introduced the "edit-entry" sub-task which performs one of these selections. Other solutions are possible.

The first two task rules each capture several simple tasks, whose action sequences bear a family resemblance close enough to be expressible in the TAG meta-language. The first rule covers the tasks of writing an entry into an empty cell, and of over-writing an already existing cell-entry, while the second one accounts for several types of editing a cell-entry. (It is arguable that these two task rules could be perceived as a family group, since both can be regarded as editing tasks, both require the selection of a single cell, and both are closed by "RETURN". Their similarities are not expressed in the TAG representation by a common task rule, however.)

The next three rules cover the tasks of erasing cell-entries, deleting cells, and inserting cells; each of these rules again captures several tasks which may vary according to the number and type of units involved (cells, rows, or columns).

The last rule, which accounts for the tasks of inserting any number of new rows or columns into the spreadsheet, sticks out as an oddity, with little resemblance to the other rules in this system or the task rules found in other Macintosh applications we have analysed. The model predicts that users versed in other Macintosh applications, such as the text editor MacWrite, would find that while the other rules could easily be guessed, this rule would need to be explained. We believe, from personal experience, that this prediction is correct.

In the second task rule, and also in the fifth task rule, the value of the features "Unit" and "Extent" of the "select" sub-task are temporarily changed (indicated by the ← operator). This deviation from a uniform replacement of feature-values throughout a rule was introduced to allow for a compact representation.

The task rules involve only three types of feature-defined sub-tasks which themselves have to be rewritten according to sub-task rules: the "select" sub-task and the "edit-entry" sub-task, and the "edit" sub-task. There are two rules for expanding the "select" sub-task. There are another two rules for rewriting "edit-entry", one of which describes the structure of insert operations while the other one describes the structure of remove and replace operations. Finally, there are five rules for rewriting the "edit" sub-task. Two of those represent operations applicable to characters only, another two, which involve the clipboard, apply to both characters and cells, while the last one is restricted to cells.

4.6 TAG as a Psychological Theory of Consistency

We have already remarked on the fundamental TAG claim that humans can perceive and utilise just those types of consistency that TAG can model. In the Multiplan example it is fairly successful, although not completely successful, in modelling the resemblances according to the authors' intuitions. Payne (1985) reports a number of laboratory studies in support of the fundamental claim, some of which are briefly described by Payne and Green (1986).

The Multiplan example only displays one type of consistency; there are, as Payne and Green point out, several other types. The older generation of interactive applications programs often relied heavily on simple mnemonics, using say the first letter of a descriptive term. Our EMACS example, Figure 4, illustrates the use of C and W as mnemonics for "character" and "word". Here we have a second type of consistency, since all the rules in that example use mnemonics of the same type. Payne and Green show that TAG can successfully model this type of consistency as well as the type seen in the Multiplan example (and BNF, of course, cannot model either type).

It must be stressed that several slightly different TAG representations of the same structure are possible. This is as it should be; if a TAG representation is intended to capture the generalisations of the user, then it should be able to capture different representations by different users. Ideally it should be possible to present a metric of "simplicity" or "compactness", with the suggestion that the most experienced users might have the most compact representations. On the other hand, we are disturbed that certain family resemblances have not been easy to capture in the Multiplan example, e.g. the similarity between the tasks of over-writing a cell-entry and of over-writing parts of a cell-entry; possibly a richer structure of semantic features and their values could cope with such phenomena, yielding further generalisations within our formalism, or possibly a more powerful formalism is needed.

A point worth emphasising is what this model does *not* exhibit. It does not exhibit the relationship between actions and system display; as far as the TAG model is concerned, the VDU screen could have been turned off. Nor does it exhibit the conceptual model. The typical Macintosh clipboard, used by Tauber (this volume, Chapter 3) as an example of the hidden conceptual model, is present in Multiplan, and the TAG shows by its feature-system which actions affect the state of the clipboard; but it does not reveal what the user's conceptual model of it might be.

4.7 TAG Descriptions as Executable Specifications

The feature grammars used in TAG descriptions correspond very closely to the "metamorphosis" or "definite clause" grammars which are easily interpreted as Prolog programs (Pereira and Warren, 1980). It is therefore possible to produce an executable version of a TAG description with minimal change to the formalism, and Green (1986) reports a general-purpose interpreter for "Prologized" TAG descriptions.

Where the correctness of a TAG description can be established by inspection, executing it adds little or nothing save confidence. Larger systems are likely to need better methods of verification than eyeball inspection, and executability is one option.

Ultimately, it may be possible also to use executable versions of models as predictors of trouble spots where slips and mistakes frequently occur, but this possibility has not yet been investigated with the TAG interpreter.

4.8 Planning and Executing Actions

The shape of a competence model constrains the implied performance model. To investigate what happens with TAG models, we considered how the user might go about planning a sequence of actions in order to accomplish a small task. We chose to work in the tradition of "planning" as formulated within artificial intelligence, starting with Newell and Simon's (1972) 'General Problem Solver' and continuing through various planning mechanisms for simulated or actual robot worlds (see Charniak and McDermott, 1985, for a review). In this tradition it is necessary to define the present state of the world, usually by a list of true propositions or "facts", and to specify the effects of each action on the world by means of a list defining the facts to be added and the facts to be deleted. Thus, if the cursor is at line N, the action "move cursor down 1 line" *deletes* the fact that the cursor is at line N and *adds* the fact that the cursor is at line N + 1. It is also necessary to state the *preconditions* for each action; in this case, the precondition is "cursor not at bottom line".

We shall not describe this work in detail here, but only list some main conclusions.

Naturally, we have assumed that the planner generates a sequence of simple tasks, which are then translated via the task-action grammar into corresponding actions. The role of the grammatical component is to reduce the clutter of detail that has to be handled by the planning component; instead of having to recall that "cursor up" is such and such and "cursor down" is something else, it can handle generalised cursor motion commands. Each *simple* task in the grammar is therefore equipped with an effects list to specify preconditions, additions, and deletions.

Normally users are in the happy position of knowing what they're doing, and it can be assumed that they possess considerable domain-specific knowledge describing the structure of their application domain - text document, spreadsheet, or whatever. It is in this area that we would place the knowledge of the structure of a shopping bill as shown in the spreadsheet example, i.e.,

Total cost = SUM [Unit-price(i) × No-of-units(i)],
i ranging over each item on the list.

The planning component therefore has the task of expressing the formula above in terms of the actions available to it. Our explorations in this area have in fact been guided so far by a graphics program, MacDraw (also for the Macintosh), rather than by the spreadsheet domain, and a typical piece of domain knowledge is that a square window might be represented as four filled squares arranged in a block. A simple planner has been written capable of generating task sequences for such goals as

"Create 4 squares, all filled with pattern A."

(The goals are not expressed in English, of course, but in a suitable formalism, in this case Prolog.)

Although we have not introduced "meta-planning" in our explorations we perceive a strong case for it. Wilensky (1983) uses this term to refer to the adjustment of plans in the light of known facts about them: a plan may be adjusted because its execution will exceed working memory limitations, for instance, or because it will be difficult to perform correctly. The latter appears to be a particular case in real life with MacDraw, where users seemingly prefer to work by "trial and correction" - draw a first attempt at a figure and then adjust it, this being one of the features supported by Mac-Draw in most circumstances. There are some figures that are hard to adjust using MacDraw, such as freehand lines. In those cases, informal observation suggests users prefer to find an alternative solution, such as drawing a polygon (which is more easily reshaped than a freehand line) and then smoothing it.

We have found it helpful to assume that the "actions" of which we have been speaking are in fact action *specifications*. These specifications, generated by the task-action grammar, are passed to an execution component which performs the actions. By this means we can also allow the planner to introduce elements of control into the plan: "Move object 1 UNTIL it touches object 2".

The idea of passing a "motor program" over to an execution component, incorporating some elements of control information among the names of actions, is not new. It has been used by Norman and Rumelhart (1981) to explain certain characteristics of typing errors, such as doubling the wrong letter ("bokk" for "book"), which suggest that the motor program is written in a code containing letter names and DOUBLE commands; doubling errors arise when the DOUBLE command has got attached to the wrong letter. However, we have not previously seen this concept extended to the planning level. We suggest that the planner is able to produce "programs" instructing the execution component to perform a sequence of actions until a simple condition is satisfied. A formalism to represent the supposed ability would be similar to a simple programming language in which no data storage was available, so that all truth-value tests would have to be tests of the current state of the world.

The rational planner will, of course, produce as short a "program" as possible, breaking the activity into bursts. Exactly such behaviour was noted by Robertson and Black (1983). Users can also take advantage of prompts from the interface to remind them to do things, rather than remembering that they have to do them. The planning structure that we have used, built round a very simple architecture, is not capable of doing that, but the "opportunistic" planner of Hayes-Roth and Hayes-Roth (1979) using a blackboard model of communication is capable, we believe.

4.9 Performance Metrics over Grammars

In Reisner's work on Robart described above, it was made an assumption that grammars with more rules were harder to learn. This is an example of a performance metric defined over a class of grammars. Another assumption which has frequently been discussed states that the more grammar rules have to be invoked to derive a particular sentence from the grammar, the harder that sentence will be - either to create, or to comprehend. This latter assumption, known as the "derivational" theory of sentence complexity, has been the bone of a certain amount of linguistic contention.

Task-action grammars can be treated in similar ways. The power of a TAG description being somewhat but not enormously greater than that of a production system description in the style of Kieras and Polson, many of the measures that they successfully used are also applicable to TAG. Important measures in their work included the number of productions fired for each unit task, which is claimed to predict the performance time; the depth of the goal stack, which is claimed to predict the working memory load; and the number of new productions that had to be learnt for each new task that was learnt, which naturally predicts the time to learn how to perform the task. These each have an analogue in the TAG description. The number of productions fired is equivalent to the number of rules used in generating the action. The depth of the goal stack is exactly equivalent between the production system and TAG.

Kieras and Polson's next measure, the number of new productions to be learnt, is trickier to duplicate in TAG, essentially because TAG makes more subtle differentiations; in particular, because TAG differentiates between simple task rules and others. We do not at present have sufficient evidence on this point but we are inclined to believe that although each would be predictive the count of simple task rules would usually be the better predictor of learning time; where many simple task rules are needed (given the same set of semantic components) the interface would, presumably, fail to supply usable generalisations to help the learner.

However, the density of the features, considered as semantic descriptors, must also be considered; a dense field will be harder to grasp, since it either makes finer distinctions or else describes a more complex task domain than a less dense field. Potentially, then, we have a more delicate set of predictors than with other models, but as yet they have not been well validated.

Kieras and Polson use the number of items in working memory as a measure of mental load. The interpretation of working memory measures in a production system is not straightforward. Working memory load measures depth of rule invocation, since one rule "calls" another by depositing an element in working memory, to be recognised by the second rule; degree of conditionality, since alternative cases are separated by working memory elements; and degree of inter-communication between rules, since this has to be performed by working memory elements. TAG, being a grammatical structure, uses separate mechanisms for these. Considerable research on the psychological interpretation of production system measures is needed before parallels can be seriously discussed.

Kieras and Polson also discuss methods to examine the "fit" between the device and the user's conceptual model of it, using the "Generalised Transition Network". We are not entirely happy with their methods, but the idea is promising. TAG representations lend themselves to a similar analysis but it has not been explored here.

Potentially useful measures, then, comprise:

- — Number of rules used per task (predicts performance time).
- — Depth of goal stack (predicts working memory load).
- — Number of task-level rules and sub-task rules (predicts learning time).
- — Number of rules common to two or more tasks (predicts transfer of learning).
- — Number of semantic features (predicts learning time).
- — Number of overlapping sequences (predicts capture errors).
- — Number of repeated or highly similar terminals (predicts response confusions).

One need hardly add that most of these need far more verification and experience in use before they can be regarded as trustworthy predictions.

4.10 How successful is TAG?

Within its intentions, of describing users' knowledge and in particular accounting for consistency effects, TAG has been more successful than its predecessors. It is compact; it gives insight into the task language; it is adequate for substantial fragments of real applications; it is individualisable for particular views of a device; and it is executable.

The formalism substantially corresponds with intuition and with empirical testing in the classes of consistency and resemblance that it expresses. However, there are still some cases of disagreement with intuition, one of which was illustrated above as part of the Multiplan example.

Limitations were deliberately accepted when TAG was devised by Payne (1985). TAG is severely limited in its description of the device, since it includes neither the external semantics nor the characteristics of the dialogue, such as the prompts and feedback given by the device.

TAG is similarly limited in its description of the user's psychology, since it does not describe the internal representation of "action programs" nor the differing properties of differing internal "storage codes", such as visual and auditory codes, and their effects on cognitive processing. Nor is there any treatment of how task-action grammars are learnt, nor of the characteristics of expertise. It has not yet been properly tied to a model of planning, but developments here look promising.

These limitations, however, should not be seen as failures to achieve its aim, but as the inevitable result of a strategy of attacking one major aspect of user knowledge at a time. We see no reason why a future generation of formalisable models should not supersede TAG by incorporating it inside a larger model which accounts for more phenomena.

5 CONCLUSIONS

5.1 The State of Formalisable Models

We believe that the models described above demonstrate that developing formalisable models is a fruitful strategy in this area, although it is clearly not the only one. We shall summarise our conclusions concerning those models, in order to clarify the requirements for a new model that will advance our thinking in new ways.

1. Low level models such as the Keystroke Level Model are clearly unable to predict conceptual difficulties.

2. Process models attempt to model "how-the-user-works" as well as "what-the-user-knows". This makes them too large and clumsy to be easily used.

3. Since these two types of modelling are mingled, we cannot know how a given detail in a performance model should be construed. The performance model of user psychology is supposed to be universal, constant across all applications, while the model of the user's knowledge about a particular system obviously differs from one application to the next. But if we cannot tell whether a given detail should be construed as part of the model of user psychology or as part of the application-specific model of user's knowledge, how can we tell whether the model of user psychology really is constant, or whether theorists have perhaps unwittingly extended their model to deal with particular difficulties?

4. What is needed, therefore, is a clear separation between the knowledge component and the performance component. Task-Action Grammar presents that separation as respectively a grammar, for the knowledge component, and a planning and execution mechanism, for the performance component (although the latter needs much more exploration). No doubt other methods are possible, and should be developed.

5. When the knowledge component of the process models we have described is singled out, it appears to be a context-free phrase structure grammar equivalent in power to BNF. The style rules and the metrics of goal depth, number of productions, etc. proposed by Kieras and Polson can be interpreted as complexity functions defined over BNF grammars.

6. BNF-equivalent models cannot explain the distributional and configural phenomena vividly expounded by Ichbaiah and empirically demonstrated by Green and Payne. A two-level representation, such as the Set Grammar, captures the syntactic aspects but not the semantic ones.

7. However, the process models do describe the task structure as perceived by the user, which is not modelled by Set Grammar. Task-Action Grammar applies grammatical machinery to the internally-perceived structure of tasks and the simple intensional semantics of features to the internally-perceived relationships between tasks.

8. Although TAG has received some measure of empirical support, it has proved necessary to make several simplifying assumptions. For instance, we initially derived predictions based on the number of rules by assuming that each rule contributes equally to the total psychological complexity. Empirical tests suggest that the number of distinct task rules is a greater factor than the number of subtask rules, but how much greater? Such questions of detail should not be investigated too closely, we suggest, until the

main framework of a formalism is very well accepted; otherwise we run the risks mentioned in our opening paragraph, of spending more effort in squeezing difficult material into shape than rethinking the system. But the existence of such questions should be noted.

9. We noted in the previous section a number of TAG's limitations. Despite these limitations, TAG's piecemeal attack on the problem, making no attempt to tackle all of user psychology in one swoop, has been profitable. It may well be that this strategy is one to adopt in the next generation of models.

5.2 Formalisable Models as Applicable Tools

It can be seen that we are optimistic concerning the future development and progress of theoretical models in this area. What is less clear is when such models will be ready to be used as tools by designers of new systems and evaluators of existing systems.

Most of the models described here appear to have been intended as applied tools, and not just as potential tools but as tools ready for immediate actual use. The Keystroke-Level Model and GOMS are presented in the context of Card, Moran and Newell's vignette of a designer swiftly calculating which of two designs will lead to better performance, which to better learning, and what the overall costs will be (1983, pp. 9-10). Kieras and Polson have put substantial effort into making their system accessible to designers and evaluators, while Reisner explictly redesigned a graphics system around her analysis. We are apparently alone in hesitating to present the models with which we have been associated, the Set Grammar and TAG models, in these terms.

Part of the reason for our hesitation and others' boldness is that the limitations of the models we have created are more clearly apparent. But there is more to it than that. It would still be premature, we believe, to claim that formalisable models are ready to contribute directly to the design process in the simple, directly evaluative terms that have been proposed. (Of course, even the present generation may contribute indirectly, by raising designers' consciousness of some important issues, but that is another story.) Our understanding of what has been achieved, and what still needs to be achieved, has been considerably advanced by our work on these models, and we shall close this chapter with a list of some of the criteria that must be met by directly-applicable formalisable models. As psychologists rather than designers this list must necessarily be tentative, but we suspect that, if anything, it is too short rather than too long.

1. The model must describe a reasonably complete psychology. (Cf. our strictures on TAG's incompleteness, above.) No major phenomena, such as the effects of consistency, must be missing from the model. This requirement has not been met by any available model. Even at the low level of typing errors, the patterns of errors recorded by Grudin (1983) cannot be predicted by existing models, because they have no representation of "action programs". Other major phenomena, such as the well-documented vagaries of working memory, are equally absent. Card et al. (1983) maintain stoutly that a successful model need only be an approximation to the truth. We agree - but existing models are not even that.

2. The model must separate the representation of the human from the representation of the design being created. At present, this has been achieved by abandoning the claim to create a performance model, but it must surely be possible to construct a modularised performance model.

3. The model must contain a representation of the external semantics, probably tied in to modern techniques for knowledge representation developed within cognitive science or to developments in the field of conceptual modelling. (See Tauber, in this volume.) At present the models available are seriously deficient.

4. The model must be usable: it must be compact, free of horrendous concepts, and appealing to the designer. Progress is being made in this direction, but there is probably room for improvement. On the other hand, designers may also need to be educated in some of the important human criteria.

5. The model must be executable, or verifiable in some other way. Descriptions of real systems rapidly become too large to be certain that they are self-consistent and correct by mere inspection. This criterion appears to be met, at least in principle, by all the models described here.

6. The model must be metricated or costed in some way; it must yield a definite evaluation. However, a "total" evaluation may not be necessary. It may be enough if the designer receives guidance over some of the human aspects - preferably the more elusive ones. The evaluations produced from

the model must receive empirical support from laboratory studies of small systems. But the model must also have been applied to several real situations, and its evaluations must have received empirical confirmation (or perhaps agree with folk wisdom). Existing models give the impression that they have abundant support, but we are sceptical about their ability to stand up to being widely used in many different situations.

Programmers are notorious for admitting candidly that their current version does not quite work, while promising wonders for the next version. We have a certain disinclination to promise that the next generation of formalisable models of user knowledge will lead to usable tools for solving designers' human factors problems. But rapid progress is clearly being made, and we are certainly hopeful.

REFERENCES

Anderson, J.R. (1982). Acquisition of cognitive skill. *Psychological Review*, 89, pp. 369-406.

Card, S.K., Moran, T.P. and Newell, A. (1983). The Psychology of Human- Computer Interaction. Hillsdale, N.J.: Erlbaum.

Carroll, J.M. and Mack, R.L. (1985). Metaphor, computing systems, and active learning. *International Journal of Man-Machine Studies*, 22 (1), pp. 39-57.

Carroll, J.M. and Thomas, J.C. (1980). Metaphor and the cognitive representation of computing systems. *Research Report RC 8303*, New York, IBM Watson Research Center.

Charniak, E. and MacDermott, D. (1985). Introduction to Artificial Intelligence. Reading, Mass.: Addison-Wesley.

Chi, U.L. (1985). Formal specification of user interfaces: a comparison and evaluation of four axiomatic approaches. *IEEE Transactions on Software Engineering*, SE-11 (8), pp. 671-685.

Gazdar, G., Klein, E., Pullum, G. and Sag, I. (1985). Generalized Phrase Structure Grammar. Oxford: Blackwell.

Green, T.R.G. (1980). Programming as a cognitive activity. *In: Human Interaction with Computers*. H.T. Smith and T.R.G. Green (eds.). London: Academic Press.

Green, T.R.G.(1986). 'Chopper', an executor for Task-Action Grammars. Unpublished MS. Cambridge, MRC Applied Psychology Unit.

Green, T.R.G. and Payne, S.J. (1984). Organization and learnability in computer languages. *Int. Journal of Man-Machine Studies*, 21 (1), pp. 7-18.

Grudin, J.T. (1983). Error patterns in skilled and novice transcription typing. *In: Cognitive Aspects of Skilled Typing*. W.C. Cooper (ed.). New York: Springer Verlag.

Harel, D. (in press). Statecharts: a visual approach to complex systems. Report CS86-02, Dept. of Applied Mathematics. Rehovot, Israel: Weizmann Institute.

Hayes-Roth, B. and Hayes-Roth, F. (1979). A cognitive model of planning. *Cognitive Science*, 3 (4), pp. 275-310.

Ichbaiah, J. and Anon. (1984). Ada: past, present, and future - an interview with Jean Ichbaiah. *Communications of the ACM*, 27, pp. 990-997.

Kieras, D.E. and Bovair, S. (1983). The role of a mental model in learning to operate a device. *Technical Report No. 12*, University of Arizona.

Kieras, D.E. and Polson, P. (1985). An approach to the formal analysis of user complexity. *Int. J. Man-Machine Studies*, 22 (4), pp. 365-394.

Moran, T. (1983). Getting into a system: external-internal task mapping analysis. *Proc. 'CHI 83' ACM Conf. on Human Factors in Computing Systems*, 45-49. New York: ACM.

Newell, A. and Simon, H.A. (1972). Human Problem Solving. Englewood Cliffs, N.J.: Prentice-Hall.

Norman, D.A. and Rumelhart, D.E. (1981). The LNR approach to human information processing. *Cognition*, 10, pp. 235-240.

Pagan, F.G. (1981). Formal Specification of Programming Languages: a Panoramic Primer. Englewood Cliffs, N.J.: Prentice-Hall.

Payne, S.J. (1984). Task-action grammars. *In: Human-Computer Interaction: INTERACT '84*. B. Shackel (ed.). Amsterdam: Elsevier.

Payne, S.J. (1985). Task action grammars: the mental representation of task languages in human computer interaction. Unpublished PhD thesis, University of Sheffield.

Payne, S.J. and Green, T.R.G. (1983). The user's perception of the interaction language: a two-level model. *Proc. 'CHI 83' ACM Conf. on Human Factors in Computing Systems*. New York: ACM, pp. 202-206.

Payne, S.J. and Green, T.R.G. (1986). Task action grammars: a model of the mental representation of task languages. *Human Computer Interaction* 2, pp. 93-133.

Pereira, F.C.N. and Warren, D.H.D. (1980). Definite clause grammars for language analysis - a survey of the formalism and a comparison with augmented transition networks. *Artificial Intelligence*, 13 (3), pp. 231-278.

Polson, P. and Kieras, D.E. (1985). A quantitative model of the learning and performance of text editing. *Proceedings "CHI-85" ACM Conf. on Computer-Human Interaction.* New York: ACM.

Reisner, P. (1977). Use of psychological experimentation as an aid to development of a query language. *IEEE Trans. Software Engineering*, SE-3, pp. 218-229.

Reisner, P. (1981). Formal grammar and human factors design of an interactive graphics system. *IEEE Trans. Software Engineering*, SE-7 (2), pp. 229-240.

Reisner, P. (1984). Formal grammar as a tool for analyzing ease of use: Some fundamental concepts. *In: Human Factors in Computer Systems.* J. Thomas and M. Schneider (eds.). Norwood, N.H.: Ablex.

Robertson, S.P. and Black, J.B. (1983). Planning units in text-editing. *Proc. "CHI-83" ACM Conf. on Human Factors in Computing Systems*, New York: ACM, pp. 217-221.

Rosenberg, J. (1983). Featural approach to command names. *Proc. "CHI-83" ACM Conf. on Human Factors in Computing Systems.* New York: ACM, pp. 116-119.

Tversky, A. (1977). Features of similarity. *Psychological Review*, 69, pp. 344-354.

van Wijngaarden, A. (1966). Recursive definitions of syntax and semantics. *In: Formal Description Languages for Computer Programming*, Steel, T.B. (ed.). Amsterdam: North-Holland.

Wilensky, R. (1983). Planning and Understanding. Reading, Mass.: Addison-Wesley.

APPENDIX: TAG description of Multiplan

LIST OF FEATURES   POSSIBLE VALUES

Unit	character cell row $\Big\}$ NOTchar column
Extent	number of Units involved in action
Layout-changed	yes (if cells are removed or added) or no
Effect	adds, replaces, or removes
Clipboard	yes (if clipboard is accessed) or no

DICTIONARY OF SIMPLE TASKS IN MULTIPLAN

1) write an entry   ::   Unit = cell, Extent = 1,
                                 Layout-changed = no, Effect = adds,
                                 Clipboard = no

2) over-write an entry   ::   Unit = cell, Extent = 1,
                                 Layout-changed = no, Effect = replaces,
                                 Clipboard = no

3) insert   ::   Unit = character, Extent = any,
    into an entry   Layout-changed = no, Effect = adds,
                                 Clipboard = no

4) over-write   ::   Unit = character, Extent = any,
    part of an entry   Layout-changed = no, Effect = replaces,
                                 Clipboard = no

5) delete   ::   Unit = character, Extent = any,
    part of an entry   Layout-changed = no, Effect = removes,
                                 Clipboard = no

6) erase cell-entries   ::   Unit = NOTchar, Extent = any,
                                 Layout-changed = no, Effect = removes,
                                 Clipboard = no

7) delete cells   ::   Unit = NOTchar, Extent = any,
                                 Layout-changed = yes, Effect = removes,
                                 Clipboard = yes

8) replace cells   ::   Unit = NOTchar, Extent = any,
                                 Layout-changed = yes, Effect = replaces,
                                 Clipboard = yes

9) insert cells   ::   Unit = NOTchar, Extent = any,
                                 Layout-changed = yes, Effect = adds,
                                 Clipboard = yes

10) insert a blank row   ::   Unit = row, Extent = 1,
                                 Layout-changed = yes, Effect = adds,
                                 Clipboard = no

RULE SCHEMAS IN MULTIPLAN

A) Task-level Rules

(1,2) 'write an entry', 'over-write an entry'

Task [Unit = cell, Extent = 1, Layout-changed = no,
Effect = adds/replaces, Clipboard = no] : =

select [Unit = cell, Extent = 1] + TYPE (?) + "RETURN"

(3,4,5) 'insert, over-write, delete part of entry'

Task [Unit = character, Extent = any, Layout-changed = no,
Effect = any, Clipboard = any] : =

select [Unit < - cell, Extent < - 1] +
edit-entry [Unit = char, Effect, Clipboard] + "RETURN"

(6) 'erase cell-entries'

Task [Unit = NOTchar, Extent = any, Layout-changed = no,
Effect = removes, Clipboard = no] : =

select [Unit = NOTchar, Extent = any] +
edit [Unit = NOTchar, Effect = removes, Clipboard = no]

(7,8) 'delete cells', 'replace cells'

Task [Unit = NOTchar, Extent = any, Layout-changed = yes,
Effect = removes/replaces, Clipboard = yes] : =

select [Unit = NOTchar, Extent = any] +
edit [Unit = NOTchar, Effect = removes/replaces, Clipboard = yes]
+ CONFIRMATION

(9) 'insert cells'

Task [Unit = NOTchar, Extent = any, Layout-changed = yes,
Effect = adds, Clipboard = yes] : =

MOUSE-POINT (?location) + MOUSE-CLICK +
edit [Unit = NOTchar, Effect = adds, Clipboard = yes] +
CONFIRMATION

(10) 'insert a blank row'

Task [Unit = row/column, Extent = any, Layout-changed = yes,
Effect = adds, Clipboard = no] : =

"SHIFT" + select [Unit = row/column, Extent = any]

B) Sub-task Rules (these occur also in many other Macintosh application programs)

select [Unit = NOTchar, Extent = 1] : = MOUSE-POINT (?unit)
+ MOUSE-CLICK

select [Unit = any, Extent = any] : = MOUSE-POINT (?unit)
+ MOUSE-DRAG (?unit)

edit-entry [Unit = char, Effect = adds, Clipboard = any] : =
MOUSE-POINT (?location) + MOUSE-CLICK +
edit [Unit = char, Effect = adds, Clipboard]

edit-entry [Unit = char, Effect = removes/replaces, Clipboard = any] : =
select [Unit = char, Extent = any]   +
edit [Unit = char, Effect = removes/replaces, Clipboard]

edit [Unit = char, Effect = adds/replaces, Clipboard = no] : = TYPE (?)

edit [Unit = char, Effect = removes, Clipboard = no]   : = "BKSP"

edit [Unit = any, Effect = adds/replaces, Clipboard = yes] : =
MENU (Edit-Paste) | "CTRL-V"

edit [Unit = any, Effect = removes, Clipboard = yes] : =
MENU (Edit-Cut) | "CTRL-X"

edit [Unit = NOTchar, Effect = removes, Clipboard = no] : =
MENU (Edit-Clear) | "CTRL-B"

C) Primitives

TYPE (?): perform typing as stored by the planning component (see 4.8)

"RETURN", "SHIFT", "CTRL-B", etc.: press appropriate keys

MOUSE-POINT (?): use the mouse to point to appropriate unit or location

MOUSE-CLICK: click mouse-button

MOUSE-DRAG (?): drag the mouse pointer across the required extent of units

CONFIRMATION: point to dialogue-button on display and click mouse-button

MENU (?): point to item on menu bar and drag to item on pulldown menu

Notation:

Task [...] Start symbol (LHS of task-level rules)
xyz [...]   Non-terminal symbol (LHS of sub-task rules)
XYZ   Primitive (action specification)
XYZ (?)   Primitive with argument
| Alternative primitives (functionally equivalent)
/   'or' (disjunction of feature-values)

KNOWLEDGE-BASED TASK ANALYSIS FOR HUMAN-COMPUTER SYSTEMS

Michael D. WILSON, Philip J. BARNARD,
Thomas R.G. GREEN* and Allan MACLEAN***

Informatics Division, Rutherford Appleton Laboratory
Didcot, Oxon OX11 0QX, U.K.

*MRC Applied Psychology Unit
Cambridge CB2 2EF, U.K.

**Xerox EuroParc, Ravenscroft House
Cambridge, U.K.

1 INTRODUCTION

The analysis of tasks is a fundamental and important process in many areas of applied behavioural science. Task analysis offers methods for exploring relationships between the properties of systems and user performance. Traditionally (e.g. see Miller, 1962), the analyst takes descriptions of the cues that should be perceived and the actions that should be performed, and maps these onto behavioural units; but working with computers presents novel problems. It is the user's conceptual skills, not the perceptual motor skills of a previous generation of technology, that must now be automated. Successful task execution now depends critically on the user's knowledge of the system, its properties, capabilities, and requirements. Units of behaviour can no longer usefully be viewed in isolation.

We shall review recent progress towards incorporating knowledge requirements into task analysis, comparing eleven forms of task analysis. All have been developed with the aim of describing knowledge intensive tasks in HCI; but naturally enough, different techniques address different aspects in differing degrees of detail, and some techniques have been more fully developed than others. The major characteristics we shall stress are the following.

1.1 Types of Knowledge Represented

As Morton et al. (1979) point out in their Block Interaction Model, many different types ('blocks') of knowledge influence the user's representation of a current problem or task. One major division separates the knowledge

47

held by the ideal user from non-ideal knowledge, such as distorted or inaccurate versions of the ideal knowledge, or input from other sources such as analogy with other systems or inferences from natural language.

1.2 User Centered Task Dynamics

We shall distinguish between analysis methods that explicitly describe the user's goals - and possibly the higher level intentions as well - and more global methods which evaluate the knowledge required to account for the user's actions without specifying any particular steps, or which concentrate on comparing the overall structure of differing methods to accomplish tasks without descending to detail.

We shall also note attempts to describe *short term* transitions in user's mental representations, such as which machine mode the user believes is currently in force; and *long term* transitions, including learning and associated changes in representations.

1.3 Cognitive Limitations on Processing

Analyses can either present functional descriptions of processing and knowledge representation, or can go further and specify limitations of the human information processing mechanism, such as constraints on memory capacities or limitations on perception, or parameters for process times.

1.4 Use of the Technique

Each section will describe how easy it is to employ an analysis technique; what knowledge the analyst would have acquire to use the technique, and what limits and cautions the analyst should be aware of when using a technique.

The eleven techniques that we shall review can be grouped under four headings, as follows:

—   Analyses of knowledge content in real world tasks. This group contains: Task Strategies approach (Miller, 1974); Task Analysis for Knowledge Descriptions (Johnson et al., 1984); Command Language Grammar (Moran, 1981).

—   Analyses designed to predict difficulties from interface specifica-
      tions, comprising External-Internal Task Mapping Analysis
      (Moran, 1983); Task Action Grammar (Payne and Green, 1986);
      The GOMS family of models (Card et al., 1983); The User-
      Device model (Kieras and Polson, 1985).

—   Analyses of users' conceptual structures: Task Analysis for Infor-
      mation Structure Description (Wilson et al., 1985); and Analysis
      of Menu Systems (Young and Hull, 1983).

—   Analyses of cognitive activities: Decomposition of mental activity
      (Norman, 1986); and Cognitive Task Analysis (Barnard, 1987).

In order to focus upon their broader properties, the descriptions of individual approaches will necessarily be brief. Likewise, several prominent analyses have not been included for lack of space (e.g. Reisner, 1981; Duncan, 1974; Bullen and Bennett, 1983; Sasso, 1985; Rasmussen, 1986). To
avoid overlap, we have also abbreviated the descriptions of Task-Action
Grammar, the GOMS family, and the User-Device model, since these are
described at length in the chapter by Green, Schiele and Payne in this
volume, and have confined ourselves to discussing the four characteristics
listed above.

2 ANALYSES OF KNOWLEDGE CONTENT IN REAL WORLD TASKS

2.1 The Task Strategies Approach

Miller (1974) created a descriptive and analytic terminology to represent
the generalised information processing functions of a highly skilled operator. The technique was developed prior to many recent developments in
HCI, but it is a useful point of departure because it was an early attempt to
bring cognitive factors into task analysis. In this approach, there is no
specific representation of knowledge or of cognitive resources.

For the purpose of analysis "a task consists of a series of goal-directed transactions controlled by one or more 'programs' that guide the operations by
a human operator of a prescribed set of tools through a set of completely or
partially predicted environmental states" (Miller, 1973, p 11). The spirit of
the analysis is captured in an example: "even a piano mover should *scan
and detect* a marble on the stairs, *interpret* its potential significance, and
devise a foot-moving *strategy* that will avoid its untoward possibilities"
(Miller, 1973, p 3). A task is described in terms of 25 task functions which

refer to possible cognitive actions (e.g. detect, transmit plan) or entities (e.g. a "message", a "goal image" or "short term memory buffer"). A complete list is given in Fleishman & Quaintance (1984). The analysis requires four stages:

— describing the task or domain content;

— identifying key aspects of the environment (e.g. goals and stressors);

— identifying what needs to be learned;

— naming the task functions.

Methods are specified for both identifying and teaching work strategies, which can be either behavioural strategies to maximise the efficiency of the operator as a resource, or task strategies to cope more effectively with the uncertainties of the environment.

Miller's approach has been used in a variety of military contexts, from rifle maintenance to the operation of office equipment. Tasks can readily be decomposed into identifiable stages, and it is possible to compare the complexity of different methods for performing a task by counting the task functions required. However, the analysis is not appropriate for describing general models.

2.1.1 Knowledge

The elemental unit of knowledge within this technique is "a message". The knowledge of a person performing a task is not the focus of the task analysis, and consequently it offers little to aid either the segregation of knowledge into any domains or any formalism for the specification of knowledge elements. The first of the four stages of the analysis requires a specification of the task or domain content, but no structure is imposed on this nor is a mechanism offered for deriving it. There is also no distinction in the analysis between an ideal set of knowledge and other knowledge.

2.1.2 User centered task dynamics

The analysis captures most aspects of the user-centered dynamics of a task. Goals are explicitly incorporated into the analysis, and there are several functions which operate on them. Although there is no specific function to account for motivational goals, a twenty-sixth function explicitly for motivation has been suggested (Fleishman and Quaintance, 1984). Since the analysis accounts for the processing of information, it explicitly addresses the short term dynamics of task performance. Long term transitions and user learning are explicitly acknowledged by the possible proceduralisation of functions as sequences are learned and by the inclusion of work strategies to account for highly skilled performance.

2.1.3 Cognitive limitations on processing and use of the technique

There are several attempts in the analysis to provide cognitively salient limitations on processing. The short term memory buffer and a "compute" task function are good examples. However, values are not specified for these limitations.

2.1.4 Use of technique

To use this approach an analyst must follow the four stages described earlier. Tools are not supplied in the approach to support the first three of these stages. Definitions and descriptions are provided which will guide the analyst, but their application is not unambiguous.

The explicit entity that an analyst is given in this technique is the set of 25 functions, and the definitions that permit their use. The specifications of the functions are detailed, but there is no indicated method for the selection of the uniquely appropriate function. This is mostly due to the overlap in the scope of several functions, which results in alternative ways of describing the same task sequence. A consequence of this is that an analyst would have to be psychologically knowledgeable in order to partition information in the world, and to select the appropriate functions based on a separate psychological view of task performance.

In fact, the first stage of the analysis advocated by Miller could well be augmented by the kind of technique outlined in the next section.

2.2 Task Analysis for Knowledge based Descriptions (TAKD)

Task analysis for knowledge based descriptions (Johnson et al., 1984; 1985) aims to make explicit the knowledge requirements for a particular world task. Whereas the task strategies approach represents a task as a series of domain independent functions, here the task is characterised by domain specific knowledge. As with the task strategies approach, TAKD involves four main stages:

— generate a task description;
— identify required knowledge in terms of objects and actions;
— classify these into generic actions and objects;
— express the task in a knowledge representation grammar (KRG).

The authors stress the use of as many sources of information as possible in the first stage of the analysis - structured interviews, direct observations of real and structured tasks, and the analysis of protocols collected during and after completion of a task by trainees, instructors and experienced users.

An initial task description generated after the first step will be a sequential plan of statements. For example, from an analysis of a joiner's order for a staircase as part of the design of a computer based ordering system (from Johnson, 1985), two steps in the task description were: (1) receive order for 15 open-plan, piranha pine staircases of design pattern p1375; and (2) check stock-list to see if supply can be met from stock (answer no).

The subsequent dictionary of identified generic objects and actions would include: CHECK: (inspect, query) SELECT: (identify, choose) TIMBER: (piranha pine; standard pine) DESIGN: (open-plan; closed) FINISH: (varnish, paint) from which valid KRG expressions would be constructed, for example:

SELECT/ a TIMBER/ for a DESIGN/with a FINISH

which could be translated as: "choose a piece of piranha pine, for an open plan design no. p1375, with a polished finish". TAKD has been used to design a syllabus for teaching information technology skills (Johnson et al., 1984) and for the generation of designs for computer programs (Johnson, 1985).

2.2.1 Knowledge

The principal objective of TAKD is to produce a specification of the knowledge required to use a system, or the knowledge that a system would have to include to perform a task. Although the methodology of TAKD will require the initial collection of both ideal and non-ideal knowledge, by the time the final specifications are produced, non-ideal knowledge will have been filtered out by the process of generification, and the KRG creation.

The method of representing knowledge elements in this technique, by action/object associations, is a relatively weak formalism since it does not distinguish between subject and object, direct and indirect objects, or instruments and agents. The power of this method is increased by the use of a knowledge representation grammar, but it is not clear that the grammar used on one occasion would be appropriate on another, any more than the knowledge suitable for one domain would be germane to another.

2.2.2 User centered task dynamics and cognitive limitations on processing

TAKD has no representation of either task dynamics or cognitive limitations.

2.2.3 Use of technique

TAKD has certain weaknesses in identifying so-called generic actions and objects and in combining them into a knowledge representation grammar. For example, from an analysis of general information technology skills (Johnson et al., 1984), 14 generic actions and 22 generic objects were derived that would underlie a syllabus structure. The recombination of these items into the KRG statements is very difficult as they overlap in scope, and their structural relationships are not made explicit by the simple dictionary structure. Consequently, it is not clear whether "type x" should be described as "insert" *with* a "textual input device" (e.g. keyboard) or "insert" *an* "alphanumeric character". If the dictionary structure were enlarged to include relationships between the objects, this confusion would not arise.

For the non-specialist, therefore, TAKD is only likely to be usable when the 'generic' actions and objects are closely related to standard English terms.

2.3 Command Language Grammar (CLG)

The Command Language Grammar was originated by Moran (1978; 1981) as a design tool to "separate out the conceptual model of a system from its command language and to show the relationship between them" (Moran, 1978, p. 5). CLG hierarchically decomposes a system's function into its objects, methods and operations. These are described in a set of definable levels which progressively specify a task in more detail.

The grammar consists of three components, each divided into two levels which are further subdivided. The Task Level describes the user's major intention. Below this are Semantic and Syntactic Levels which focus on the objects and actions the user employs to accomplish the task. The Semantic level contains a conceptual model composed of objects and operations that may be performed on them, and semantic methods for accomplishing the tasks of the previous level. The Syntactic Level describes the command language structure, discriminating between commands, arguments, descriptors and command contexts. At the Interaction Level below this, the dialogue must be mapped onto a sequence of physical actions, e.g. key presses. The lowest two levels are the Spatial Layout Level, where the physical layout of the input/output devices are specified, and the Device Level, where the remaining physical features are defined.

The important feature of CLG is that its several levels of description are designed to correspond to the levels of representation held by users. CLG maintains that users need not represent all knowledge at all levels - some knowledge (especially at lower levels, but also higher) will be held as procedures whilst other knowledge will be declaratively represented. CLG implies that users can operate efficiently with only the Interaction Level methods. However, users who have not come to represent the higher levels will probably be at a loss when something goes wrong. For example, they will not possess the appropriate concepts to make sense of an error situation. Conversely, users may know their objective but may not know what commands to use to reach it; that is, they know the semantic method, but not the syntactic method.

CLG has been used as a design tool to develop the structure of computer programs (Moran, 1981) and as a method for evaluating interfaces (Davis, 1983), for which it was only moderately successful.

2.3.1 Knowledge

Non-ideal knowledge is not an important part of CLG and its inclusion depends on the analyst, so inconsistencies between interface terms or differences between interface terms and natural language terms may well go unobserved. CLG offers a symbolic notation, and a grammar for describing knowledge which permits the relationships between knowledge to be expressed. This is a more powerful formalism than the use of object/action pairs which only permit a relationship between two items. The limitation on the use of the formalism is in the identification of the knowledge to be represented. Once knowledge has been specified, relationships and conflicts can be captured by the grammar.

2.3.2 User centered task dynamics and cognitive limitations on processing

The CLG grammar rules are not a performance theory and their structure does not capture user centered task dynamics or cognitive processing limitations. While the different levels for the representation of knowledge in CLG have psychological credibility, it is unfortunate that no mechanism is provided to select which knowledge exists at which level.

2.3.3 Use of the technique

CLG guides designers by placing an order on the decisions they must make. It also enables the designer to maintain consistency throughout this process, and suggests the stages at which reduction in the elements should take place, but the analyst/designer must invent each new element. This is a slow and laborious process. Without a tool such as CLG the process results in many inconsistencies and the design must be checked and changed as conflicts and errors are discovered by chance. However, CLG is a cumbersome tool if used only to explicate consistency; other methods for this are more easily managed - for example, TAG, discussed below. CLG can only aid the designer in making design and trade off decisions if the rules of how to design user interfaces are included in it as originally planned (Moran, 1978).

3 ANALYSES DESIGNED TO PREDICT DIFFICULTIES FROM INTERFACE SPECIFICATIONS

The next four techniques focus on capturing knowledge of systems from designs and specifications to assess complexity, learnability, transfer or performance times.

3.1 External-Internal Task Mapping Analysis (ETIT)

The purpose of the External-Internal Task Mapping Analysis (Moran, 1983) is to assess the complexity of learning a system for a naive user and the potential transfer of knowledge from one system to another.

The user comes to a system with a task to perform which is defined for ETIT in terms of the external task space (e.g. reports, chapters) and not in terms of the internal task space (e.g. directories, files, editing commands). The complexity of the relationship between these two spaces will reflect the difficulty found in using the system and especially in learning to use it.

ETIT compares representations of these two spaces, assuming the user's knowledge of a system's properties is either complete or nil. For a text editing task, the external task space can be taken as the set of core editing tasks defined by Roberts and Moran (1983). They reduced 212 tasks which text editors could potentially perform to "the minimal subset of an editor's functions" (Roberts, 1979, p. 8). That is, the 37 tasks which all of a sample of editors actually performed. Each task (e.g. Remove-Word) consists of a function term and a task term. This external task space for editing tasks was built from eight editing functions and five types of text entities. The internal task space for a display editor (Moran, 1983) may have only one entity - a character string - and three functions - Insert, Cut and Paste. To map from the external to the internal task space requires a set of ten rules. One of these would translate all text entities into strings, another would map Remove-Word from the external space into Cut-String in the internal space of the editor commands. In contrast to this straightforward mapping, a line editor (Moran, 1983) may require 15 mapping rules which would be more complex than those for the display editor. Therefore the complexity of the mapping rules reflects an increased complexity in using one system over another.

Transfer from one system to another can be assessed as the number of common rules between the systems. For example, every display editor rule exists for the line editor, therefore the transfer would be easy. The converse is not true. This analysis assumes that learning will not necessarily be facilitated by any form of similarity between commands or command sequences in different systems. Rather, the key factor is the similarity in mapping rules from the internal to external task spaces for the two systems.

ETIT has only been used for the demonstration examples of a line and text editor summarised above from Moran (1983), and in Douglas's (1983) thesis to account for several aspects of the Roberts and Moran (1983) learning data for different text editors. Outside the area of text editing there are no available applications, and there are no available specifications of the external task space other than that of Roberts and Moran (1983).

3.1.1 Knowledge

The internal task space captures the ideal knowledge of the system. The external task space captures knowledge of the world version of the task domain. Some aspects of knowledge of other devices and systems can be identified by the comparison of the ETIT mapping rules for two systems. This comparison will not show how this knowledge will interfere with the ideal knowledge of any system under consideration, although it will show where the knowledge overlaps. Knowledge of natural language is not caught by the analysis unless this is incorporated in either the external or internal task space.

The level of description of elements of knowledge used in the example external task space is of actions and objects. This matches the simple "function and one object" command languages used on the systems investigated. For other external task spaces other descriptions may have to be derived.

3.1.2 User centered task dynamics and cognitive limitations on processing

This analysis only captures goals to the extent that they represent nodes in the external or internal task space. There are no dynamic properties to this analysis and therefore no cognitive limitations on it. ETIT does not address the problem of interference or negative transfer effects.

3.1.3 Use of the technique

To use ETIT the analyst must code a system specification into an internal task space and code domain knowledge into an external task space, and then produce mapping rules between these spaces. The construction of the internal task space from a system specification can be performed by a non-specialist.

The development of a representation of tasks in the real world as an external task space is more problematic. ETIT is presented as two example analyses using the same external task space provided by Roberts and Moran (1983). The mechanism used for establishing this external task space appears to establish the common internal task space of a set of computer systems designed to perform the same task. To accurately reflect the performance of individuals, the external task space ought to be an individual's conceptual model of the task which would be susceptible to influences from that individual's general knowledge. There is no simple method of assessing this, therefore one must use a representation of the task abstractly presented in the world. Whether the external task space produced by any method is sufficiently close to a user's conceptual model for an analyst's purposes can only be judged by empirical investigation. Consequently, although an internal task space may be easy to construct, the correct method for constructing an external task space is uncertain.

3.2 Task Action Grammar (TAG)

Task-Action Grammar (Payne and Green, 1986) attempts to model the user's knowledge of the mappings from tasks to actions, and to predict learnability by capturing all the generalities that the user may be aware of. Green et al. give a detailed account of TAG in this volume.

An analysis of a computer version of a task into a TAG requires its decomposition into "simple tasks". A simple task is "any task that a user can routinely perform" or which can be accomplished with no problem solving component or control structure; they may be at a very low level, for novices, or for more experienced users they may be compiled (Anderson, 1983) into larger groupings. For example, "move cursor one character upward" may require several actions, but after practice it would equate to a single command and therefore to one "simple task". Higher levels of planning, requiring several "simple tasks" are modelled by a separate planning component, left unspecified.

TAG offers two mechanisms for capturing the generalities within command languages. Firstly, simple tasks may be defined as having the features of another simple task, but with one or more specifically different. For example, "move cursor one character down", could be described as having the features of "move cursor one character upward" with the "direction" specifically set to "down". The second mechanism allows TAG to capture different forms of general semantic knowledge in separate rules. For example, when the command term "UP" is the token used in the command language, it is not an arbitrary symbol - it draws on knowledge of natural language. TAG is able to express the notion that a command language token is based on the presumed natural language knowledge of the user. Rules of this sort (which can apply to other domains besides natural language) give TAG a powerful mechanism to capture information relevant to the interaction which are not specified in the language itself.

TAG has been used (Payne, 1985) to describe the languages used in several experiments (e.g. Carroll, 1982) and its predictions are consistent with the experimental findings. It has also been used to describe various systems such as MacDraw and Multiplan which are described in the chapter by Green et al., in this volume.

3.2.1 Knowledge

Like ETIT, TAG captures other knowledge in addition to ideal system knowledge. However, TAG goes further, in showing where non-ideal knowledge interferes with system knowledge. One of the benefits of TAG is its ability to capture influences from natural language which ETIT and CLG could not. TAG can therefore indicate potential user errors due to the choice of command names or command ordering. For example, abbreviating the commands UP, NEXT and DELETE to their first letters (U, N, D) may unfortunately lead users to enter "D" when they want to move "down" because of the relationship between up and down in natural language. Knowledge of other systems or of world domain versions of tasks could also be entered into TAG representations to show effects of interference from these knowledge sources. As yet, however, none of the presented examples of TAGs include these components.

One problem is that the choice of features may be unstable. This is because the set of features that defines a simple task depends on the contrast within the set of simple tasks chosen for consideration. For example, one set of directional features suitable for contrasts between movement tasks which vary in direction and magnitude will be inappropriate for comparing a variation between functions such as "move" and "copy". This mechanism has the advantage that no absolute set of all the features need be specified, but it has the disadvantage that the feature set for a command must be changed or increased to capture new contrasts. Unless the analyst has thought of all possible contrasts which may occur in the analysis, errors due to unsystematic changes to the feature sets are likely.

3.2.2 User centered task dynamics and cognitive limitations on processing

TAG claims to be a "cognitive competence" model, not a performance model. It does not explicitly account for any dynamics of the user's representation or processing. User goals can be equated with "simple tasks" in TAG, but there is no mechanism to chain "simple tasks" and there is no precise definition of what a "simple task" is or how a system's language should be segmented into them. There is also no attempt to capture higher level goals or motivations.

As a competence model TAG proposes a more powerful view of users' competence than is usually adopted. Most models are presented as though users were unable to perceive the "family resemblances" that TAG uses to give a structuring to the command language.

3.2.3 Use of the technique

The TAG analyst must re-code an ideal representation of a computer interface dialogue into a task dictionary and rule schemata. Other information must also be coded into the same form, and the analyst must attempt to minimise the number of schemata required for the TAG description.

The re-coding of a well-specified system description into a TAG description is comparatively simple, but the selection of what other (non-ideal) information to encode relies on the analyst's intuition and observation. This can lead to difficulties in comparing two interfaces.

Complexity metrics can only be comparative between TAGs for different systems where the same non-system knowledge is included in all analyses. If there were specified psychological constraints in the model there might be a simple route for deriving a complexity metric by which to judge the rules derived by the analysis. Without these the scope of the predictions from any analysis are limited to comparative judgments of the complexity of different systems.

3.3 The GOMS Family of Models

The purpose of the GOMS analysis (Card, Moran and Newell, 1980; 1983) is to generate useful engineering models to predict the time to complete tasks. Different members of the GOMS family incorporate different grains of analysis. A technique of sensitivity analysis (Card et al., 1983) can be used to assess the grain of analysis which is most appropriate for describing observed behaviour. Two of the specific models in the family will be considered: the GOMS model itself, and the Keystroke model. Further details, together with examples, are given in the chapter by Green et al. in the present volume.

The GOMS model provides a simple view of mental processes in terms of "goals", "operators" for achieving those goals, "methods" which are sequences of operators, and "selection rules" for choosing between alternative methods. The task to be analysed is decomposed into successively smaller sub-tasks until the level of "unit tasks" is reached. This is the level that drives the mechanisms in GOMS and for which the user is assumed to know particular methods (e.g. a "line feed" method for locating a line); in the task of editing, the unit task can be equated with a particular correction on a manuscript. Within the task a user is driven by a series of goals. The top level goal (e.g. EDIT-MANUSCRIPT) would create a sub-goal to perform each "unit-task" (e.g. EDIT-UNIT-TASK) which would be repeated until no more unit tasks remain to be performed.

The Keystroke Level model is based on the GOMS model but its role is purely to predict "the time an expert user will take to execute the task using the system, providing he uses the method without error" (Card et al., 1983, p 260). The user's task is again divided into "unit tasks" but instead of being decomposed into goals and methods, the time to perform each is directly the sum of three components: an "acquisition time" (computed at 1.8 seconds); a performance time which is the sum of the times to execute the keystrokes in the commands (dependent on the user's typing speed); and times for mental operations (computed at 1.4 seconds). The model incorporates a set of rules for the application of mental operators such as adding times for each "cognitive unit" (approximately a command string).

The Keystroke Level model is only intended to give quantitative predictions of the performance time for error free expert performance. In doing this, it assumes the shortest sequence of commands is used to perform a task, although evidence suggests that even experts do not always use the technique that is either fastest (e.g. MacLean et al., 1985) or has fewest keystrokes (Embley and Nagy, 1982). Additionally, Roberts and Moran (1982), found that major errors (those that took more than a few seconds to correct) occupied between 4 and 22 per cent of testing; Allen and Sczerbo (1983) report that the average time spent correcting errors was 20.1 per cent of the time not involved in errors. Considering this, it is remarkable that the Keystroke Level model appears to generate fairly good predictions.

Roberts and Moran (1983) present a comparison of nine text editors using the model and performance tests. Although the values generally follow the predictions, the editor predicted to be fastest by the model was only found to be sixth fastest in practice. The model is reported as being accurate to a standard error of 21% over a variety of different tasks and systems (Card et al., 1983, p 297). The model's predictions should be adjusted by a factor of 1.4 (1.1 to 2.0) to fit true performance (Roberts and Moran, 1982).

3.3.1 Knowledge

These analyses seek to predict performance times assuming ideal system knowledge. They do not attempt to capture other knowledge. Most of this ideal system knowledge is contained within the system specification, but in addition the models use individual typing speed estimates, determined from performance, and in the case of GOMS individual selection rules are also determined from performance.

3.3.2 User centered task dynamics

GOMS incorporates task goals in the analysis, but not motivational goals, which are assumed to be constant. Since the technique is limited to predictions for expert users, the goals and sub-goals are derived from stored (learnt) plans, rather than being generated through problem solving. The analysis is also greatly limited by being unable to account for learning, since it assumes that the user has optimal system knowledge. GOMS can, however, describe the short term dynamics of the interaction to some degree, depending on the grain of the operators used. The more the processing operators used are based on the human information processing system, the more exact the account of the dynamics of processing.

The only aspects of the dynamics of processing which the Keystroke Level model attempts to capture are the times for the action and mental operators. This is reasonable since its sole purpose is to predict the times for expert error free performance on a system. However, it has been suggested (Allen and Scerbo, 1983) that the error margin that exists for these predictions is due to inadequacies in the rules for the application of mental operators.

3.3.3 Cognitive limitations on processing

The very limited degree to which this analysis involves any psychological process model can be assessed from the amount of psychological reasoning behind it. The analysis is based on two basic principles of psychology. Firstly, that people act so as to attain their goals through rational action given the structure of the task, and secondly, that problem solving activity can be described in terms of a set of knowledge states; operators for changing states; and control knowledge for applying knowledge.

Since "Operators are elementary ... information processing acts, whose execution is necessary to change any aspects of the user's memory ..." (Card, 1978, p 58) the model has the potential for employing psychologically salient operators, to represent short term processing operations (e.g. the perception of salient cues). Card et al. (1983) present a model incorporating such operators (the Model Human Information Processor) which is used to derive action performance times, but these operators are not included in the example analyses using GOMS.

3.3.4 Use of the technique

The Keystroke Level model is a concise engineering formula which is obviously predictive of approximate performance times from a design description and is also comprehensible to the non-specialist. The only parts of the model which are not explicit are the definitions of the "unit-task" and the "cognitive unit". The approximation of these units to system commands is workable, but limited by the analyst's intuition. This problem arises because the units of representation chosen in the model are those of the system (optimal methods and keystrokes) rather than psychologically motivated units of representation. It could be avoided if the model were more strongly motivated by a cognitive theory which specified cognitively salient units, or if the units were based on user performance. However, it is unclear that a sufficiently detailed cognitive theory exists to make predictions, and if assessments were made of user performance, time predictions would be redundant and the model's applicability would be severely reduced.

The usability of the GOMS analysis is far more constrained by the problem of defining the "unit task". For applications where there is an established body of previous computer versions of the domain application, the approximation to a command sequence may be acceptable. In other applications, the analyst must rely heavily on his own intuition in dividing the task into units. It would also be difficult for a non-psychologist to estimate the correct range for the operators in an application. In many cases, it may be necessary for any analyst to attempt several grains of operator before accepting one as appropriate. It is also necessary for any potential users of the GOMS family of tools to decide the extent to which predictions of times for optimal error free performance may in fact be useful for their situation.

3.4 The User-Device Model

Kieras and Polson (1985) present a two-component approach to assess the effects of transfer of knowledge from one system to another, the complexity of devices, learning and performance times, and error frequencies. This approach is described at length elsewhere in this volume, in the chapter by Green, Schiele and Payne, and will only be outlined here.

The first component is a production system model of the user's how-to-do-it knowledge of system use, based on the GOMS representation. The user's goal structure is derived using a mechanism similar to that in GOMS, with the addition that active goals are represented in working memory. In this model, one measure of user complexity is the depth of the goal stack during operation - a more complex method for achieving a task will require a deeper goal stack than a simple method. Another measure of complexity is the number of productions required to represent a method for achieving a task. Performance time predictions can also be made from the number of productions fired.

The second constituent of the approach is a Generalised Transition Network (GTN) model of the device - that is the computer interface, showing the system's possible states, the possible actions the user can take in that state, and a connection to the next state that will result from that action. Whereas the production system model captures the how-to-do-it knowledge this model can be viewed as capturing how-it-works knowledge. This representation is comparable to other formal grammars of devices, with the advantage that it is visually more appealing.

The description of a device and a task using these formalisms offers the opportunity for running computer simulations of task performance. A simulation has been presented for the IBM Display-writer (Kieras and Polson, 1985) which appears to predict the learning rate and performance time for the device with some accuracy (Polson and Kieras, 1985).

Production rules are assumed to be single units that are learnt on an "all or none" basis, and rules already learnt for one "task" or "method" can be incorporated when a new one is learnt. Therefore if two methods (e.g. how to delete a word, and how to delete a character) have some production rules in common, learning one method will make it easier to learn the other. In the same way, knowledge which the user possesses prior to learning a particular device is "device independent" and therefore has no learning cost; "device dependent" information does carry a learning cost. There is no formalism for assessing the device independence of knowledge, although if the knowledge is employed in a domain outside that of the device then it is assumed to be device independent.

3.4.1 Knowledge

This technique incorporates a representation of the ideal knowledge of the system, but not any non-ideal knowledge. The technique does permit the comparison of ideal knowledge of different systems. Although not yet implemented, this approach is potentially capable of capturing other "device independent" knowledge such as that from a domain version of a task. The technique contrasts with ETIT where transfer of knowledge between systems is assessed, not by the overlap in representations of methods from different systems, but in the mapping rules from those methods to a third user representation. ETIT attempts to incorporate knowledge of a task outside any system whereas this technique only incorporates knowledge of systems.

3.4.2 User centered task dynamics

The production system component of the technique has many of the properties and drawbacks of the GOMS approach on which it is based. The generalised transition network, however, presents one element of task dynamics which none of the other techniques discussed in this chapter do. It presents what information is on the screen at any time. This permits the analyst to assess the consistency of use of system prompts etc. When this component of the approach is linked to the production system, it will offer a starting point for assessing the perceptual and attentional aspects of an interaction. At present, although rules can contain conditionals on the perceptual cues required for a method, no mechanism is provided to account for the effort of discriminating these salient cues from other objects in the environment.

3.4.3 Cognitive limitations on processing

Kieras and Polson's model places few limitations on cognitive processing abilities. When modelling experts, working memory is used as an infinitely large, non-decaying goal stack. Novice-level users are assumed to test all goals that are in working memory, to explicitly attend to feedback information and verify each step they take, so production rules to model novices are written in a constrained style. It is not clear how these views relate to other views of working memory in the human information processing system (e.g. Baddeley, 1983) where capacity and decay constraints are applied. Constraints on these aspects could be added to the tool in the future, but are not at present included.

3.4.4 Use of the technique

The analyst would have to encode a system specification into two formalisms, one for each component of the model. Both these formalisms are complex to use, and production systems are generally cumbersome to construct and maintain.

Programming style determines the number of production rules used to represent a method. The analyst must therefore take care to maintain a strict consistency of style so that a count of productions can be used as a complexity metric. Various metrics of performance and transfer are available with this technique and the choice of the "best" one for any circumstances cannot be guided until more experimental data is available (but see Polson, 1987). If an assessment was to involve rules of different flavours (e.g. rules for natural language or the work domain version of a task) then a more complex metric than mere rule counting would have to be employed. This metric would have to incorporate some psychologically based balance between the different rule types.

4 ANALYSES OF USERS' CONCEPTUAL STRUCTURES

The next two techniques are empirically based analyses of the knowledge actually possessed by users, not the idealised knowledge presented in design specifications.

4.1 Information Structure Description

Wilson et al. (1985) used a task analysis to classify user errors, so that the knowledge elements or "information structures" supporting actual user performance could be derived. A second purpose was to describe long term transitions in learning as knowledge structures evolve.

This approach makes use of two levels of task description. One level describes the overall process of controlling a dialogue sequence in terms of attempts to satisfy task goals. The other specifies particular "information structures" or "meta-information structures" that make up the knowledge called upon to achieve those goals. Performance protocols are analysed with respect to these two levels.

The process of controlling a dialogue sequence is described as a simple goal structure, consisting of a major goal (e.g. edit-manuscript) subdivided into individual goals approximately equivalent to individual editing instructions. It is assumed that for each goal the user makes an attempt to achieve it and tests to see whether the attempt succeeded: an attempt-test cycle.

The attempt-test cycle for the example study involved four stages: one of attempt specification (a mental event) and three of action with contingent tests on that action - establishing a command context, the performance of a command specific procedure, and termination of a command sequence. The definiton of these three latter stages was derived from a syntactic analysis of the particular menu interface examined.

At each stage the test could either be passed, and the attempt continued as specified; failed resulting in a local correction (e.g. deleting the last character typed) or, failed resulting in the specification of a new attempt or goal. There were also special cases for passing a test and the user assuming the attempt was completed so a new goal was prematurely attempted. This analysis permits a complete classification of user performance (both correct and erroneous), to arcs connecting the four stages of the attempt-test cycle, that is, a description that is sensitive to the device specification.

When tasks are performed in an optimal fashion it can only be assumed that users possess ideal task knowledge. When errors arise, non-ideal knowledge can be inferred or a performance breakdown assumed. The second level of the analysis involves a specification of the user knowledge required to support the analysed performance. Two classes of information structure are incorporated in this analysis: Meta-Information Structures, or general rules of system performance, and Information Structures, or specific fragments of performable methods. Information structures for an expert user are similar to the methods (or task-action mappings) used in GOMS, however for other users these will account for the partial knowledge they hold of the system.

The changes that take place during a user's learning are viewed as changes in a repertoire of these information structures. Early in learning, the repertoire contains a small number of both types, some of which may accurately and completely specify appropriate task-action mappings, or general characteristics of system operation. Other members will be inaccurate, incomplete or contradictory with each other. As practice continues, inaccurate or incomplete information structures may become inaccessible with the addition of new members. Expert status may be achieved when the content of knowledge within the repertoire stabilises, and is in accord with, the system requirements for the tasks that that user needs to undertake.

As the process of learning progresses, information structures are derived from more general meta-information structures which are themselves also generated. An illustrative model has been presented that could account for this process but it will not be described here.

Particular information structures and meta-information structures can be inferred from the analysis of user performance provided by the first half of the technique. This enables the system knowledge held by users at different stages of learning to be characterised without merely assuming it to be none for a novice and "complete" for an expert. This allows the designer to be aware of user difficulties and to support performance at different stages of knowledge development, and for different types of user.

4.1.1 Knowledge

This technique attempts to capture the knowledge involved in actual error prone performance. Consequently, it captures both ideal system knowledge and the non-ideal knowledge which a user may have acquired. The information structures and meta-information structures derived from performance can contain influences from natural language, the task domain and other devices and systems.

The information structure terminology provided by this technique is powerful enough to capture consistencies and structured relationships between knowledge at various levels. The information structures are written as informal English phrases embedded within a bracketing notation. Mismatches between the knowledge assumed for actual system use and idealised system use emerge in the context of the bracketing of sequences which actually occur.

4.1.2 User centered task dynamics

The first level of the analysis captures the goal structure of a task in a tree. The top level of the tree in the example analysis did not capture high level motivations, but these could be represented in the same way as other goals if required. All actions by the user and changes in the system state are specified in this technique. Therefore the task model developed in the example analysis permits the capture and structuring of all short term transitions both in the system and in the user's mental representations. Since the system state is described and the user's representation, the technique permits the mismatches between between the two to be identified.

The area where this analysis differs from most of the others, is that it captures not only the short term transitions but also the long term transitions in the user's representations. The description of a repertoire of information structures which changes as knowledge develops permits the analyst to investigate the interaction of the various knowledge sources for maturing user populations.

4.1.3 Cognitive limitations on processing

This analysis does not assert that the inferred information structures have absolute psychological saliency. These structures are taken to represent the "content" of knowledge held by users but not necessarily the "form" in which that knowledge is represented. The analysis characterises the set of information structures that might need to be generated to support the task-action mappings performed by users. Beyond these qualities of the representations, there are no other information processing constraints included in the analysis on the processing of user knowledge.

4.1.4 Use of the technique

To use this technique analysts must describe the optimal method to achieve a task. Then they must specify the stages of the attempt-test cycle for that task. They can then assign user actions to arcs in that cycle. Having identified the sites of major deviations from the optimal method, analysts must hypothesise the knowledge held by users which led them to these deviations. Where performance is studied for a sufficient period, the analysis can be used to identify the changes that take place in a repertoire of knowledge as learning progresses.

The technique has been described for a single system, and much of its application is heuristic rather than formalised. The major drawback with using this analysis is the time and effort required to assign individual user actions to the possible arcs of the fully specified attempt-test cycle. The original analysis was performed to give example mismatches between actual user knowledge and idealised knowledge in order to motivate further experimental research. For these purposes the significant effort required is often worthwhile (e.g. Wilson, Barnard and MacLean, 1985). However, for more practical system evaluations, problems can be identified with much less effort (e.g. Hammond et al., 1983) and progress may depend upon automating the more sophisticated scoring schemes such as that deployed with this technique.

4.2 An Analysis of Menu Systems

Few of the previous analyses attempt to account for problem solving during performance. The next method of task analysis (Young and Hull, 1982; 1983) explicitly addresses real-time problem solving during a search for target information, and illustrates how the performance of users can be based on the effects of their deep mental models (Carroll, 1984) - both of the system and of the domain of the information presented on-screen.

Young and Hull analysed the use of a hierarchical page-based viewdata system (Prestel). In this system each page, or frame, provides information and a menu leading to other frames. The user's task, at each step, is to select the appropriate item from the menu; that is, to match a menu item with a hypothesis about the route leading eventually to the target information. Young has analysed examples of user's performance on the menu search task and has suggested an implicit relation between the overall topic of a menu frame and the individual options on its menu, and the way these relations can constrain the way that users can process the frame. Each menu presents a categorisation of a domain into subsets. Different "categorisation structures" require users to adopt correspondingly different decision strategies in order to handle them correctly. Young attempted to develop a taxonomy of "categorisation structures" for menu systems giving the prototypical decision strategy for each. Examples of these structures include partitioning the topic into non-overlapping subsets; the "N + Other" structure, with a series of specific choices followed by a catch-all category; categorisation by multiple bases or dimensions, forcing the user to first pick the appropriate dimension, then to choose within it; overlapping categories; and structures based on analogies to other sources of information, such as newspaper layout. Each of these requires a different user strategy.

In relation to this partial taxonomy Young presented a tentative process model for menu selection. In this "the decision making is opportunistic, driven strongly by the particulars of each choice, so that the decision 'method' emerges as a product of the interplay between the context, the user's query, and the details of the frame itself" (Young and Hull, 1983).

4.2.1 Knowledge

This technique recognises that the knowledge used to construct a hypothesis or understand a menu frame could originate from any source available to the user - not just the "idealised" knowledge of how to find the target. Thus it captures aspects of the general knowledge brought to bear by users which other analyses have not considered.

4.2.2 User-centered task dynamics and cognitive limitations on processing

Young's process model is restricted to cases where the user's main goal is always constant and neither higher motivational goals nor lower goal nestings need be considered. The process model presented does not attempt to include any cognitive limitations on processing.

4.2.3 Use of the technique

This analysis is simply an example of one analysis of a particular task which results in a partial taxonomy of menu structures. It serves as an illustration and a reminder of the shortfall of many other analysis techniques, but as it stands it does not generalise further.

5 ANALYSES OF COGNITIVE ACTIVITIES

The last two approaches are analyses of the cognitive processing which occurs during task performance. These complement the analyses outlined in the previous sections which emphasised the knowledge requirements of tasks.

5.1 Decomposition of Mental Activity

Norman (1984, 1986) describes an analysis based upon the decomposition of a task into different mental activities. The description of mental activities is intended to help analysts understand the cognitive consequences of design features. The analysis requires mapping from system variables to psychological ones.

The user approaches a system with a set of goals to achieve, yet these goals must be realised through physical actions at the terminal. The gap between goal formation and action is what Norman calls "the gulf of execution". Bridging that gulf requires three types of mental activity: forming an intention to act; specifying an appropriate action sequence; and executing that action sequence.

Once an action sequence has been executed, there is a corresponding "gulf of evaluation" because the user must relate the system's response to the original goal. This is again bridged by three complementary types of activity: perceiving the physical properties of the system state; interpreting them; and evaluating those interpretations in relation to the original goal.

Taking these stages together with the initial formation of a goal gives seven stages of mental activity:
1. Establishing the Goal.
2. Forming the Intention.
3. Specifying the Action Sequence.
4. Executing the Action.
5. Perceiving the System State.
6. Interpreting the State.
7. Evaluating the System State with respect to the Goals and Intentions.

In real tasks the stages need not necessarily occur in strict sequence and some may even be omitted. The definition of stages represents an approximate theory of action which itself is undergoing evolution (the number and definition of stages may change). In practice, the analysis "must be used in ways appropriate to the situation" (Norman, 1986, p. 42). The system designer can tackle substantial gulfs of execution or evaluation by making the system more like the user's psychological needs. Alternatively, the user may have to create plans and and carry out action sequences that meet the requirements imposed by the physical system. These action sequences can, of course, be developed through experience and supported by training until they feel almost part of the system.

Different aspects of system design support different stages of activity, and designers can use this analysis to assist their choices. In many cases, design decisions are really trade-offs between supporting one stage or another. Menus, for example, can assist the stages of intention formation and action specification. However, if many sequential selections are required, menus may slow down the stage of action execution. In contrast, command languages may support rapid execution of action but create problems in action specification and so on.

Such an analysis helps us to understand the benefits that arise from direct manipulation interfaces or from providing a consistent and explicit system image. Menus and pointing devices combined with immediate visual feedback can help to reduce the gulfs of execution and evaluation. Likewise, a consistent model can help support the user during phases of activity that involve a strong problem-solving component.

5.1.1 Knowledge and user centered task dynamics

This analysis makes frequent reference to the use of knowledge, both correct and incorrect, during the various stages of activity. No formalism is offered for specifying or analysing that knowledge. Rather, analysts must draw their own inferences about how and when particular forms of knowledge are relevant.

Similarly, the approach incorporates an analysis of goals during task performance, and also allows for the construction of plans during performance - in fact, it emphasises plan construction. As with the case of knowledge, no explicit mechanisms are provided to guide more detailed analyses or for assessing their relation to higher motivations.

By simply identifying attributes of the gulf between the state of the user and the state of a system, the approach allows the analyst to be aware of where learning would be required by the user. Once again, the technique does not specifically address how longer term changes in user representations might come about.

5.1.2 Cognitive limitations on processing

The seven stages suggested are all forms of cognitive processing that are required to map a mental representation onto a physical system. In this respect, the approach provides a means of thinking about the likely complexity of that mapping. In its current form the analysis does not seek to specify constraints on mental representations, mental capacity or mental processing in exact form. As an "engineering approach" it makes use of approximate representations drawn more generally from the science base of psychology - such as known attributes of cognitive skills (e.g. perceptual search, the motor control of typing), or of underlying processing constraints (e.g. the approximate capacity of human short term memory).

5.1.3 Use of the technique

Users of this analysis technique need to divide the user's tasks into the seven stages and see what support the system gives to each stage. The mappings from the system to the users' model must be as direct as possible, so designers will often have to choose between supporting one stage or another. Approximate tools for assessing the value of these trade offs are also suggested but they are outside the scope of this review. At present, the technique is best viewed as a tool for thought rather than a rigorous form of task analysis. Since the technique clearly requires a basic knowledge of cognitive psychology, users of the technique will need a working knowledge of cognitive skills and capabilities relevant to the tasks and systems being analysed. Although not as explicit as some of the analyses presented in earlier sections, it does provide a way of representing what a user might actually being doing. In this respect, human factors specialists have commented that this form of analysis makes contact with their immediate concerns more readily than more formal approaches (e.g. Whiteside and Wixon, 1987).

5.2 Cognitive Task Analysis (CTA)

Like Norman's approach, Cognitive Task Analysis (Barnard, 1987) focuses on the nature of mental activity rather than on tasks themselves. The general idea is that a theoretically based decomposition of cognitive resources can be used to describe mental activity associated with dialogue tasks.

Following the Interacting Cognitive Subsystems (ICS) approach to human information processing (Barnard, 1985), it is assumed that the cognitive system is divided into subsystems, each of which processes information in a particular mental code (e.g. propositional). Each subsystem has associated with it a local "image record" which stores representations in its own code. A subsystem also contains translation processes that recode its input into the codes that are used by other subsystems or by specific effectors.

Sensory subsystems (e.g. visual, acoustic) generate codes that can be processed by representational subsystems, which in turn handle higher level descriptions of linguistic and visual structure, as well as meaning and its implications. Effector subsystems (e.g. articulatory, limb) translate the representational codes into codes for controlling particular effectors (e.g. hands, speech musculature).

The description of mental activity contains four components: the mental processes required; the procedural knowledge embodied in those processes; the contents of relevant memory records that may be accessed; and the way in which the cognitive mechanism will be dynamically controlled during task execution.

The first component, the *configuration of processes*, does no more than describe what is required for a given phase of cognitive activity. In reading, for example, a visual representation is translated into an object encoding, which is subsequently recoded through a representation of linguistic form into a propositional representation of the meaning of the information and so on. The set of processes required defines the configuration for reading. A different set of processes would define the configuration for say typing text.

The second component, *procedural knowledge*, describes the properties of each individual process within the configuration. For example, this component would specify whether or not fully automated procedures existed to carry out a particular mental recoding required by the task. So, linguistic processes cannot automatically recode novel command words (e.g. BLARK) into a propositional representation of their meaning.

The third component, *record contents*, specifies the properties of memory records that are likely to be accessed during task execution. This includes a representation of the task to-be-performed. In some circumstances users may rely on a semantic form of encoding (e.g. a propositional representation). Under these circumstances they may confuse elements with similar meaning (such as "Display" and "Show") and have trouble resolving the sequencing of dialogue constituents. In other circumstances they may rely on a representation of linguistic form which specifies sequencing but which is open to confusions between constituents that sound similar (such as the filenames "Nine.txt" and "Mine.txt").

The first three components describe properties of processes and representations. The fourth component, *dynamic control*, describes the flow of information among processes. This component specifies both the nature and extent of the transactions among processes that occur during task execution. Thus, the generation of a dialogue sequence may require resolving the identities of constituents and their order. This may be achieved by inferential activity or by recovering specific memory records or by some combination of both.

The description of dynamic control is arrived at by applying rules which interrelate the components. These rules are derived from empirical phenomena of system use (e.g. Barnard, 1987). For example, where the knowledge required for a task is incompletely proceduralised, or where record contents have a high degree of order uncertainty associated with them, then the complexity of dynamic control will increase and may take on a different form.

The complete four component description makes up a cognitive task model and the attributes of such models are used to predict user behaviour at novice, intermediate, and expert levels. The complexity of dynamic control required by a task is, for example, assumed to relate to overall ease of learning and performance.

This form of task analysis is based upon a theoretical decomposition of cognitive resources and heuristic principles which describe their functioning. Both the decomposition and the principles can be explicitly represented in the knowledge base of an expert system. Hence, the process of analysis and prediction can be automated (see Barnard et al., 1987). To date, illustrative principles have been derived to deal with a limited range of issues associated with command names, structures and menu dialogues.

5.2.1 Knowledge

In Cognitive Task Analysis knowledge is described in two forms - the form required for mental recodings (procedural knowledge) and the form required to represent task specific concepts and sequences (record contents). The analysis can therefore take into account a broad range of user knowledge, including knowledge of other systems, natural language, and domain versions of tasks. The important feature of this analysis is that knowledge is described in an approximate form in a way that relates directly to mental codes and to features of the use of the knowledge (such as the pragmatic resolution of order uncertainty via inference). It seeks to represent the *use* of knowledge in performance rather than providing a formalism for representing the *structure* of required system knowledge. Task action grammars, in contrast, attempt to represent the structure rather than the use of knowledge.

5.2.2 User centered task dynamics

The CTA is capable of characterising most aspects of task dynamics. Goals are implicitly specified in this model as information structures held in propositional memory records. Short term aspects of task dynamics are captured in terms of phases of cognitive activity and their contents. Longer term changes that take place during skill acquisition are dealt with by building different models for novice, intermediate and expert users.

5.2.3 Cognitive limitations on processing

CTA is first and foremost a means of making relationships explicit between approximate knowledge representations and cognitive limitations on their mental processing. The characteristics and limitations are specified in terms of the properties of mental codes; restricted capabilities for coordinating and controlling processes which handle those codes; and more specific limitations such as recency and description effects in memory retrieval. The approach essentially provides a language in which such constraints can be specified. The language refers to processes and coded mental representations which can be described in terms of their attributes. In its present form, only a limited range of attributes and constraints are actually utilised. They can, however, be added to as further analyses of user performance and provide additional empirical justification for extending that range.

5.2.4 Use of the technique

CTA can be used in two ways by different kinds of analysts. One class of analyst needs to analyse tasks in detail and establish the principles which interrelate the four components of the task model (cf. Barnard, 1987). Clearly, this type of analyst needs both to be a specialist in the cognitive sciences and to have a detailed working knowledge of the model-building process. The products of this class of usage are principles of cognitive task modelling; mappings from those principles to particular classes of application or system; and mappings onto properties of user behaviour. These principles and mappings can then be incorporated in the knowledge base of an expert system, as has been shown by Barnard et al., 1987.

The second class of analyst is the user of the resulting expert system. One of the attractive features of this approach is that the expert system users do not need detailed knowledge of the model building process. They simply need to be in a position to answer the particular queries for information that the expert system needs in order to build its model (Barnard et al., 1987). In its present form, the expert system user does need a working knowledge of cognitive psychology in order to answer all the queries in an appropriate manner. Hence, this type of user has been referred to as a behavioural analyst rather than a system designer.

The authors see this approach as the most extreme position yet reached in a trend that will affect other models. Understanding human behaviour requires detailed consideration of many different processes. The underlying models therefore become increasingly detailed and accessible only to specialists. While one solution is to look for powerful approximations (such as the GOMS approach), our belief is that it will be more successful to develop intelligent design aids, such as the expert system tool that is under development via this technique.

6 CONCLUSIONS

At the start of this chapter we observed that the interaction of people with computers offers novel problems for task analysis, and in the course of this chapter we have reviewed the various attempts at solving these new problems. The eleven techniques of task analysis summarised in this chapter are not simple rivals, all trying to achieve the same results in the same ways with varying degrees of success. Although, for expository purposes, they have been grouped into four groups according to the starting points they take for their analysis, the techniques differ also in their focus, their output, and their usability to the non-specialist. There is no single "best" technique. As Olson (1987) has pointed out, we have fragments of the kinds of representations required to meet the full needs of researchers and practitioners.

Users of task analysis do, nevertheless, have to choose among the fragments to get the form of representation that best suits their particular requirements. But is any method acceptable at present? Despite the wide variety, there are obvious and important problems that none of these techniques satisfactorily address at present, so we shall start this final section by reviewing some shortcomings and conclude with some remarks concerning future prospects.

6.1 Shortcomings of Present Techniques

None of the techniques discussed provides very much in the way of a treatment of *cognitive strategies* or *individual differences*. This is likely to be an important area of development since there is a body of research (e.g. Egan and Gomez, 1985; Green et al., 1988) which suggests that there are different learning styles between individuals as well as differences in various cognitive abilities. TAG, for example, explicitly excludes any mechanism to describe how users choose their strategy to achieve their goals. In contrast, GOMS provides at least some basis for strategic variation via selection rules based on actual user preferences incorporating empirical data. There is a clear need to develop analyses which can more readily cope with individual and strategic variation.

Similarly, *user motivation* - including the social motivations to work - is ill-represented, as are the constraints of office and organisational life (but see Olson, 1987; Malone, 1987). Studies of office automation have demonstrated that the attitudes of workers to the introduction of technology affect how that technology is used (e.g. Long et al., 1983; Macaulay et al., 1985), yet only one of the analyses considers higher-level motivations in any significant degree.

Assessments of *reliability* and *validity* are another weak spot. Where predictions are offered there is little data as yet on the general validity. In addition, most of these techniques have only been used by their originators.

How would they fare in other hands? Would other people produce the same analyses, and hence the same predictions? An example of the problem can be found in the analysis method used by Kieras and Polson, where the number of production rules is one of the metrics of complexity. Here the style in which the rules are written determines their number. Unless the style can be acquired by other analysts, the methodology will be difficult to standardise.

Finally, different techniques require different *analytical skills*. Some techniques are expected to be easy for designers to use, e.g. the Keystroke Level Model; but others, notably the Young/Hull analysis and Wilson et al., effectively require training in cognitive science. This makes it hard to transfer methodologies from the research community to the design community, who are the potential users of these techniques. One solution may be to automate them as executable formalisations, as Kieras and Polson have done and as the authors of TAG are currently doing, or as automated decision aids, as is being done with CTA. The use of intelligent interfaces to these techniques (see Barnard et al., 1987) may offer the best hope of making the more complex techniques directly available to designers rather than indirectly through behavioural specialists.

6.2 Pragmatic Issues

Choice of a technique must also be influenced by such pragmatic issues as ease of use, and sometimes a balance must be struck between pragmatic and conceptual advantages. For instance, there are two techniques aiming at knowledge specifications, TAKD and CLG. Of these, TAKD is more general and less cumbersome; but it also less formalised, and unlike CLG it does not include specific components to help in the structuring of design specifications.

Similarly, within the group of four techniques aiming at complexity predictions, increase in conceptual power must be balanced against predictive tightness. At one end, GOMS uses only the knowledge in the design, and produces absolute estimates of performance time - "It will take 3.45 seconds for a skilled user to perform this task using this system". Kieras and Polson increase the conceptual power by including knowledge of other systems, to estimate times for transfer of learning as well; ETIT tries to capture world knowledge of the task and makes estimates of comparative complexity of learning systems. At the far end, TAG introduces knowledge of natural language and of family resemblances between commands, but is limited to estimates of relative difficulty in learning systems - "This system will be harder to learn than that".

6.3 Choice of Focus

The techniques we have surveyed have, broadly speaking, three kinds of focus: ideal knowledge representation, user-centered task dynamics with less than ideal knowledge, and cognitive activities. We are now in a position to offer some observations on these possibilities.

A focus on knowledge representation seems to lead to techniques which are relatively quick to apply but are limited in predictive range. The simplest body of knowledge on which to base an analysis is the ideal knowledge of a system design. This clearly restricts predictions to error-free optimal performance. Introducing other types of knowledge requires more time and effort to verify the knowledge, and its completeness is always doubtful, so that increasing generality also leads to increased uncertainty. These approaches use models of performance which collapse over short term transitions in processing so that they cannot predict which particular errors will be made, only that one system will be more complex than another and hence that "more" errors will be made or that "more time" will be spent learning it.

However, these estimates of performance time and judgments of complexity can be used as soon as a design is available; they do not have to be based on a running system, and they are comparatively quick to use, so they can be applied early in the design cycle and their output can be used to guide design decisions before the systems are programmed (cf. Card et al., 1983).

A focus on user-centred task dynamics, associated in this survey with the work of Miller, Young & Hull, and Wilson et al., gives a more detailed understanding of why particular errors occur. As such these techniques can potentially provide more directive input concerning design attributes. However, they are time consuming, since they are based on actual behaviour, and they also require a running system, a simulation, or a comparable product for data collection. (Note that even if a prototype is used, it must still present a very accurate version of the intended user interface.) The time and effort required during the design cycle may not be worthwhile (Hammond et al., 1983).

A focus on the constraints of the human information processing system is given by the work of Norman and of Barnard. At present these are best described as conceptual frameworks which require considerable development to produce mature design aids.

6.4 Prospects

In the last analysis, user-system behaviour must be determined by a combination of task requirements and the ways in which the human information processing system copes with them. Accordingly, it seems vital to develop integrated approaches that can encompass different forms of knowledge requirements as well as information processing activity (Barnard, 1987): and if the techniques are to be useful outside the laboratory, mature ways of transferring the required skills and knowledge to the design community or to others who wish to use the techniques.

For the knowledge based techniques to move towards integration, they must identify sources of knowledge which are likely to interfere with ideal system knowledge during task performance. Then they must specify this in a way that does not rely on experts' abilities to identify relevant information for each analysis. Having done this, they require a mechanism to describe the user's mental processing that takes place during performance so that they can predict which errors will occur as well as offer comparative judgements of complexity.

At present, the choice of a technique requires a balance between the purpose, the starting point required by its techniques, and the form of its output. To these must be added the more pragmatic concerns of the requirements for particular skills, knowledge and effort. Little enough attention has been paid to these pragmatic considerations to date. Before the discipline can be called mature, we shall need to study these pragmatic issues in far more depth.

References

Allen, R.B., and Scerbo, M.W. (1983). Details of command-language keystrokes. *ACM Transactions on Office Information Systems*, 1, pp. 159-178.

Anderson, J.R. (1983). The Architecture of Cognition. Mass: Harvard University Press.

Baddeley, A.D. (1983). Working memory. *Philosophical Transactions of the Royal Society*, Series B, 302, pp. 311-324

Barnard, P.J. (1985). Interacting cognitive subsystems: a psycholinguistic approach to short-term memory. *In: Progress in the Psychology of Language*, A. Ellis (ed.). Vol II. Hillsdale, N.J.: Lawrence Erlbaum Associates, pp. 197-258.

Barnard, P.J. (1987). Cognitive resources and the learning of human-computer dialogues. *In: Interfacing Thought: Cognitive Aspects of Human-Computer Interaction*, J.M. Carroll (ed.). Cambridge, Mass.: MIT Press, pp. 112-158.

Barnard, P.J., Wilson, M.D. and MacLean, A. (1987). Approximate Modelling of Cognitive Activity: towards an expert system design aid. *In: Proceedings of CHI + GI 1987 (Toronto April 5-9)*, New York: ACM, pp. 21-26.

Bullen, C.V. and Bennett, J.L. (1983). Office workstation use by administrative managers and professionals. IBM Research Report RJ 3890.

Card, S.K. (1978). Studies in the psychology of computer text editing systems. Report no: SSL-78-1. Palo Alto, Calif.: Xerox Corp.

Card, S.K., Moran, T.P. and Newell, A. (1980). Computer text-editing: an information processing analysis of a routine cognitive skill. *Cognitive Psychology*, 12, pp. 32-74.

Card, S.K., Moran, T.P. and Newell, A. (1983). The Psychology of Human-Computer Interaction. Hillsdale, N.J.: Lawrence Erlbaum Associates.

Carroll, J.M. (1982). Learning, using and designing command paradigms. *Human Learning*, 1, pp. 31-62.

Carroll, J.M. (1984). Mental Models and software human factors: an overview. IBM Watson Research Centre, Research Report RC 10616 (47016).

Davis, R. (1983). Task analysis and user errors: a methodology for assessing interactions. *International Journal of Man-Machine Studies*, 19, pp. 561-574.

Douglas, S.A. (1983). Learning to text edit: semantics in procedural skill acquisition. PhD. dissertation, Stanford University.

Duncan, K.D. (1974). Analytical techniques in training design. *In: The Human Operator in Process Control*. E. Edwards and F.P. Lees, (eds.). London: Taylor & Francis.

Egan, D.E. and Gomez, L.M. (1985). Assaying, isolating, and accommodating individual differences in learning of complex skill. *In: Individual Differences in Cognition*, R.F. Dillon, (ed.). Vol 2. London: Academic Press, pp. 174-217.

Embley, D.W. and Nagy, G. (1982). Can we expect to improve text editing performance? *In: Human Factors in Computer Systems*, (Gaithersburg), New York: ACM, pp. 152-156.

Fleishman, E.A., and Quaintance, M.K. (1984). Taxonomies of Human Performance. San Diego, Calif.: Academic Press.

Green, T.R.G., Schiele, F. and Payne, S.J. (1988). Formalisable models of user knowledge in HCI. This volume.

Greene, S.L., Cannata, P.E., Gomez, L.M. and Devlin, S.J. (1987). A novel interface for database query: no IF's, AND's or OR's. *In: Proceedings of Bellcore Database Symposium* (Sept 15-17, 1987), Bellcore Special Report.

Hammond, N., MacLean, A., Hinton, G., Long, J., Barnard, P. and Clark, I.A. (1983). Novice use of an interactive graph plotting system. *IBM Hursley Human Factors Report HF083*. IBM UK Laboratories Ltd., Hursley Park, Winchester, UK.

Johnson, P. (1985). Towards a task model of messaging: an example of the application of TAKD to user interface design. *In: People and Computers: Designing the Interface*. P. Johnson and S. Cook (eds.). Cambridge: Cambridge University Press, pp. 46-62.

Johnson, P., Diaper, D. and Long, J.B. (1984). Tasks, skills and knowledge: task analysis for knowledge based descriptions. *In: Human-Computer Interaction - INTERACT '84*. B. Shackel (ed.). Amsterdam: North Holland, pp. 499-503.

Johnson, P., Diaper, D. and Long, J.B. (1985). Task analysis in interactive system design and evaluation. *Paper presented to the IFAC/IFIP conference on Design and Evaluation Techniques for Man-Machine Systems*, Italy.

Kieras, D.E. and Polson, P.G. (1985). An approach to the formal analysis of user complexity. *International Journal of Man-Machine Studies*, 22, pp. 365-394.

Long, J., Hammond, N., Barnard, P. and Morton, J. (1983). Introducing the interactive computer at work: the user's views. *Behaviour and Information Technology*, 2 (1), pp. 39-106.

Maclean, A., Barnard, P.J. and Wilson, M.D. (1985). Evaluating the human interface of a data entry system: user choice and performance measures yield different tradeoff functions. *In: People and Computers: Designing the Interface*. P. Johnson and S. Cook (eds.). Cambridge: Cambridge University Press, pp. 172-185.

Macaulay, L.A., Fowler, C.J.H. and Porteous, R. (1985). What do clerical workers think about computers? *In: People and Computers: Designing the Interface*. P. Johnson and S. Cook (eds.). Cambridge: Cambridge University Press, pp. 290-298.

Mack, R., Lewis, C. and Carroll, J. (1983). Learning to use word processors: problems and prospects. *ACM Transactions on Office Information Systems*, 1, pp. 254-271.

Malone, T.W. (1987). Computer support for organisations: towards an organisational science. *In: Interfacing Thought: Cognitive Aspects of Human-Computer Interaction*. J.M. Carroll (ed.). Cambridge Mass: MIT Press, pp. 294-324.

Miller, R.B. (1962). Task description and analysis. *In: Psychological Principles in System Development*. R.M. Gagné, (ed.). New York: Holt, Rinehart, & Winston.

Miller, R.B. (1967). Task taxonomy: science or technology? *In: The Human Operator in Complex Systems*. W.T. Singleton, R.S. Easterby and D.C. Whitfield (eds.). London: Taylor & Francis.

Miller, R.B. (1973). Development of a taxonomy of human performance: Design of a systems task vocabulary. *JSAS Catalog of Selected Documents in Psychology*, 3, pp. 29-30 (Ms. No. 327).

Miller, R.B. (1974). A method for determining task strategies (*Tech. Rep. AFHRL_TR_74_26*). Washington, D.C.: American Institutes for Research.

Moran, T.P. (1978). Introduction to the Command Language Grammar. *Report no: SSL-78-3*. Palo Alto, Calif.: Xerox Corp.

Moran, T.P. (1981). The Command Language Grammar, a representation for the user interface of interactive computer systems. *International Journal of Man-Machine Studies*, 15(1), pp. 3-50.

Moran, T.P. (1983). Getting into a system: external-internal task mapping analysis. *In: CHI '83 Conference on Human Factors in Computing Systems* (Boston). New York: ACM, pp. 45-49.

Morton, J., Barnard P.J., Hammond N.V., and Long J.B. (1979). Interacting with the computer: a framework. *In: Teleinformatics* E.J. Boutmy and A. Danthine (eds.). Amsterdam: North- Holland, 79, pp. 201-208.

Norman, D.A. (1984). Stages and levels in human-computer interaction. *International Journal of Man-Machine Studies*, 21, pp. 365-375.

Norman, D.A. (1986). Cognitive engineering. *In: User Centered System Design*, D.A. Norman and S.W. Draper (eds.). Hillsdale, N.J.: Lawrence Erlbaum Associates, 31-62.

Olson, J.R. (1987). Cognitive analysis of people's use of software. *In: Interfacing Thought: Cognitive Aspects of Human Computer Interaction*, J.M. Carroll (ed.). Cambridge Mass: MIT Press, pp. 260-293.

Payne, S. (1984). Task-action grammars. *In: Human-Computer Interaction - Interact '84*, B. Shackel (ed.). Amsterdam: North Holland, pp. 527-532.

Payne, S. (1985). Task-action grammars: the mental representation of task languages in human-computer interaction. Unpublished PhD. Dissertation, University of Sheffield, U.K.

Payne, S. and Green, T.R.G. (1986). Task-action grammars: a model of the mental representation of task languages. *Human Computer Interaction*, 2 (2) pp. 93-133.

Polson, P. (1987). A quantitative theory of human-computer interaction. *In: Interfacing Thought: Cognitive Aspects of Human-Computer Interaction*, J.M. Carroll (ed.). Cambridge Mass: MIT Press, pp. 184-235.

Polson, P.G. and Kieras, D.E. (1985). A quantitative model of the learning and performance of text editing knowledge. *In: Proceedings of CHI '85 Human Factors in Computing Systems* (San Francisco), New York: ACM, pp. 207-212.

Rasmussen, J. (1986). Information Processing and Human-Machine Interaction. Amsterdam: North Holland.

Reisner (1981). Formal grammar and design of an interactive system. *IEEE Trans. Software Engineering*, 7, pp. 229-240.

Roberts, T.L. (1979). Evaluation of computer text editors. PhD. Dissertation, Stanford Univ., Stanford, Calif.

Roberts, T.L. and Moran, T.P. (1982). Evaluation of text editors. *In: Proceedings of Human Factors in Computer Systems* (Gaithersburg). New York: ACM, pp. 136-140.

Roberts, T.L. and Moran, T.P. (1983). The evaluation of text editors: methodology and empirical results. *Communication of the ACM*, 26 (4), pp. 265-283.

Sasso, W.A. (1985). A comparison for two potential bases for office analysis: function and organizational unit. Dissertation from the Graduate School of Business Administration, the University of Michigan.

Whiteside, J. and Wixon, D. (1987). Discussion: improving human-computer interaction - a quest for cognitive science. *In: Interfacing Thought: Cognitive Aspects of Human-Computer Interaction*, J.M. Carroll (ed.). Cambridge, Mass: MIT Press, pp. 353-365.

Wilson, M.D., Barnard, P. J. and MacLean, A. (1985). User learning of core command sequences in a menu system. *IBM Hursley Human Factors Report HF114*. IBM United Kingdom Laboratories Ltd., Hursley Park, Winchester, UK.

Young, R.M. and Hull, A. (1982). Cognitive aspects of the selection of viewdata options by casual users. *In: Pathways to the Information Society*. M.B. Williams (ed.). Amsterdam: North Holland, pp. 571-576

Young, R.M. and Hull, A. (1983). Categorisation structures in hierarchical menus. *In: Proceedings of the the Tenth International Symposium on Human Factors in Telecommunications*, Helsinki, pp. 111-118.

ON MENTAL MODELS AND THE USER INTERFACE

Michael J. TAUBER

Department of Computer Science
University of Pittsburgh, USA

1 INTRODUCTION

This chapter addresses a fundamental problem in theoretical HCI. It has now become widely accepted that when a person uses a device, part of that person's knowledge about the device includes a "mental model", as described below, but the range and variety of the mental models postulated in the literature has been diverse and untrammelled. This exuberant approach to theorising seems false; theorists have acted as though there were no bounds whatever on the possible mental models, and that the mental model formed in one situation had nothing at all in common with the model formed in another situation. Not just the topic of the mental model, but also the form of the mental model has been treated in a thoroughly ad hoc, arbitrary manner.

It is our aim to propose a unifying description. We shall argue for the existence of a "language in the head" in which all conceptual structures can be represented. The most effective means to argue this position, and to demonstrate its relevance to HCI, is to show how such a "language in the head" can be formally represented, and to use the formalism to rephrase one of the existing accounts of a user's knowledge about a device. Two formalisms have been worked out which are candidate accounts of the "language in the head", one by Klix (1984) and one by Jackendoff (1983). In each case, the claim is that all knowledge - and therefore, a fortiori, "mental model" knowledge - is represented in a form that can be described using the formalism. However, there has been no previous attempt to rephrase any of the existing mental models postulated in the literature in terms of either of these formalisms.

We shall adopt Jackendoff's account and will use it to present a reformulation of Payne and Green's (1986) "Task-Action Grammar", TAG. Task Action Grammar is presented in detail elsewhere in this volume, by Green et al., and it is an attempt to give a formal description of the knowledge held by the user of a device. Our reformulation, Extended TAG or ETAG, not only places TAG on a more stringent theoretical basis, but also allows the theory to be extended to cover more of the underlying semantics than was previously possible. An important result from the development of ETAG is that we have been able to describe some of the consequences of design decisions that were not treated by the original version of TAG - especially decisions about how much information to reveal to the user. To demonstrate this, we shall investigate a particular example in some depth.

The structure of this chapter therefore is as follows. First we shall briefly describe the essentials of the particular program that is to be used as an example. Then we shall introduce the notion of "mental model" and show why it is important to seek formal descriptions of such models. Next we shall put mental model theory into the context of general model theory and show that to understand the architecture of mental models, it is necessary to obtain an account of the tasks that the user intends to accomplish. We shall then introduce Jackendoff's theory of conceptual structure and use it to develop ETAG.

2 A CASE FOR ANALYSIS: MacWrite

Throughout this chapter we shall make repeated reference to a particular application program as a concrete example on which to test our ideas, finishing in the Appendix with a worked-out analysis using the concepts we shall introduce. This program is a simple word-processing program named MacWrite, developed by the Apple Computer Co. The most important features for our purposes are (a) that it uses mouse actions and menu commands, and (b) the way that cut-and-paste works. A brief description is in order.

To cut a text section out, it is "selected" by locating the cursor at one end, depressing the mouse button, and moving the cursor to the other end, keeping the button depressed; this action highlights the text, and when the button is released the highlighting remains to show what text has been selected. Then the menu command "cut" is used, and the text disappears. It is now on the *clipboard*.

To paste a previously-cut-out section into the text, it is only necessary to locate the cursor at the desired point and use the menu command "paste". Whatever material was most recently sent to the clipboard will be copied into the text at that point. The clipboard itself is not altered and the same text can be inserted at many different points.

It must be observed that the clipboard itself is not visible to users of MacWrite, except by using a special command; and that when a further "cut" command is issued, the first contents of the clipboard are replaced by the new contents, without warning. This aspect is, no doubt, the result of a design decision: and it is on this point that we shall focus most of our analysis.

3 MENTAL MODELS, THEIR NATURE AND IMPORTANCE

It is obvious that users frequently do not fully understand the machines they use. Sometimes they are unaware of the existence of certain components or facilities; sometimes, to help themselves explain how a machine might work, they invent extra components that do not exist in reality. Even the parts that users do understand may be conceptualised in an unexpected way - "a file system is like a flower bed where you can plant new flowers or dig them up". All these aspects are represented by the term "mental model". To help control discussion about this difficult term, Norman (1983) distinguished between four kinds of model of a target system, t, as follows:

— the user's mental representation of the system, $M(t)$;

— the designer's conceptual framework for the description of the system, $C(t)$;

— the image the system presents to its users, $S(t)$;

— and the psychologist's conceptual model of the user's mental model, $C(M(t))$.

While this framework does not exhaust the possibilities, it suggests many important points. Mental models are owned by individuals. Usually, they are incomplete, partially wrong, and different from person to person. Norman's "conceptual model" can be regarded as the complete and correct mental model of a hypothetical ideal user. Since a user's mental model should be in accordance with the conceptual model, the designer must take into consideration the mental model he ideally requires of the future user. The system's image should also be consistent with the conceptual model, which means that it should properly communicate the conceptual aspects of the system to the users so that they can acquire a mental model which is in accordance with the conceptual model.

The question arises, however, of whether the term "mental model" refers to a particular manifestation of the general principles of human knowledge representation and acquisition, or whether it is something special and unique. Both views have been supported in the literature, but the position taken here is that mental models are simply a particular form of knowledge representation. What is particular about them is not their structure or form, but their topic: they describe things that people interact with.

> "In interacting with the environment, with others, and with the artefacts of technology, people form internal, mental models of themselves and of the things with which they are interacting. These models provide predictive and explanatory power for understanding the interaction." (Norman, 1983).

In similar vein, Bayman and Mayer (1984) write:

> "In the course of learning to use a new computer language .... the user may develop a "mental model" of the machine. A mental model is a metaphor consisting of the components and the operating rules of the machine. A mental model of a calculator allows the user to conceive of "invisible" information processing states (such as contents of internal registers) and "invisible" transformations (such as moving the contents of one register into another) that occur between input and output. Mental models are particularly important when users will have to guess the current state of the machine, or have to make inferences about how a given sequence of commands produces a certain output."

(Terminological note: Some researchers speak of a user's conceptual model instead of a user's mental model (Moran 1981, Young 1983). This usage of the term "conceptual model" should not be confounded with the designer's conceptual model, as introduced by Norman).

With this framework, Norman challenged interdisciplinary research in psychology and informatics to develop the strong design methods needed for the specification and realisation of user-oriented software. He points out:

> "In the ideal world, when a system is constructed, the design will be based around a conceptual model. This conceptual model should govern the entire human interface with the system, so that the image of that system seen by the user is consistent, cohesive and intelligible. I call this image the system image to distinguish it from the conceptual model upon which it is based, and the mental model one hopes the user will form of the system. The instruction manuals and all operation and teaching of the system should then be consistent with this

system image. The conceptual model that is taught to the user must fulfil three criteria: Learnability, Functionality, Usability." (Norman, 1983).

Such a framework allows us to define the cognitive ergonomics approach to the design of human-computer interfaces as follows:

— designers should specify their envisaged system by means of a conceptual model;

— a conceptual model describes the system in terms of an ideal user's mental model;

— the Human-Computer Interface in the narrow sense (the interaction language, information conveyed by the system, what is visible on the screen) must be based on the conceptual model;

— teaching about the system by means of manuals, help systems, or tutorials must be based on the conceptual model (van der Veer, Tauber, Waern and Muylwijk, 1985).

4 MENTAL MODELS AND MODEL THEORY

Research in cybernetics has established a "general model theory" in which the concept of a mental model or a conceptual model can be embedded (Klaus, 1969; Stachowiak, 1973). Rohr and Tauber (1984) applied general model theory to the concept of a model in HCI. They point out that it is necessary to distinguish between the model, M; an object O, modelled by M; and the person S using the model for definite purposes. Models can exist for such purposes as manipulating, planning, constructing, predicting, or explaining, and each different purpose may require a different aspect in the model.

M, the model, is built from a "substratum" which may be material (as in a model boat) or ideal (as in a mental model). Ideal models may be "internal" or "external"; mental models are ideal internal models, while sign systems and formalisms are ideal external models.

In order to represent mental models by a sign system, first we need sign systems which model the human cognition in general. In creating such a sign system, one must distinguish carefully between the mental model postulated by a theory and its representation by a sign system. Mac an

Airhinnigh (1985) usefully distinguishes between an entity, e, a user's conceptual model of that entity, M(u,e), and the scientist's representation R(M(u,e), F) of that model using the formal language F. Therefore, in order to work out strong foundations of a theory of mental models, first we need useful scientific models of the human cognitive structure and then we need formal description languages for the notation of mental models.

It is essential that such a description language is both highly formal, to enable its use as a precise specification language for designers, and also sufficiently wide in scope.

5   MENTAL MODELS OF SYSTEMS

One of the first papers on mental models of systems was published by Young (1983). He introduced two types of mental models of a system: *surrogates* and *mappings*. Surrogates are models of a system's behaviour and Young defines them as follows (M stands for the surrogate and D stands for the device): "M is a physical or notational analogue of the mechanism of D, and can be used to answer questions about D's behaviour." Caroll (1984) presents a very similar definition: "A surrogate M is a conceptual analysis that perfectly mimics the target system's D input/output behaviour." (Caroll, 1984). Although such definitions show the general idea of what a surrogate model is, they tell us nothing about the conceptual framework that humans use in their surrogates. Moreover, the surrogates that ordinary users have may well be very different from those formed by designers or engineers.

Whereas surrogates are a form of analogue, mappings, as defined by Young, are mental models which map different tasks to different aspects of a system. Task action mappings, for example, model a mental representation of a direct connection between, on the one hand, a mentally represented task, and on the other hand, how to perform that task by actions on the physical surface of a system.

Mappings claim to model a strongly task-oriented view which does not need any surrogate model of the internal working of the system. These claims are questionable when we consider the concept of the MacWrite *clipboard*, introduced above. Task action mappings would ignore the existence and the behaviour of the clipboard; a user who employed only task action mappings would not be able to take full advantage of the clipboard. A surrogate model, especially one of the invisible components of the system, makes better sense. The question is, in what conceptual framework will the model be constructed? Would it be constructed in implementation terms? Not at all. In order to take advantage of a surrogate it must be represented in concepts which help to locate some parts of the task; the system components must be described in terms of the roles or purposes they can serve. The clipboard, for example, should be conceptualised as an *object where a string can be placed and a copy of it can be inserted into the text*. There also should be conceptualised invisible machine operations like the *movement of a string from the text to the clipboard by replacing the old string on the clipboard* if there is any.

As this example demonstrates, a mental model is neither a pure surrogate nor a pure mapping. The task comes first. The mental model can then be considered and analysed with respect to that task. Two cases of rather useless mental models may illustrate the dominance of the task for the discussion and evaluation of a mental model. An actually used task action mapping, for example, can hide some important aspects of virtual internals of the system which when known would facilitate the human task performance. Or a surrogate used for the machine is so far removed from the concepts by which the task is represented that the usefulness of the surrogate must be in doubt.

Formal grammars have recently been introduced for the representation and notation of mental models. Green et al.'s chapter in this volume provides a broad view ranging from Reisner's Action Grammars to the Task-Action Grammars suggested by Payne and Green (1986). Production systems are a further formalism for the representation and notation of a mental model, also discussed in that chapter.

In the sense of the above required general model of human cognition and its notation, no current formal descriptions are sufficiently worked out. In Reisner's last version of the Action Grammar, for example, cognitive and motor actions are taken equally as terminal symbols in the formal grammar. On the one side, it is easy to decide for primitive motor actions like PRESS A KEY, DRAG THE MOUSE, or MOVE A CURSOR. On the other side, what kind of cognitive terminals should be taken? In the absence of any well-developed theory of conceptual structures and their place in human cognition the choice of which actions to call "cognitive" is more or less arbitrary. So we have to make the theory explicit.

As long as the task concept is not strongly based on a model of human cognition and the mental representation of a task, neither action grammars like
that introduced by Reisner nor production systems as used by Kieras and
Polson (1985) can be regarded as notating a mental model of a user. The
choice of the symbols in a formal grammar - or, equivalently, the content
of the working memory in a production rule system - will be arbitrary. It
must be noted, however, that the use of those notational systems is promising. Experimental evidence has confirmed that these notations reflect what
a user perceives as complexity, and so they bear on the problem of how to
predict a user's cognitive effort in learning the system, using the system
and mapping tasks to the system (Tauber & Rohr, 1986).

As mentioned above the task is the dominant aspect which requires the user
to build up mental models of a system. A task is a mental concept reflecting
how to reach the goals and what must be done. How can we incorporate
models of human cognition which are strongly based on theory and validated by psychological experiments into a notational framework for the
description of a mental model? In what follows we shall investigate the possibility of a formal system, in this case a grammar, that starts from *tasks*
rather than from a description of the system.

By introducing the idea of a task action grammar (TAG), Payne (1984) and
Payne and Green (1986) recognised the need to incorporate theoretical
assumptions about human representation of tasks into the notation of mental models. Payne refers to the model presented by Rosenberg (1984), in
which a task is mentally represented as a concept determined by features
with feature values. In TAG, the notation starts with the definition of the
mental dictionary defining the task-relevant features with the related sets of
feature values; the dictionary of the so-called primitive tasks can then be
defined. A primitive task is represented by its individual features and
feature values. A detailed account of TAG is given in Green et al.'s
chapter.

The TAG approach demonstrates the general architecture of notational systems for mental models:

1. The task is to be described in terms of a general model of human cognition.

2. The components defining the task are to be used in the formal grammar
   or the production rule system. The rules model the process by which
   the understanding of the task is decomposed into motor actions.

The essential point for any notational system is that the conceptual space by which the task is represented must be predefined and then a grammar or production rule system can be embedded in this conceptual context. Like a type definition in a programming language, a conceptual framework for the definition of a conceptual context is needed.

In fact, all the notations can describe a particular and even incomplete mental model of a particular user if this mental model can be elicited by experiment. However, the methodological problems of experimental investigation of an individual mental model are not part of this paper and are not solved yet. We shall instead restrict ourselves to discussing ideal and complete mental models. Such ideal models describe the knowledge of an ideal and competent hypothetical user. This ideal mental model acts as the designer's conceptual model in the sense of Norman: the system to be designed requires specific conceptual knowledge.

In the next two sections, an extension of TAG is proposed. This extension is based on a more detailed theory of human concept building.

6 A MODEL OF HUMAN COGNITION AND CONCEPTUAL STRUCTURE

6.1 Semantic Memory and Conceptual Structure

In psychology, there are several theories of human concept building and mental representation which can contribute to an extension of the promising TAG approach. One is the theory on the architecture of the *semantic memory* which is regarded as a knowledge base with concepts as its constituents (Klix, 1984). Between the concepts represented by the semantic memory, two different types of relationships, inner-concept relationships and inter-concept relationships, are postulated. The inner-concept relationships are relations established between a concept and its features but there also are concepts describing events which are characterised by inter-concept relationships. In the terminology of Klix, such relationships can be, for example, LOCATION, OBJECT, INSTRUMENT, or ACTOR. The representation of events, which are important concepts for the understanding of the operation of a system, are not covered by the pure feature approach. However, the remarkable fact about Klix's theory is, it is based upon, and supported by, the findings of psychological experiments.

A somewhat similar approach is the theory of human conceptual structure proposed by Jackendoff (1983). Like the semantic memory component of Klix's theory, conceptual structure is taken as the central level of mental representation on which linguistic, sensory, and motor information are made compatible. Also like the theory of Klix, Jackendoff suggests some relationships between concepts which cannot be directly modelled by features and feature values; but, unlike Klix, he gives the inter-concept relationships the dominant role (since they are developed in human evolution by conceptualising events in the outside world) and explains the feature-based concepts by means of those. Apart from its similarities to the theory of Klix, which is strongly determined by experimental work, and some first results from experiments of Rohr (1986), Jackendoff's theory is not yet supported by a broad range of experimental evidence. Nevertheless, since Jackendoff's theory looks very promising for modelling the user's mental knowledge of some important classes of tasks in human-computer interaction (especially object-manipulation tasks), we hope for more experiments in this direction.

6.2 Conceptual Structure and the Notation of Mental Models of Systems

We now introduce a blend of Jackendoff's theory of innate conceptual structure with some aspects of a user's mental model. In Jackendoff's theory, concepts are the constituents of the mental representation of the outside world. What Jackendoff calls a concept is a complex relationship between different concepts, and he applies an ontological approach to mental structure when he suggests that some ontological categories are *high level concept types* to which concepts belong as subtypes. Concepts are notated by [ ] and the name inside is the type label of the concept. The basic spatial ontological category is the concept [THING] or [OBJECT]. There are other ontological categories like [PLACE], [PATH], [STATE], or [EVENT] which all are based on the [OBJECT] concept.

A [PLACE] points to a region defined with respect to an [OBJECT] (the *reference object*) and enables human conceptualisation of the location of another [OBJECT] (the *theme object*). *Place-functions* map an [OBJECT], acting as a reference, onto a [PLACE]. In the sense of Jackendoff, we define the following replacement rule:

[PLACE] ::= [place.FUNCTION ([OBJECT])]

In the MacWrite example (see above), the clipboard ([CB]) as an [OBJECT] provides a [PLACE] for a [STRING]. Since the clipboard has only one type of a [PLACE], the place.FUNCTION is place.ON:

[place.ON ([OBJECT = CB])]

where place.ON is a place.FUNCTION mapping the reference [CB] onto a particular [PLACE]. In our notation, the ontological category (concept supertype) is restricted to the particular concept type.

A [PATH] is defined by a *path-function* and a [PLACE]. A [PATH] is a reference to either an object's location or else an object's movement. Depending on whether the [PLACE] is an ending point (a *bounded path*), is elsewhere on the [PATH] (a *route*), or would belong to the [PATH] if it were extended (a *direction*), different PATH-FUNCTIONS like path.TO([PLACE]), path.VIA([PLACE]), or path.TOWARD([PLACE]) can be employed for the description of a [PATH]. Following the informal description of the [PATH] concept, a [PATH] is defined by

[PATH] ::= [path.FUNCTION ([PLACE])]

and the [PLACE] concept is extended to

[PLACE] ::= [place.FUNCTION ([PATH])]

A [STATE] is defined by a *state.function* which has an [OBJECT] and a [PLACE] as its arguments.

[STATE] ::= [state.FUNCTION ([OBJECT], [PLACE])]

A basic state.FUNCTION is state.BE. The invisible but conceptually known fact *string X is on the clipboard* is described by

[state.BE ([OBJECT = STRING],
[place.ON ([OBJECT = CB])])].

An [EVENT] is notated by an event.FUNCTION which maps an [OBJECT] and a [PATH] to it:

[EVENT] ::= [event.FUNCTION ([OBJECT], [PATH])]

The movement of an [OBJECT] to the clipboard, an [EVENT] which is also invisible, can be notated by

[event.GO ([OBJECT = STRING],
[path.TO ([place.ON ([OBJECT = CB])])])]

However, there also is a side effect to this movement which is discussed later.

Besides their concepts of the *location* of an [OBJECT], users also have concepts of the *existence* of an [OBJECT]. This fact can be modelled by a concept [EX] as a special reference for an [OBJECT] which is interpreted as being in existence (an existential state), or coming into existence (an

existential event), or being non-existent, or going out of existence.
[OBJECTS] also may have [PROPERTIES] but these are not discussed
here; we shall restrict ourselves to very basic spatial concepts which are
typical concepts for some tasks in human-computer interaction (Rohr,
1986).

6.3 The User's Virtual Machine

If people use spatial concepts to represent knowledge of task related aspects
of a system how can we describe and specify the conceptual model of this
system in terms of the basic concept types just introduced? Tauber (1985,
1986a and b) has suggested the *User's Virtual Machine* (UVM), as a general descriptional framework in which the structure of knowledge needed to
understand the task related work of a system can be specified. The basic
idea of the UVM is similar to, but more general than, the concept of the
black box inside the glass box (du Boulay et al., 1981). In our model, it is
assumed that the user's understanding of both programming and task solving with application software can be modelled as the building up of concepts on a virtual machine.

The concept of the clipboard, for example, is part of a UVM representing
knowledge of MacWrite and is a concept of an invisible object in the black
box inside the visible glass box. Surrogate models can be defined by concepts pertaining to an invisible but task relevant virtual machine, the
UVM. However, visible components of a system also are interpreted by
conceptual knowledge. So these concepts also contribute to the definition of
the UVM. What is made visible and what is hidden does not make any
difference in defining the concepts a user must employ. The presence or
absence of visibility is a design decision regarding the perceptible surface of
a system linking it to the UVM behind. A direct manipulation interface
usually visualises and conveys most of the conceptual world, whereas a typical command language interface to an operating system requires a lot of
concepts describing the invisible and virtual work of the machine.

A UVM models the black box inside the glass box if there is any. Otherwise it models the concepts of the visible operations of the system. What is
the general structure of a spatially conceptualised UVM? In the sense of
the theory of Jackendoff and some experimental findings, the following general architecture of a spatial UVM is suggested:

–   The UVM is a complex [OBJECT] conceptualised as the overall
        OBJECT SPACE.

—   In the *OBJECT SPACE*, there are different types of [OBJECTS].

—   Each of them provides particular [PLACES] for the location of other [OBJECTS].

—   Each [OBJECT] type has one or more individual objects defined by the type's denotation.

—   [OBJECTS] may have [PROPERTIES] comparable to features with feature values.

—   Basic *OPERATIONS* establish the types of [EVENTS] which are possible in the UVM.

All [OBJECTS] in a UVM must be task relevant. For MacWrite, for example, the following [OBJECTS] and [PLACES] are part of the *OBJECT SPACE*:

[OBJECTS] :

[WORD], [STRING], [RULER], [TEXT], [CB]

[PLACES] :

[place.ON ([OBJECT = CB])],

[place.ON-POINT.(i,j) ([OBJECT = TEXT])],

[place.ON-REGION.[OBJECT = STRING] ([OBJECT = TEXT])]

An [OBJECT] defining a [PLACE] acts in the role of a reference for another [OBJECT], the theme, possibly located on that [PLACE]. In working with a spatially conceptualised system, a user focuses upon *theme-reference relations* like ([STRING], [CB]) and wants to change them. The space of the possible theme-reference relations is defined by the typology of the object space of the UVM. In addition to changes regarding theme-reference relationships, there also may be assignments of property values to [PROPERTIES]. Changes of the UVM *OBJECT SPACE* are conceptualized as [EVENTS] and a set of particular [EVENTS] defines a UVM's *OPERATIONS*. Those [EVENTS] are either initiated by the user or by the system. In order to realize an [EVENT] in the UVM, a user must use the interaction language as defined in the user interface. So the basic specifications in terms of the interaction language determine with their meaning the set of *OPERATIONS* of the UVM. A command with its argument or a direct manipulative action like *mark the object and move it with the mouse* are examples of the specifications of basic [EVENTS] in a UVM.

An example may illustrate that the degree of simplicity (or complexity) of those primitive [EVENTS] triggered by basic specifications in terms of the interaction language varies from system to system. In several versions of the Unix 'mail' command, the *save* command **s** (if applied when working with the public mailbox located in /usr/spool/mail) has the following conceptual effect:

— an [OBJECT = MESSAGE] is copied to
   [place.TAIL ([OBJECT = FILE])]

— a [PROPERTY = TO-BE_DELETED] has assigned the property value "YES"

So the [OBJECT = MESSAGE] is still in the public mailbox, but it is now marked for deletion. But that deletion will take place only if the mailing environment is left with the command **q**. If one wants to see the headers of the messages which are still in the mailbox, by using the command **h**, messages which are marked for deletion by the command **d** are not displayed, but messages which are copied with the command **s** and also are marked for deletion are displayed labelled with *. This conceptual context, which one should control when using the save command, is rather complex: but it is, nevertheless, a "simple" basic [EVENT] assigned to a basic command. So a conceptual description of this [EVENT] is part of the *OPERATIONS* of the UVM of Unix mail. Another user interface to the same conceptual world as provided by Unix mail might have a copy command, a move command, and a delete command. In this case we have three different basic [EVENTS] provided by these three commands.

The same *OBJECT SPACE* can have different *OPERATIONS*. For a unified conceptual description of all the different basic *OPERATIONS* on the same *OBJECT SPACE* we need *conceptual primitive operations* in a spatial UVM. With those primitive operations or combinations of them, any basic operation provided by the interaction language must be describable. In Tauber (1986b), we introduced the following conceptual primitive operations:

— the *locational operations* PLACE and UNPLACE

— the *existential operations* CREATE, DUPLICATE, CREATE-FROM, and DESTROY

— the *property setting operation* SETPROP

In terms of functions, the primitive operations return results and may have side effects. Results are particular [OBJECTS], while side effects change the current state of the overall *OBJECT SPACE*. In detail, the conceptual primitive operations represent the following primitive [EVENTS]:

PLACE ([OBJECT], [PLACE]) <->
[event.GO ([OBJECT], [path.TO ([PLACE])])]
returns: nil
side effect: [state.BE ([OBJECT], [PLACE])] is set
(*PLACE locates [OBJECT] on [PLACE]*)

UNPLACE ([OBJECT], [PLACE]) <->
[event.GO ([OBJECT], [path.FROM ([PLACE])])]
returns: [OBJECT]
side effect: [state.BE ([OBJECT], [PLACE])] no longer valid
(*UNPLACE removes [OBJECT] from the [PLACE]*)

CREATE ([OBJECT])
returns: [OBJECT]
side effect: nil
(*the new [OBJECT] is introduced into the overall *OBJECT SPACE**)

DUPLICATE ([OBJECT]) <->
[event.GO ([OBJECT], [path.TO ([EX])])]
returns: [OBJECT]
side effect: nil
(*the existing [OBJECT] is duplicated and a new individual is introduced*)

DESTROY ([OBJECT]) <->
[event.GO ([OBJECT], [path.FROM ([EX])])]
returns: nil
side effect: nil
(*the [OBJECT] is destroyed*)

SETPROP ([OBJECT], [PROPERTY], [VALUE])
returns: nil
side effect: [VALUE] set for [PROPERTY] of [OBJECT]
(*the [OBJECT] has [VALUE] for [PROPERTY]*)

Existential and locational operations can be composed to yield descriptions of typical situations:

PLACE (UNPLACE ([OBJECT], [PLACE:*y]), [PLACE:*x])
for movements, or
PLACE (DUPLICATE ([OBJECT]), [PLACE])
for copy to, or
PLACE (CREATE ([OBJECT]), [PLACE])
for the location of new objects.

In many tasks, particular [PLACES] have generic properties with respect to their use in the locational operations PLACE or UNPLACE. Again the clipboard with the

[PLACE = ON_CLIPBOARD] :: =
[place.ON ([OBJECT = CB])]
for holding a [OBJECT = STRING]

can be taken as an example. An [OBJECT = STRING:*y] moved to the [CB] causes a further side effect: an [OBJECT = STRING:*z] already located on the [PLACE = ON_CLIPBOARD] is replaced by [OBJECT = STRING:*y] and so destroyed. Those generic properties of a [PLACE] with respect to PLACE/UNPLACE are called *PLACE PARADIGM*, or *UNPLACE PARADIGM*. The notation [CONCEPT:*x] is equivalent to [CONCEPT] but with *x an arbitrary instance of this concept is explicitly addressed. This notation is helpful when a concept has more than one occurrence and the instances should be the same.

For the examples in the chapter, we need

— the *von Neumann paradigm*,
— the *dynamic paradigm*, and
— the *dynamic-replace paradigm*.

The first paradigm says that in the case of PLACE, an [OBJECT] already on the [PLACE] will be replaced, and in the case of UNPLACE only a copy of the [OBJECT] can be removed. The clipboard [CB], for example, uses this paradigm for all kinds of [OBJECTS] it can hold and for both operations PLACE and UNPLACE.

The second paradigm describes the insertion or removal of an [OBJECT], into or from a dynamic structure. The location of an [OBJECT] on a [PLACE] changes the location of the [OBJECT] on the [PLACE] and of many other [OBJECTS]. The insertion of an [OBJECT = STRING] on a [place.POINT.(i,j) ([OBJECT = TEXT])] can be taken as an example: characters on and after the [PLACE] are shifted. Removal can be similarly described.

The third paradigm is a *PLACE PARADIGM* and is described by the effect of replacing an object in a dynamic structure - e.g. the replacement of a string in a text, in 'insert'.

This sketch of the structure and specification of a spatial UVM may illustrate how a task related surrogate can be described. Looking back to Norman's conceptual model, the UVM is the conceptual model of a system acting as the mental model of an ideal and competent user. Ideal, since this user's conceptual architecture is as described by Jackendoff and competent, since she or he knows all task relevant components of the machine.

6.4 The UVM and TAG: ETAG

As demonstrated surrogate models can not be separated from the task. Rather they describe how the task is represented by the system. A user's tasks need to be mapped to basic system tasks which constitute the internal, system-related task space. As a surrogate model a UVM represents the conceptualisation of the internal basic tasks. Even if many task-relevant processes of the system are not made visible, the user needs knowledge of the UVM in order to perform proper actions on the surface of the user interface. Basic actions can be defined as mapped from the internal basic tasks. In summary, a competent user's representation of a task to be accomplished with a system consists of:

— a representation of the task;

— knowledge of internal, basic tasks in terms of the UVM;

— and mappings of the internal, basic tasks to the actions to be performed.

With Extended Task Action Grammars (ETAG), we introduce a type of mental grammar, combining the UVM as a description of the structure of a surrogate model with the TAG approach. An ETAG is a semantic grammar producing actions to tasks represented in terms of the UVM. A more complete definition is given in Chang, Tauber, Yu and Yu (1987). The main components of an ETAG are:

(1) the *UVM DESCRIPTION,*

(2) the *TASK DICTIONARY,* and

(3) the *REPLACEMENT RULES.*

The *UVM DESCRIPTION* replaces the mental dictionary of the TAG. It specifies the type of the *OBJECT SPACE,* and the type of [OBJECTS], [PLACES], their PLACE/UNPLACE paradigms, and their [PROPERTIES]. The description of the UVM will not be discussed in the body of this chapter. An example of a UVM definition is given in the appendix.

The *TASK DICTIONARY* contains the basic, internal tasks of the system as determined by the basic *UVM OPERATIONS* which are made accessible through the interface. These operations are conceptualised as [EVENTS] in the *UVM OBJECT SPACE* and are either conceptual primitive operations or composed of those primitive operations. Each task listed in the task dictionary has a *name* representing the type of the [EVENT], a *conceptual description* in terms of the concepts introduced by the UVM, an *attributed symbol* used in the replacement rules, and concepts associated with this symbol. A *where-clause* provides information on the conceptual context in which the conceptual description of the [EVENT] is embedded. Concepts associated to a symbol are subtypes to the supertypes which may be used in the grammar. Supertypes are either the ontological categories like [OBJECT], [PLACE], or [PATH] or special concept types needed to understand the interaction language. [SYMBOL], for example, is a concept indicating that some special command symbols are to be used for the interaction with the system. Subtypes are the specific concepts constituting a particular task. Only those concepts which directly contribute to the understanding of an action are associated to a task symbol. So an entry in the task dictionary consists of the following components:

- name,
- conceptual description,
- where-clause,
- attributed-symbol,
- comments.

The basic task *copy an object from the text to the clipboard* is taken as an example of an entry in the *TASK DICTIONARY*. In this entry the name of the event is "COPY_TO_CB", the conceptual description says that a duplicate copy of an object is moved to a place which is the clipboard, the where-clause says that the object to be duplicated may be a string, a word, or a ruler. The object must come from a place that exists and is a text region. The attributed symbol is **T1**, to be defined for the replacement rules.

ENTRY 1:

name:[EVENT = COPY_TO_CB],

conceptual description:
    [event.GO ([OBJECT = DUPLICATE ([OBJECT:*x])],
    [path.TO ([place.ON ([OBJECT = CB])])])])]),

where-clause:
    [OBJECT:*x] = ONE-OF {[STRING], [WORD], [RULER]}
    AND
    [state.BE ([OBJECT:*x],
    [place.ON-REGION.[OBJECT:*x] ([OBJECT = TEXT])])],

attributed symbol:
    T1 [OBJECT = ONE-OF {[STRING], [WORD], [RULER]}],

comments:
    "copy an object from the text to the clipboard".

The conceptual description of the [EVENT] may also be described by the conceptual primitives, but for use in ETAG we prefer the above description. It provides a better view of the concepts which constitute the representation of the task and the subset of them which is associated to the task symbol as relevant for the actions to be performed.

Besides the concepts which primarily constitute the task, a complete understanding of the task requires knowledge of the context in which the task is embedded. In the sense of a surrogate model, this context knowledge is determined by the structure and processes defining the UVM. For the sample task, this context knowledge comprises the knowledge of the specific nature of the clipboard defined by the *PLACE PARADIGM* saying that an [OBJECT] located at the [CB] will be replaced. So in a particular task a user may want to control which [OBJECT] is on the clipboard before it is replaced by a new one. This kind of knowledge is part of the surrogate model a user has of the system. A surrogate model guarantees the understanding of how a task is represented by the system but it also supports a user in planning a particular task and in controlling its accomplishment. A task action grammar, however, describes only how a task, once decided upon, is to be specified to the system.

The *REPLACEMENT RULES* model the mappings from the conceptually represented task to the actions needed to accomplish it. ETAG is a generative grammar producing actions to achieve the tasks of the *TASK DICTIONARY*. There is a starting symbol **T** with a related replacement rule collecting all basic tasks listed in the *TASK DICTIONARY*, and there are other non-terminal symbols modelling the decomposition of the task. Terminal symbols represent physical actions to be performed by the user. Concept types associated with the symbol of the left side of a replacement rule are associated to one or more symbols in the right hand side. The following replacement rule for the sample basic task *copy to the clipboard* is taken as a first example.

T1 [OBJECT = ONE-OF {[STRING], [WORD], [RULER]}] :: =
    select [OBJECT] + **select** [SYMBOL = EDIT]
    [SYMBOL = COPY]

The concept [OBJECT] is associated to **T1** in the left side of the rule and also to **select** in the right side. An ETAG replacement rule can be regarded as a metarule producing replacement rules. The rule above produces three individual rules for each type ([STRING], [WORD], [RULER]) included within the supertype [OBJECT]. In a replacement rule, the relevant types need to be defined only when they first occur. Thereafter the types are inherited by any occurrence of this supertype.

A further point demonstrated by the example is the possibility of introducing new concepts in the right hand side of a replacement rule. [SYMBOL = COPY] and [SYMBOL = EDIT] are used only in the right side of the rule. Those concepts are introduced by a particular interface, and not primarily established by the conceptual structure of the task. Rather they are established by the type of interaction and presentation provided by the user interface. In the example, [SYMBOL] stands for command names used in the menus. However, they can be regarded as contributing to the explanation of the left side symbol. In the MacWrite example, [SYMBOL = EDIT] groups together all the operations in which the clipboard is involved, and [SYMBOL = COPY] is a specification for the conceptual [EVENT] defining the task **T1**.

The next example illustrates a replacement rule with more than one concept associated to the left side symbol and associated with some right side symbols. The rule defines the decomposition of the *placement of a new string* into the specification of the [PLACE] and the construction of the [OBJECT].

T4 [OBJECT = STRING] [PLACE = ONE-OF {
        [place.ON-POINT.(i,j) ([OBJECT = TEXT])],
        [place.ON-REGION.[OBJECT = ONE-OF
            {[STRING], [WORD]}] ([OBJECT = TEXT])]}] :: =
    select [PLACE] + **construct** [OBJECT]

Some rules bridge the gap between conceptual aspects and the physical actions needed to specify the concepts to the system, as illustrated by the following:

select [OBJECT = WORD] :: =

       MOUSE-POINT (VIS [OBJECT]) +
       MOUSE-BUTTON-DOUBLE-CLICK

Those rules describe how the concepts are specified by the actions. Since the MacWrite interface makes some concepts visible and provides the possibility of working with the visual representation of these concepts the rule above is based on a relationship ([*concept*], *VIS* [*concept*]), where VIS is the visual representation of a concept. Those relations between meaning and visual representation are discussed by the concept of a generalised icon (Chang, 1987).

7 DISCUSSION

We want to suggest a unified task-oriented approach to surrogates and mappings by combining the UVM concept with the TAG approach. This first design of an ETAG, however, needs more detailed discussion and formal definition of this type of semantic grammar (see also Chang et al., 1987). Examples of details still to be worked out are the relationship between concepts and their visible images, or the types of dialog-specific nonterminal symbols which can be used in such a grammar.

Previous grammar oriented approaches to task-action representations claim to provide predictive power with respect to a user's effort to learn or to use a system (see Green et al.'s chapter). The predictive power of ETAG needs to be determined and experimentally demonstrated. Besides this necessary research, ETAG also seems to open the possibility for some qualitative evaluations of the specified system which can be derived from the overall structure of the *UVM DESCRIPTION*, the *TASK DICTIONARY*, and the *REPLACEMENT RULES*. Those evaluations, for example, can be done by asking:

—   How far is the entire conceptual structure of a task inherited from the decomposition modelled by the replacement rules?

—   Which concepts required by the user are made visible, and which are left to be inferred and how complex are these concepts?

- To what degree is the conceptual context of a task explicitly associated with the symbols in the replacement rules?
- How simple or complex are the basic tasks?

In order to answer those questions, we need to compare ETAG descriptions of different systems with different types of user interfaces, different types of visual representations, and different types of interaction styles. Additionally, this comparison must be accompanied by psychological experiments.

REFERENCES

Bayman, P. and Mayer, R.E. (1984). Instructional Manipulation of User's Mental Models for Electronic Calculators. *International Journal of Man-Machine Studies*, 20, pp. 189-199.

Caroll, J.M. (1984). Mental Models and Software Human Factors: An Overview. *Research Report RC 10616*, Yorktown Heights: IBM Watson Research Center.

Chang, S.K. (1987). Icon Semantics - A Formal Approach to Icon System Design. *Proceedings of the International Conference on Chinese Computing*. Singapore, August 1987.

Chang, S.K., Tauber, M.J., Yu, B. and Yu J.-S. (1987). The SIL-ICON Compiler - An Icon-Oriented System Generator. *In: Proceedings of the IEEE Workshop on Languages for Automation*. S.K. Chang, H. Schauer and M.J. Tauber (eds.). Computer Society Press of the IEEE, Washington, D.C. pp. 17-22.

du Boulay, B., O'Shea, T. and Monk, J. (1981). The Black Box Inside the Glass Box: Presenting Computer Concepts to Novices. *International Journal of Man-Machine Studies*, 14, pp. 237-249.

Jackendoff, R. (1983). Semantics and Cognition. Cambridge Mass: MIT-Press.

Kieras, D.E. and Polson, P.G. (1985). An Approach to the Formal Analysis of User Complexity. *International Journal of Man-Machine Studies*, 22, pp. 365-394.

Klaus, G. (1969). Wörterbuch der Kybernetik. Frankfurt am Main: Fischer Bücherei.

Klix, F. (1984). Gedächtnis, Wissen, Wissensnutzung. Berlin: Deutscher Verlag der Wissenschaften.

Mac an Airchinnigh, M. (1985). Report on the User's Conceptual Model. *In: User Interface Management Systems*. G.E. Pfaff, (ed.). Berlin, Heidelberg, New York, Tokyo: Springer-Verlag.

Moran T.P. (1981). The command language grammar: a representation for the user interface of interactive computer systems. *International Journal of Man-Machine Studies*, 15, pp. 3-50.

Norman, D.A. (1983). Some Observations on Mental Models. *In: Mental Models*. D. Gentner and L.A. Stevens, (eds.). Hillsdale, New Jersey: Lawrence Erlbaum Associates.

Payne, S.J. (1984). Task-Action Grammars. *Interact' 84. Proceedings of the first IFIP-Conference on "Human-Computer Interaction"*. 4-7 September, London, IFIP, pp. 139-144.

Payne, S.J. and Green, T.R.G. (1986) Task-action grammars: a model of the mental representation of task languages. *Human-Computer Interaction*, 2 (2), pp. 93-133.

Reisner, P. (1981). Formal Grammar and Human Factors Design of an Interactive Graphic System. *IEEE Transactions on Software Engineering*, SE-7, (2), pp. 229-240.

Reisner, P. (1984). Formal Grammar as a Tool for Analyzing Ease of Use: Some Fundamental Concepts. *In: Human Factors in Computer Systems*. J.C. Thomas and M.L. Schneider, (eds.). Norwood, New Jersey: Ablex Publishing Corporation, .

Rohr, G. and Tauber, M.J. (1984). Representational Frameworks and Models for Human-Computer Interfaces. *In: Readings on Cognitive Ergonomics - Mind and Computers*. G.C. van der Veer, M.J. Tauber, T.R.G. Green and P. Gorny, (eds.). Berlin, Heidelberg, New York, Tokyo: Springer-Verlag.

Rohr, G. (1986). Using Visual Concepts. *In: Visual Languages*. S.K. Chang, T. Ichikawa, P.A. Ligomenides (eds.). New York: Plenum Press.

Rosenberg, J. (1984). A Featural Approach to Command Names. *In: Human Factors in Computing Systems*. A. Janda, (ed.). Proceedings of the CHI'83, Boston, December 1983, pp. 116-119, Amsterdam: North Holland.

Stachowiak, H. (1973). Allgemeine Modelltheorie. Wien, New York: Springer-Verlag.

Tauber, M.J. (1985). Top Down Design of Human-Computer Systems from the Demands of Human Cognition to the Virtual Machine - An Interdisciplinary Approach to Model Interfaces in Human-Computer Interaction. *In: Proceedings of the IEEE Workshop on Languages for Automation*, Palma de Mallorca, Spain, June 28-29, 1985, IEEE Computer Society Press, Silverspring.

Tauber, M.J. (1986a). An Approach to Metacommunication in Human-Computer Interaction. *In: Man-Computer Interaction Research MACINTER I*. F. Klix and H. Wandke (eds.). Amsterdam, New York: North Holland, pp. 35-50.

Tauber, M.J. (1986b). Top-Down Design of Human-Computer Interfaces. *In: Visual Languages*. S.K. Chang, T. Ichikawa, P.A. Ligomenides (eds.). New York: Plenum Press.

Tauber, M.J. and Rohr, G. (1986). Zur Gestaltung von Mensch-Maschine Schnittstellen unter Berücksichtigung des Mentalen Modells. *In: Die Zukunft der Informationssysteme - Lehren der 80er Jahre*. A. Schulz, (Hrsg.), Berlin, Heidelberg, New York: Springer-Verlag, pp. 565 - 575.

van der Veer, G.C., Tauber, M.J., Waern, Y. and Muylwijk, B. (1985). On the Interaction between Systems and User Characteristics. *Behaviour and Information Technology*, 4 (4), pp. 289-308.

Young, R.M. (1983). Surrogates and Mappings: Two Kinds of Conceptual Models for Interactive Devices. *In: Mental Models*. D. Gentner and A.L. Stevens, (eds.). Hillsdale, New Jersey: Erlbaum.

Appendix: ETAG-Description for Some Basic Internal MacWrite Tasks

1. The UVM - Object Structure and Object Types

DEFINE ([UVM-MACWRITE], .)
  NAME: "MacWrite Subset"
  SPATIAL FIELD
    supports: [TEXT], [CB]
    structure: SET-OF {[TEXT], [CB]}
  END SPATIAL FIELD
END [UVM-MACWRITE].

DEFINE ([CB], [UVM-MACWRITE])
  NAME: "Clipboard"
  card: 1
  SPATIAL FIELD
    supports: [STRING], [WORD], [RULER]
    structure: SINGLE-PLACE-OBJECT FOR
        [WORD], [STRING], [RULER]
    place.FUNCTIONS: place.ON ([OBJECT = CB])
         FOR [WORD], [STRING], [RULER]
    place-paradigm: von Neumann
    unplace-paradigm: von Neumann
  END SPATIAL FIELD
END [CB].

```
DEFINE ([TEXT], [UVM-MACWRITE])
   card: 1
   SPATIAL FIELD
      supports: [STRING], [WORD], [RULER]
      structure: BOX (I,J) OF [STRING], [WORD], [RULER]
      place.FUNCTIONS:
      ON-POINT.(i,j) ([OBJECT = TEXT]) FOR [STRING], [WORD]
               place-paradigm: dynamic-insert
               unplace-paradigm: dynamic-remove |
      ON-REGION.[OBJECT = ONE-OF {
                  [STRING], [WORD]}] ([OBJECT = TEXT])
               FOR [STRING], [WORD]
      place-paradigm: dynamic-replace
      unplace-paradigm: dynamic-removement
   END SPATIAL FIELD
END [TEXT].

DEFINE ([WORD],[TEXT])
   SPATIAL FIELD
      supports: nil
   END SPATIAL FIELD
END [WORD].

DEFINE ([STRING], [TEXT]/[CB])
   SPATIAL FIELD
      supports: nil
    END SPATIAL FIELD
END [STRING].

DEFINE ([RULER], [TEXT]/[CB])
   SPATIAL FIELD
      supports: nil
   END SPATIAL FIELD
END [RULER].
```

2. The Task Dictionary TD

TD = {[EVENT = COPY_TO_CB], [EVENT = MOVE_TO_CB],
      [EVENT = COPY_FROM_CB], [EVENT = TYPE_STRING],
      [EVENT = DELETE_FROM_TEXT]}

ENTRY 1:

name: [EVENT = COPY_TO_CB],

conceptual description:
    [event.GO ([OBJECT = DUPLICATE ([OBJECT:*x])],
    [path.TO ([place.ON ([OBJECT = CB])])])],

where-clause:
    [OBJECT:*x] = ONE-OF {[STRING], [WORD], [RULER]}
    AND
    [state.BE ([OBJECT:*x],
    [place.ON-REGION.[OBJECT:*x] ([OBJECT = TEXT])])],

attributed symbol:
    T1 [OBJECT = ONE-OF {[STRING], [WORD], [RULER]}],

comments
    "copy an object from the text to the clipboard".

ENTRY 2:

name: [EVENT = MOVE_TO_CB],

conceptual description:
    [event.GO ([OBJECT:*x],
    [path.FROM (
        [place.ON-REGION.[OBJECT:*x] ([OBJECT = TEXT])])],
    [path.TO ([place.ON ([OBJECT = CB])])])],

where-clause:
    [OBJECT:*x] = ONE-OF {[STRING}, [WORD], [RULER]},

attributed symbol:
    T2 [OBJECT = ONE-OF {[STRING], [WORD], [RULER]}],

comments
    "move an object from the text to the clipboard"

ENTRY 3:

name:[EVENT = COPY_FROM_CB],

conceptual description:
    [event.GO ([OBJECT = DUPLICATE ([OBJECT:*x])],
    [path.TO ([PLACE = ONE-OF {
        [place.ON-POINT.(i,j) ([OBJECT = TEXT])],
        [place.ON-REGION.[OBJECT:*y]
          ([OBJECT = TEXT])]}])])],

where-clause:
    [state.BE ([OBJECT:*x], [place.ON ([OBJECT = CB])])]
    AND
    [OBJECT:*y] = ONE-OF {[WORD], [STRING]},

attributed symbol:
    T3 [PLACE = ONE-OF {
        [place.ON-POINT.(i,j) ([OBJECT = TEXT])],
        [place.ON-REGION.[OBJECT:*y] ([OBJECT = TEXT])]}],

comments
    "copy an object from the clipboard into the text".

ENTRY 4:

name: [EVENT = TYPE_STRING],

conceptual description:
    [event.GO ([OBJECT = STRING:*x],
    [path.TO ([PLACE = ONE-OF {
        [place.ON-POINT.(i,j) ([OBJECT = TEXT])],
        [place.ON-REGION.[OBJECT:*y]
          ([OBJECT = TEXT])]}])])],

where-clause:
    [OBJECT:*y] = ONE-OF {[WORD], [STRING]}
    AND
    [STRING:*x] = CREATE,

attributed symbol:
    T4 [OBJECT = STRING] [PLACE = ONE-OF {
        [place.ON-POINT.(i,j) ([OBJECT = TEXT])],
        [place.ON-REGION.[OBJECT:*y] ([OBJECT = TEXT])]}],

comments
    "placement of a new string".

ENTRY 5:

name: [EVENT = DELETE_FROM_TEXT],

conceptual description:
    [event.GO ([OBJECT:*x],
    [path.FROM (
            [place.ON-REGION.[OBJECT:*x] ([OBJECT = TEXT])])],
    [path.TO ([PLACE = NON-EX])])],

where-clause:
    [OBJECT:*x] = ONE-OF {[STRING], [WORD], [RULER]},

attributed symbol:
    T5 [OBJECT:*x],

comments
    "delete an object in the text".

3. The Replacement Rules

(I) Top Level Replacement Rule

T ::=**T1** [OBJECT = ONE-OF {[STRING], [WORD], [RULER]}] |
    T2 [OBJECT = ONE-OF {[STRING], [WORD], [RULER]}] |
    T3 [PLACE = ONE-OF {
            [place.ON-POINT.(i,j) ([OBJECT = TEXT])],
            [place.ON-REGION.[OBJECT = ONE-OF
                {[STRING], [WORD]}] ([OBJECT = TEXT])]}] |
    T4 [OBJECT = STRING] [PLACE = ONE-OF {
            [place.ON-POINT.(i,j) ([OBJECT = TEXT])],
            [place.ON-REGION.[OBJECT = ONE-OF
                {[STRING], [WORD]}] ([OBJECT = TEXT])]}] |
    T5 [OBJECT = ONE-OF {[STRING], [WORD], [RULER]}]

(II) Basic Tasks with the Clipboard

T1 [OBJECT = ONE-OF {[STRING], [WORD], [RULER]}] ::=
    select [OBJECT] + **select** [SYMBOL = EDIT]
            [SYMBOL = COPY]

T2 [OBJECT = ONE-OF {[STRING], [WORD], [RULER]}] :: =
    select [OBJECT] + **select** [SYMBOL = EDIT]
        [SYMBOL = CUT]

T3 [PLACE = ONE-OF {
        [place.ON-POINT.(i,j) ([OBJECT = TEXT])],
        [place.ON-REGION.[OBJECT = ONE-OF
            {[STRING], [WORD]}] ([OBJECT = TEXT])]}] :: =
    select [PLACE] + **select** [SYMBOL = EDIT]
        [SYMBOL = PASTE]

(III) Basic Tasks without the Clipboard

T4 [OBJECT = STRING] [PLACE = ONE-OF {
        [place.ON-POINT.(i,j) ([OBJECT = TEXT])],
        [place.ON-REGION.[OBJECT = ONE-OF
            {[STRING], [WORD]}] ([OBJECT = TEXT])]}] :: =
    select [PLACE] + **construct** [OBJECT]

T5 [OBJECT = ONE-OF {[STRING], [WORD], [RULER]}] :: =
    select [OBJECT] + **key** [LABEL = BACKSPACE]

(IV) Action Rules

select [OBJECT = STRING] :: =
        MOUSE-POINT (FIRST (VIS [OBJECT])) +
        MOUSE-BUTTON-PRESS +
        MOUSE-DRAG-TO (LAST (VIS [OBJECT])) +
        MOUSE-BUTTON-RELEASE |
        MOUSE-POINT (VIS [OBJECT]) +
        MOUSE-BUTTON-CLICK

select [OBJECT = WORD] :: =
        MOUSE-POINT (VIS [OBJECT]) +
        MOUSE-BUTTON-DOUBLE-CLICK

select [OBJECT = RULER] ∷=

    MOUSE-POINT (POINT-AREA (VIS [OBJECT])) +
    MOUSE-BUTTON-CLICK

select [PLACE = ON-POINT.(i,j) ([OBJECT = TEXT])] ∷=

    MOUSE-POINT (VIS [PLACE]) +
    MOUSE-BUTTON-CLICK

select [PLACE = ON-REGION.[OBJECT:*x] ([OBJECT = TEXT])] ∷=

    select [OBJECT:*x]

construct [OBJECT = STRING] ∷= **TYPE** (VIS [OBJECT])

select [SYMBOL:*x] [SYMBOL:*y] ∷=

    MOUSE-POINT (VIS [SYMBOL:*x]) +
    MOUSE-BUTTON-PRESS +
    MOUSE-DRAG-TO (VIS [SYMBOL:*y]) +
    MOUSE-BUTTON-RELEASE

key [LABEL] ∷= **HIT** (KEY [LABEL])

SECTION 2

EMPIRICAL EVIDENCE IN COGNITIVE ERGONOMICS

Whereas section 1 was concerned with issues in the theory of HCI at the level of interface design, this section addresses the more general area of Software Engineering and the '*other interface*' of systems design, analysis and procurement. Strategies for attacking disparate strands of the software life cycle are presented by Potts (*requirements specifications*), Lanzara and Mathiassen (*project management*) and Hoc (*planning aids*). All are described within the overall structure of the conceptual modelling schema presented by Traunmüller in his critical overview of the methodologies of information systems design.

This first chapter lays the foundation for the introduction of cognitive ergonomic interests to the design and development of the applications systems and environments which constitute the backbone of the computers we work with.

Potts, in chapter 5, describes and critiques the methodologies of design specifications in common use and discusses the accompanying role played by such specifications in the software development process and the client-contractor relationship. In keeping with the orientation of this book, a descriptive analysis of techniques is accompanied by the presentation of specific examples of usage in real-world situations. The author's own prescriptive method is described and an outline of its use fully covered. The use of such techniques as a communicative medium is one which is highly pertinent to cognitive ergonomics and is discussed in the light of new ways of presenting formal specifications and dynamic interactions such that the human considerations become paramount.

The area of systems development projects and effective programme management is the subject under consideration in chapter 6 by Lanzara and Mathiassen. A discussion of tools, techniques and strategies employed by the actors in these situations is followed by a presentation of the authors' own tool to allow exteriorisation and intervention by participants in order to develop and formalise internalised knowledge, much as in the formal descriptions of user's '*how to do it*' knowledge of the previous section. A full description of the 'mapping' technique when used in a system development situation in a Danish company is a major contribution, together with the prescriptive details of the tool's implementation.

Hoc, in the final chapter in this section, discusses the notion of planning behaviour in programming and developmental environments, such as those advocated by Potts and Traunmüller. This is a crucial feature in systems design and the cognitive ergonomic aspects addressed by Hoc center on an investigation of the computer aids available for planning within the framework of psychological and AI theory. An experimental investigation is presented and described in full, providing the applications orientation of this chapter and making specific recommendations for this category of planning tools as aids to planning strategies.

CONCEPTUAL MODELS FOR DESIGNING INFORMATION SYSTEMS

Roland TRAUNMÜLLER

Johannes Kepler Universität Linz
Institut für Informatik, Austria

Abstract

Although the roles played by both programmers and end-users have attracted a great deal of attention in Human Factors research, those of the Systems Analyst and Designer still await investigation. The following paper addresses this issue when considering basic conceptual models of Information Systems Design.

The Introduction describes the design of information systems in general while the major part of the paper deals with the different conceptual models existing in Information Systems Design. A number of fundamental methods are presented and examples from a Higher Education Planning System and some common application packages are given.

1 THE DESIGN OF INFORMATION SYSTEMS

1.1 Scope and Aspects of Information Systems Design

Information systems are socio-technical systems designed for the storage, processing, display, and distribution of information. Information systems encompass the whole information structure of business and organisations. The design of such systems is a global task dealing with many different constraints and criteria, and so is quite different from the task of constructing individual programs. This difference in scope has been reflected by the two separate professional profiles which have evolved for systems analysts and for programmers.

The main ways in which Information Systems Design differs from computer programming are the following:

- Information System Design starts with the goals and needs of the organisation in question.

- In Information Systems, design of the database is of paramount importance.

- Information Systems Design encompasses a multitude of individual programs, connected via a common database.

- Information Systems Design ends with the specification of the required programs. Procedural details are often delegated to programmers.

- In Information Systems, the social context and the security and social compatibility of the system are dominant parameters.

Three disciplines in computer science are closely related to Information Systems Design: those of Systems Analysis; Database Design, and Software Engineering. A synonymous use of these terms is misleading because there are very particular points of difference:

- Systems Analysis may be the closest synonym to Information Systems Design, and most professionals occupied in the design of systems hold a position as a Systems Analyst. The term in itself is somewhat narrow because it neglects the large element of synthesis and construction involved in the work.

- Although Database Design is the main task in Information Systems Design, the two are not identical: Database Design in general is too restricted to particulars of the database itself, and does not include the major tasks of obtaining user and system requirements.

- Software Engineering has a scope which is quite different from that of Information Systems Design. In Software Engineering a neat set of requirements is assumed as given as a prerequisite and programs are specified and written to fulfil those requirements. In contrast, Information Systems Design starts with a fuzzy descriptions of needs, wishes, and problems, and in many cases, the crucial part comes in actually determining specific requirements.

The term "design" is also itself ambiguous: it can mean the "blueprint" of a product, as well as describing the actual process which eventually leads to that blueprint. Initially, the design aspect in Information Systems Design was used in the first context. This is in close correspondence with other technical disciplines (e.g. as in house building, or industrial engineering).

Later, the focus of interest of computer scientists moved to that of the process of design itself, which was originally regarded as a highly organised activity. Subsequent attention was centered on the following particular aspects of design:

— design as a technique;
— design on a methodological basis;
— design which could be supported by the computer itself;
— design as a cognitive process.

1.2 The Evolution of Techniques, Methods, and Tools

The evolution of techniques, methods, and tools reflects the transition of Systems Analysis and Design from an artistic metier to the level of computerised production.

Systems Analysis and Design were originally treated as artistic skills but task performance has since merged into technique, and so correspondences can be drawn between design and craftsmanship. Recognised design techniques became part of the designer's repetoire and design reached the level of "craftsmanship". In establishing a theoretical basis, these techniques were transformed into methods, and with a well-defined methodology, design had reached the level of industrial-like production. At this point, in a perfect analogy with industrial production, these methods are now sustained by computerised support tools.

Intrinsic forces and constraints controlled these transitions since the resulting Information Systems had to be technical products of a high standard, and production had to be based on some objective mechanism in order to minimise reliance on any one individual systems designer. The use of formalised methods allows for planning of resources, time and costs while the identification of clearcut divisions makes it possible to subdivide the whole task between individuals or teams, with well-specified interfaces between the various parts.

In addition, only sound methodologies can improve testing and enforce provability: in Computer Aided Design it is possible to lower costs by rationalisation, and, with computer assistance, documentation becomes a by-product. Computerised design leads to the development of methods that can be concatenated and brought together to reduce overheads.

1.3 Conceptual Models for Information Systems Design

The large number of available methods and the pace of development have, however, resulted in some problems. The terminology of the few established methods is ill defined and makes for confusion when different terms are used for the same notion, and vice versa (e.g. there is not even a common concept for the term "phases"). Some methods cover only small sectors of the life-cycle while others have a rather small methodological basis, and are rather more pure techniques than methodologies as such.

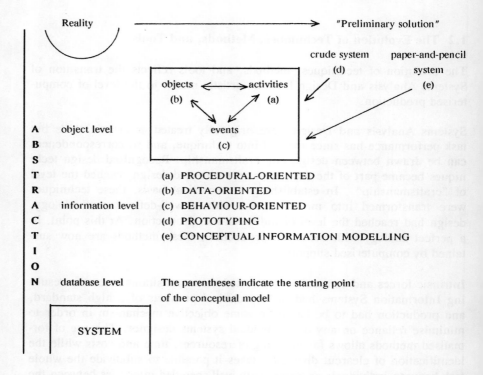

Figure 1.   Principal approaches to leading conceptual design models
of information systems

In consequence, a Review Committee (in which the author participated) performed a comparison of such methods. The results have been published by IFIP (Olle, Sol and Verrijn-Stuart, 1982; Olle, Sol and Tully, 1983). In the following Section the different methods highlighted by these reviews can be assumed to be representative of the principal approaches to design.

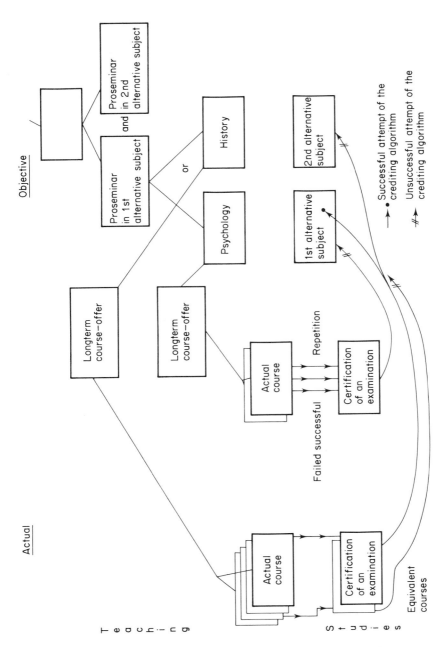

Figure 2.   Basic schema for the Higher Education Planning System

In subsequent sections of this chapter, five conceptual models which underly such methods are given. Figure 1 illustrates some of the main ways in which design can be approached. As an example, a Higher Education Planning System (OECD-CERI, 1974; Strigl and Traunmüller, 1976) is described in Figure 2. Further examples stress the analogies to such common applications as spreadsheets.

1.4 Computer Assisted Design and Support Environments

From the very beginning, technical progress has been accompanied by the development of tools. In data processing the tool of utmost importance is the computer itself - the use of compilers in bootstrapping complicated machine-code programs is one of the best known examples.

In Information Systems Design this tendency is reflected by research into software tools and design support environments. In such environments, the crucial element is the use of a coherent set of methods and tools sustaining a fan of targets including the modelling of objects and activities; design of the database at various levels; specification of software and hardware interfaces; prototyping of human-computer interfaces; simulation of logical constraints, and scheduling the project and its resources.

The state of the art for methods and tools can be assumed to be fairly advanced (Verrijn-Stuart, Sol and Olle, 1986; Lockemann and Mayr, 1986). For support environments which have to provide a maximum of synergy between human and computer, aspirations to be fulfilled are high and current status is still at the level of fundamental research (Bretton Woods, 1986).

1.5 Human Factors During the Design Process

Understanding the Human Factors of the Information Systems Design process has become a research issue due to two recent converging developments. On the one hand, the scope of Human Factors research has been expanding to include the analysis and design processes, and on the other, Information Systems Design has been widening its perspective.

The discipline of Cognitive Ergonomics is now investigating the work of Systems Analysts and Designers (Van der Veer, Tauber, Green and Gorny, 1984). Those previously targeted by Human Factors research were the end-users of Information Systems such as databases and decision support systems; and subsequently individual, and then teams of programmers (due to the need for efficient software production).

In Information Systems, interest originally focused on design as a product, and on the methods and intermediate stages which lead to that product. Interest in design as a process came about by investigating the basic concepts of life-cycle, project-organisation, and data abstraction. These concepts were esteemed as self-evident and were not questioned. Nowadays, more attention is paid to the question of understanding the design process and to investigating what it is that designers actually do.

This new trend in Information Systems Design has been reflected in a recent IFIP conference (Bretton Woods, 1986) and a Working Group (WG 8.1, 1986) has been set up to concentrate on three points:

— communication of problems and solutions (design products) between the different groups involved (e.g. designer, manager, end-user, acceptor, programmer, co-operating designer etc.);

— the Cognitive Ergonomics of design methods and tools;

— creative synthesis and its role in finding novel and technically feasible solutions.

2 THE PROCEDURE-ORIENTED DESIGN MODEL

2.1 Description

As shown in Figure 1, a consideration of the system at the level of objects identifies three basic categories: objects, activities, and events. Different approaches can be classified according to the point of departure when attempting to describe real-world events.

In a procedure-oriented design model, the starting point is a description of current activities. The operations of the business or organisation in question (also named business procedures or business functions) are broken down hierarchically while functions described globally at higher levels are detailed at lower levels. The resulting design is presented as graphs and tables. All-in-all, the procedure-oriented approach can be classified as being heavily rooted in classical Systems Analysis techniques.

The process of abstraction which is applied follows the infological model as first formulated by Langefors. It comprises the following steps:

— Business activities are considered first;

— Descriptions of the objects involved are added next;

— An information flow is constructed between these points;

— A data model is extracted and composed from detailed functional descriptions.

2.2 Examples

There are two well known methods which employ the procedure-oriented approach - SADT (Ross and Schoman, 1977) for early development, and ISAC (Lundeberg, 1982), which is very close to the infological model.

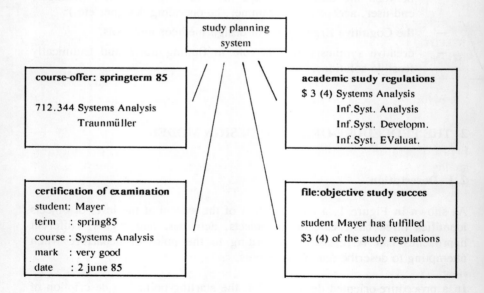

Figure 3.   Decomposition in basic activities for the example of Study Planning in the Higher Education Planning System

Figure 3 sketches the decomposition of activities using the example of a Higher Education Planning System (OECD-CERI, 1974; Strigl and

Traunmüller, 1976). The highest level of activities (comprising the procedures: course-offer; examinations; crediting; and confirmation) will be broken down in analogous descriptions.

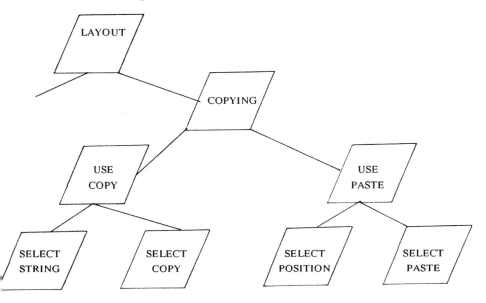

Figure 4.   Copying in a layout system as an example for a functional decomposition

Figure 4 gives a functional decomposition of a layout system, stressing the analogies to a similar analysis in the Appendix to Tauber's contribution in this volume.

2.3 Evaluation

The procedure-oriented models mainly reflect the requirements point of view, have proven to be an excellent means of communication with laymen, and have been successfully employed in many projects during the past decade. From an outcome point of view, procedure-oriented models deserve high marks (Verrijn-Stuart, Sol and Olle, 1986).

There is, however, a weakness evident in the lack of formalisation. As a consequence, it is very hard to derive specifications directly from the stated requirements and automation of the process is therefore placed out of reach. Tools are available to support graphic representations but because of the low level of formalisation, these tools have not yet achieved significant impact.

3 THE DATA ORIENTED DESIGN MODEL

3.1 Description

The data-oriented design model has its origins in research on database design. In a complementary manner to the procedure-oriented approach, the prime consideration is the modelling of objects as data. The modelling mechanism itself comprises the following sequence:

— modelling of the real world as interpreted (also called the Universe of Discourse);

— structuring of the object system by creating an abstraction system;

— representing the abstraction system in a conceptual schema and filling the database with recorded facts by modelling the object system.

3.2 Examples

Database research has promoted a number of design facilities ranging from simple techniques and methods to sophisticated tools and support environments: Some of these are:

— entity-relationship-diagrams (Chen, 1976) as techniques;

— models for normalisation as methods (Codd, 1982);

— NIAM as a binary data model with some tool assistance (Verheijen and van Bekkum, 1982);

— self-contained support environments for database design (DDEW, in progress);

— NF2-models as high level semantic data models (Pistor and Traunmüller, 1985).

NF2-models have particular advantages in representing real-world structures since they combine the tabular view of a relational model with a subtle structuring in hierarchies. Figure 5 describes some details from the

Higher Education Planning System and Figure 6 stresses the similarity to spreadsheets (cf. the Appendix to the contribution by Green, Schiele and Payne, this volume).

Study Progr.	Subjects					
	Subject	Hours reqd.	Courses			
			Course	Hours	Compuls.	Prereq.
Computer Science	Commercial Programming Languages	4	Cobol	2	yes	-----
			APG 3	2	no	Cobol
			PL/1	4	no	Cobol
	Scientific Programming Languages	4	Fortran	2	no	-----
			PL/1	4	no	Cobol
			Prolog	2	yes	-----
	Systems Analysis	4	Inf.Syst.Analysis	2	no	-----
			Inf.Syst.Developm.	2	no	Inf.Syst.Anal.
			Inf.Syst.Evaluation	2	no	-----
	Databases	2	DBMS-1	2	yes	-----
			DBMS-1	2	no	DBMS-1

Figure 5. NF2-Datamodel for the example of Study Planning in the Higher Education Planning System

3.3 Evaluation

The sequence of steps mentioned above is usually made more complex because the multitude of users participating in the design process have divergent viewpoints. Despite this diversity, database design has to arrive at a single conceptual schema comprising the totality of views. As a consequence, the amalgamation of different views within such a conceptual schema is an iterative task. Additionally, the intrinsic properties of the data have to be considered when normalising the relationships - a substantial difference between theory and outcome exists in the data-oriented model.

There are a large number of methods and tools resulting from current database research (Brodie, Mylopoulos and Schmidt, 1984) but, despite this progress, usage of such methods in real-life projects is limited (Verrijn-Stuart, Sol and Olle, 1986).

FAMILY ALLOWANCE						
		CHILDREN				
NAME	DOMICILE	NAME	AGE	SCHOOL		
				LOCATION	MONTH	FRACTION
PISTOR	LEIMEN	FLORIAN	13	HEIDELBERG	12	100
				HEIDELBERG	11	50
				SANDHAUSEN	11	50
				SANDHAUSEN	10	0
		GEREON	10	ST.ILGEN	12	100
				ST.ILGEN	11	100
TRAUNMUELLER	THALHEIM	ROLAND	14	LINZ	12	70
				WELS	12	30
				WELS	11	100
		LUCIA	10	THALHEIM	12	20
				THALHEIM	11	100

Figure 6.   Spreadsheet-like table from an administrative application
representing requests for Family Allowances

4 THE BEHAVIOUR-ORIENTED DESIGN MODEL

4.1 Description

In behaviour-oriented design models the basic concept is the event which
triggers the transition between states on certain conditions. In more detail,
the following sequence of phenomena occur:

—   Events trigger operations.

—   Operations modify objects.

—   Objects are ascertained by events.

Behaviour-oriented modelling has communalities with both the procedural
and the data-oriented approach but there are points of difference to be
noted.

In a data-oriented model there is a common emphasis on transitions
between states and attention is paid only to those transitions which are
relevant to the representation of business functions. In the behaviour-
oriented approach the totality of conceivable transitions is investigated. As a
consequence, the method produces a very voluminous documentation.

In the procedure-oriented approach there is a common emphasis on transactions. Activities viewed from the business point-of-view, however, are very macroscopic in comparison with activities which are actually transactions on a database.

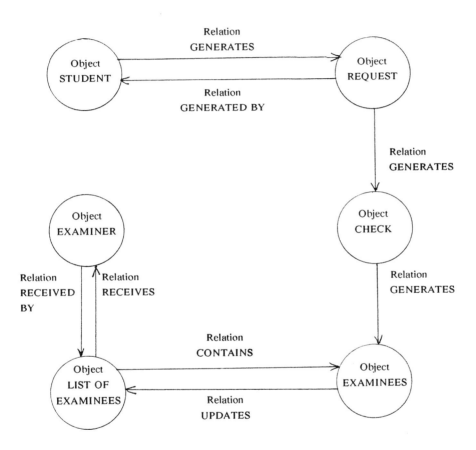

Figure 7.   Modelling the establishment of a list of examinees with PSL/PSA

4.2 Examples

There are several methods which can be judged as behavioural, though often with a bias to either the procedural or to the data-oriented model:

- PSL/PSA (Teichroew and Hershey, 1977) is a very early fore-runner and dates back to the late sixties, having gained a reputation through its pioneering role.

- IML (Richter and Durchholz, 1982) is quite the opposite, a high-level attempt based on net formalisms.

- REMORA (Roland and Richard, 1982) is a comprehensive engineering approach with some tool support.

- ACM/PCM (Brodie and Silvan, 1982) is a database approach tending towards the behavioural.

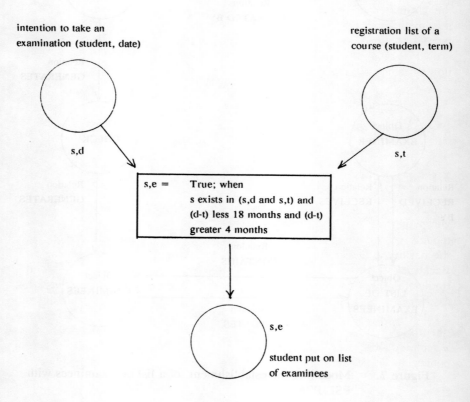

Figure 8.   Modelling the constraints for putting a student on the list of examinees in IML

To give a flavour of these systems, the same example is described using PSL/PSA and IML respectively. Figure 7 shows the rich repertoire of the former while Figure 8 gives some impression of the logical conditions necessary for transition.

4.3 Evaluation

As regards the "theory versus outcome" perspective, a sharp distinction has to be made between simple and sophisticated methods. On the one hand, broad experience can be claimed in the use of PSL/PSA, most especially in the United States where it is widely used. On the other hand, interest in this method has faded because of its poor theoretical foundations. Experimental background on the more sophisticated methods is scarce but some growth is evident in particular fields - IML is being used in office information systems (Wisskirchen, 1983).

5 PROTOTYPING AS A DESIGN MODEL

5.1 Description

Prototyping is guided by a design philosophy which is quite different to the views which characterise the previously mentioned models. All of these models (procedure-oriented, data-oriented, or behaviour-oriented) rely on the basic assumption that, in principal, the design process is a linear one. Backtracking loops due to the detection of flaws do occur but do not contradict this assumption of a linear process. In prototyping, the underlying assumption is that no accurate and final design can be achieved from scratch and, in a two-step process, a crude version is built first. Subsequently, precise specifications and requirements can be extracted from it for a second, more sophisticated and elaborate version. Later, by discussing a concrete running system, end-user involvement and participation can be made more efficient.

5.2 Examples

There are many ways in which prototyping can be achieved. Examples range widely according to intention:

- USE (Wasserman, 1982) is a theoretically sound method with a heavy emphasis on obtaining precise specifications.

- BOP (Jordanger, 1981) is a package of APL modules which focus mainly on the advantage of rapidly achieving a crude version that can then be discussed with end-users.

- particular languages such as APL and PROLOG are suited to building rapid prototypes.

- mask-generators can be used to build an experimental end-user interface.

The breakdown between prototyping methods is mostly procedural (cf. Figures 2 and 3) and hinges on attempts to use prefabricated modules. There are many contributions in this volume which present tools for visualisation and so an example is given only for USE. Figure 9 describes a dialogue by transition diagrams.

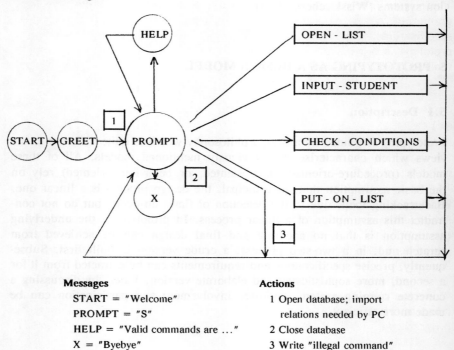

Messages

START = "Welcome"
PROMPT = "S"
HELP = "Valid commands are ..."
X = "Byebye"

Actions

1 Open database; import
   relations needed by PC
2 Close database
3 Write "illegal command"

Figure 9. Transition diagram in USE in a dialogue for a list of examinees

5.3 Evaluation

Two main advantages ensue from the procedure of building a first prototype:

Since users are unlikely to be capable of adequately expressing their requirements at the beginning of a project, prototyping will reduce the necessity of re-designing a system during the course of development. This is an important aspect because any later shift in requirements may have a disastrous impact on both time and manpower. On the technical level it has not been possible, up until now, to construct adequate forms of visual representation for Human-Computer Interaction without prior experimental trial and error. These factors do bring advantages but problems are also likely, and the two have to be circumnavigated like Scylla and Charybdis:

There is an inherent temptation to misuse prototyping as a pretext for programming in a quick and dirty way. It is difficult to later extract accurate specifications from sloppy prototypes. It may also be counter-productive if a prototype is too elaborate: in that instance management may not want to replace a prototype which already fulfills the job in question.

6 LOGICAL MODELLING AS A DESIGN MODEL

6.1 Description

It is evident that some of the advantages of prototyping may also be achieved by inspecting the logical structure of the system in question at the conceptual level. Conceptual information modelling (CIM) has been suggested as a mechanism for "mental prototyping" during early stages of design.

There are close links between CIM as a design method and logic programming as advocated for Artificial Intelligence: logical modelling resembles programming in PROLOG and there are also some notational similarities.

There is, however, a caveat for holding them as synonyms: CIM is a design method encompassing a broad view of design and belongs to the early phases of a project while PROLOG is a programming language and can play only a minor part in the process of phasewise designing a system.

6.2 Examples

Logical modelling at the conceptual level was first suggested by Bubenko - he was also responsible for developing CIM as a particular method (Bubenko et al., 1982). Currently, the building of computer-assisted tools is under way so that it may be possible to do these checks automatically in the near future.

entity	**STUDENT**
identifier	name
	study programme
	term
entity	**COURSE**
identifier	title
	subject
	term
function	**REGISTRATION**
domain	s: student
	c: course
	t: term
definition	A function REGISTRATION is true
	when t1 = t2 and
	the subject is within the study programme.
event	**EXAMINEE**
identifier	name
identifier	course
	date
occurrence	external

Figure 10.   Logical modelling of functions and events in CIM

A detail from the Higher Education Planning System can be seen as an example in Figure 10. Many features can be checked at the conceptual level:

—   Are there contradictory exclusion rules?

—   Is there deadlock in the necessary prerequisites?

- Are there enough courses offered for credits?
- What credits can be maintained after changing from one study programme to another?

6.3 Evaluation

Paper-and-pencil prototyping has advantages which can be ranked highly since the very time-consuming stage of building the actual prototype can be abandoned and, as a consequence, a number of different versions and drafts can be inspected thus widening the range of solutions to be considered.

In the last resort, however, it is necessary to balance the pros and cons: both users and managers have more opportunity to verify their requirements with an actual prototype than with its paper-and-pencil version (having omitted the stage of building of a prototype there is no way of actually checking the user interface).

7 THEORY VS. OUTCOME: A RESUME

From the state-of-the-art point of view, both the theory and the practice of Information Systems Design have provided excellent examples, based on firm theoretical foundations and grounded in practical usability.

However, this progressive image is less convincing if individual methods are critically examined. For each particular method the balance between theory and practical outcome remains a sensitive one. As shown in the course of discussion, the various methods of Information Systems Design demonstrate no common excellence in theoretical foundation and acceptance in practice.

Future efforts, therefore, have to focus on the borderline between the two. There are four trends which will govern the course of development:

- Computer assistance will be a necessary condition for all methods in question.
- Methods, tools and techniques have to merge in future support environments.

—   CAD-like design, allowing visualisation of the design in its various
     stages and versions will be of paramount importance.

—   Visualisation of results must be combined with a high degree of
     formalism in methodologies (this may be the most difficult prob-
     lem).

Summarising the overall situation, Information Systems Design might be
judged to be a successful discipline but more effort is needed before it can
reach the mature state of Software Engineering.

REFERENCES

Bretton Woods (1986). IFIP-TC8 Conference: Information Systems Sup-
    port Environments, Bretton Woods (N.H.), September 1985, A.
    Wasserman and P. Lockemann, (eds.). Amsterdam: North-Holland.

Brodie, M. and Silvan, E. (1982). Active and Passive Component Model-
    ling: ACM/PCM. *In: IFIP-TC8 Conference: Comparative Review On
    Information Systems Design Methodologies - A Comparative Review.*
    T.W. Olle, H. Sol and A.A. Verrijn-Stuart (eds.). Amsterdam, New
    York: North-Holland.

Brodie, M., Mylopoulos, J. and Schmidt, J. (1984). On Conceptual
    Modelling. New York, Berlin, Heidelberg, Tokyo: Springer-Verlag.

Bubenko, J.A., Karlsson, T. and Gustaffson, M.R. (1982). A Declarative
    Approach to Conceptual Information Modelling. *In: IFIP-TC8 Confer-
    ence: Comparative Review On Information Systems Design Methodologies
    - A Comparative Review.* T.W. Olle, H. Sol and A.A. Verrijn-Stuart
    (eds.). Amsterdam, New York: North-Holland.

Chen, P.P. (1976). The Entity-Relationship Model - Towards a Unified
    View of Data. *ACM Transactions on Database Systems,* 1, pp. 9-36.

Codd, E. (1982). Relational Data Bases: A Practical Foundation of Pro-
    ductivity. *Communication of the ACM,* 25.

DDEW (In progress). Database Design and Evaluation Workbench Project.
    Computer Corporation of America, Cambridge (MA).

Jordanger, O. (1981). BOP Prototyping User Guide. SINTEF-Report
    STF17 A811012, INTEF, Norway.

Lockemann, P. and Mayr, H.C. (1986). Information Systems Design, Techniques and Software Support. *In: IFIP-86 Conference*, Dublin. To be published by North-Holland.

Lundeberg, M. (1982). The ISAC Approach to Specification of Information Systems and its Application to the Organization of an IFIP Working Conference. *In: IFIP-TC8 Conference: Comparative Review On Information Systems Design Methodologies - A Comparative Review.* T.W. Olle, H. Sol and A.A. Verrijn-Stuart (eds.). Amsterdam, New York: North-Holland.

OECD-CERI (1974). Measuring Student Success. OECD-Document, Paris.

Olle, T.W., Sol, H. and Verrijn-Stuart, A.A. (eds.) (1982). IFIP-TC8 Conference: Comparative Review On Information Systems Design Methodologies - A Comparative Review. Amsterdam, New York: North-Holland.

Olle, T.W., Sol, H. and Tully, C. (eds.) (1983). IFIP-TC8 Conference: Comparative Review On Information Systems Design Methodologies - A Feature Analysis. Amsterdam, New York: North-Holland.

Pistor, G. and Traunmüller, R. (1985). A Database Language for Sets, Lists, and Tables. IBM Science Centre Heidelberg, TR 85.10.004.

Richter, G. and Durchholz, R. (1982). IML-Inscribed High-level Petri Nets. *In: IFIP-TC8 Conference: Comparative Review On Information Systems Design Methodologies - A Comparative Review.* T.W. Olle, H. Sol and A.A. Verrijn-Stuart (eds.). Amsterdam, New York: North-Holland.

Roland, C. and Richard, C. (1982). The Remora Methodology for Information Systems Design and Management. *In: IFIP-TC8 Conference: Comparative Review On Information Systems Design Methodologies - A Comparative Review.* T.W. Olle, H. Sol and A.A. Verrijn-Stuart (eds.). Amsterdam, New York: North-Holland.

Ross, D.T. and Schoman, K.E. (1977). Structures Analysis of Requirements Definition. *IEEE Transactions on Software Engineering.*

Strigl, K. and Traunmüller, R. (1976). Institutionalisierte Messung des Studienerfolges. Wien, New York: Springer-Verlag.

Teichroew, D. and Hershey, E.A. (1977). PSL/PSA: A Computer-Aided Technique for Structured Documentation and Analysis of Information Processing Systems. *IEEE Transactions on Software Engineering.*

Van der Veer, G.C., Tauber, M.J., Green, T.R.G. and Gorny, P. (eds.) (1984). Readings on Cognitive Ergonomics - Mind and Computers: Second European Conference on Cognitive Ergonomics. Berlin, Heidelberg, New York, Tokyo: Springer-Verlag.

Verheijen, G.M.A. and Bekkum, J.van (1982). NIAM: An Information Analysis Method. *In: IFIP-TC8 Conference: Comparative Review On Information Systems Design Methodologies - A Comparative Review.* T.W. Olle, H. Sol and A.A. Verrijn-Stuart (eds.). Amsterdam, New York: North-Holland.

Verrijn-Stuart, A.A., Sol, H. and Olle, T.W. (eds.) (1986). IFIP-TC8 Conference: Comparative Review on Information Systems Design Methodologies - Improving the Practice. Amsterdam, New York: North-Holland.

Wasserman, A.I. (1982). The User Software Engineering Methodology: An Overview. *In: IFIP-TC8 Conference: Comparative Review On Information Systems Design Methodologies - A Comparative Review.* T.W. Olle, H. Sol and A.A. Verrijn-Stuart (eds.). Amsterdam, New York: North-Holland.

WG 8.1-Task Group (1986) Human Factors During Information Systems Design, to be formed 1986.

Wisskirchen, P. et al. (1983). Informationstechnik und Burosysteme.

THE OTHER INTERFACE:
Specifying and Visualising Computer Systems

Colin POTTS

Dept. Computing, Imperial College of Science and Technology
London, U.K.

1 INTRODUCTION

Human-computer interaction is often taken to refer exclusively to interaction between end users and computer systems, and recently a great deal of well-placed effort has been spent in studying the design of user interfaces. There is, however, another 'interface' of arguably greater importance to the acceptability of any computer system. This is the 'procurement interface' between client and developer. Both parties must understand and agree upon a description of the envisaged system. The client must know what he is going to get (and pay good money for) and the developer must know what he is being paid to do. If the procurement interface fails and undetected misunderstandings arise some of the classic and well-documented symptoms of the 'software crisis' result.

Software developers seldom have knowledge of and expertise in the application domain to match that of the client. Their skills lie elsewhere. But a detailed knowledge of the application domain may be neccesary for a developer to understand the client's requirements. Consequent communication failures can range from simple misunderstandings over terminology - because the developer interprets in its everyday sense a word that has a more precise domain-specific meaning - to a failure to appreciate fully the implications of a requirement because the developer cannot conceptualise application knowledge as richly as the client.

Another problem associated with the procurement interface is the complexity of the information that passes across it. Even if the developer and client can communicate effectively and reliably, the size and inter-relatedness of the total set of requirements for an industrial computer system is such that careful attention must be paid to its organisation and representation. Everyone knows how complicated and difficult to understand even an existing, working system can be. It is far more difficult to come to a thorough understanding of a non-existent, planned system from a complex description.

The cognitive ergonomic implications of these observations about the procurement interface, unlike those pertaining to the design of user interfaces, have received only unsystematic and anecdotal attention. It is the purpose of this chapter to explain the various approaches to specifying systems from such a perspective. It is hoped that this chapter will help readers with a background in psychology to be able to make more sense of the software engineering literature on specification. Likewise, software engineers should be encouraged to see the issues discussed in an unfamiliar but profitable light.

1.1 Specification and Design

A specification serves several functions. First and foremost it is a definitive statement of requirements which can be used by client and developer alike as a reference source when they have any queries about what is being developed. Ultimately this may be disputed in a court of law, and it is the specification which forms the technical (non-financial) part of the contract.

Related to this function is the role that specifications play in defining acceptance tests. Indeed, the litigious mind would say that software specifications do not specify the software itself but its conditions of acceptance.

A specification is also the starting point of the design and implementation process, but it is not a design in its own right. If I go to a restaurant and ask for a particular dish I am communicating a specification, and if in return I receive a something different then, as a client, I have every reason to complain. I have no right, however, to dictate to the chef how to cook my meal. Cooking is a design issue and as it is not my business I should not meddle. The specification is my business, however; I may not know much about Indian food but I know what I like.

Software development can be regarded as a sequence of transformations between representations, the first of which is the specification and the last of which is the executable program (Lehman, Stenning and Turski, 1984). According to this rather purist view, what constitutes a specification depends on where you are standing: if you were a compiler, you would think of programs as specifications. Abstract though it is, this notion carries weight and while no one would normally regard programs as specifications neither is the term restricted only to the first representation of the proposed system. For example, many companies make a distinction between a representation known usually as the 'system requirements' and an ensuing representation known usually as the 'software specification'. This is partic- ularly common in the procurement of embedded real-time systems (e.g. avionics or process control systems) because only some of the system will be implemented in software and will be sub-contracted out to other sup- pliers than the main system contractors. For the purpose of this chapter, we need maintain no such rigid distinction, as the comments made apply equally at the 'system' and 'software' level. Whether the distinction is necessary is a matter of some controversy anyway.

The distinction between specifications and designs is often discounted in industry despite the fact that almost everybody pays lip service to it. One reason is that the distinction between system and software requirements, if complied with, implies some design decisions must already have been made in the software specification.

Another is that the structure of a specification is always different from the structure of well-structured designs. (If solutions always had the same structure as problems, problem solving would be much easier). Despite this, software specifications frequently have structures that are more appropriate for an elegant design than for an intelligible specification. The structure of such a specification aids the project manager by identifying work packages and minimises and controls the interfaces between the design components it describes. It may be very difficult, however, to read such a structured specification and understand what the specified system will do in certain circumstances - precisely the reason why lots of clients and developers get nasty surprises when systems are delivered.

Structuring software specifications according to the system's functional architecture rather than a premature design is not without its dangers, how- ever, simply because it is an unusual and unfamiliar practice. The author knows of one avionics system for which the software was specified in terms of communications, user interface, navigation, etc. Very sensibly these clear functional components were defined in separate chapters of the software specification. Not knowing any better, the project manager duti- fully assigned software engineers to communications, user interface, and navigation teams. Unfortunately, these clear functional categories did not map onto clear design modules: in Myers' (1975) terminology the modules' coupling was high and their cohesion low. As a result each team had to liaise with the others to a far greater extent than should be neces- sary, with the attendant communication overheads and potential dangers of making faulty assumptions about what the others were doing.

Finally, however clean and desirable the specification-design split may be in theory, in the heat of the software engineer's kitchen the boundary is blurred. Clients' requirements continually change throughout the course of design and implementation - particularly in the early stages. If one were to wait for an ultimately definitive statement of requirements one would never stop waiting. In practice, however, it is just not possible to keep the requirements fluid and what happens is that there comes a time, ideally before design and implementation commence but in practice after, when the specification is frozen and subsequent changes are deemed post-implementation modifications or "maintenance". Alternatively the system may be implemented in releases, in which case later specification modifications can often be incorporated into subsequent releases before much work has been done on them.

In addition, therefore, to serving as a communication medium across the procurement interface between client and analyst, the specification also serves as a communication medium between the activities of specification or analysis and design. These activities are often performed by different people (system analysts and designers or programmers), who have different perspectives on the system building process and different ways of looking at the specification. Misunderstandings can occur across this interface as well.

Thus it should be clear that specifications have many functions. Structuring mechanisms that may be appropriate for one (for example initiating design) may not be appropriate for another (for example, envisaging the consequences of a certain environmental event).

This brings up the question how to resolve these conflicts: what media and structuring mechanisms are, or should be, used to specify large software systems?

2 TEXTUAL SPECIFICATIONS

The traditional procurement cycle involves a large amount of natural language documentation, and the agreed description of the planned system takes the form of a textual specification.

Natural language is the type of language with which we are most familiar and good reasons are required to depart from it as a medium for expression of requirements. Unfortunately, there are many such reasons. The most often cited is the ambiguity of natural language. Indeed, it is its very familiarity, and the facility with which people think they communicate with each other using it as a medium, that makes possible the kinds of misunderstandings between client and developer discussed above.

Another, less often appreciated, and perhaps more significant, shortcoming of natural language is the static structure of text. While the structure of a specification may be rational, it is inevitable that any structuring principle will cut across and hide inter-relationships between requirements that may be inadvertent and should be understood. The size of industrial specifications is a genuine impediment to the detection of such consquences: in practice, the real specification for a large industrial system may run into hundreds of pages with many volumes of supporting material (e.g., explaining application-specific technical details and documenting current working practices and standards). We do not learn at school how to navigate such huge textual sources, and in the face of such magnitude and complexity the familiarity and cosiness of natural language appears more apparent than real.

It was emphasised above that a specification ideally needs to be structured differently for different purposes and to answer different questions. It is not that natural language specifications are more poorly structured than they would be in another medium, but that the intractability of natural language makes restructuring a specification an onerous and error-prone task. In practice one has to make do with the existing structure and use whatever navigation aids one can. Traditionally these have been limited to the rigorous use of hierarchical paragraph numbering schemes with the provision of cross-references. Even this has been slow in coming, however, because indexing a specification relies upon software tool support of greater sophistication than generic word processing, tool support that is not widely available.

Another aid to textual navigation may be the use of study strategies developed in educational research. Some of these (see Holley and Dansereau, 1984) have excited the interest of the IKBS (intelligent knowledge based systems) community as potential tools for knowledge elicitation from textbooks. They also appear promising in orthodox systems analysis for acquiring application domain knowledge from reference texts, but it is unlikely that they will be of much assistance in the interpretation of

specifications themselves (Finkelstein and Potts, 1985), because such strategies are intended to help the reader to extract the thematic structure of the
text, not the detailed inter-relationships of a large number of low-level facts.

Thus it appears that natural language is a weak and potentially misleading
medium for expressing requirements. Indexing schemes and the use of
study strategies may shore up the practice of specifying natural language
but cannot prevent the occasional collapse. But are there any superior alternatives to natural language?

3 FORMAL SPECIFICATIONS

An extreme alternative to the use of natural language specifications is to
adopt rigorous, or even fully formal, logical and mathematical methods.
The justification for these methods is that the full ramifications of different
requirements can only be checked by formal consequence generation techniques ('theorem proving') and that an implementation can only be verified
as correct if there is a formally unambiguous statement of what it should
do.

Software is becoming increasingly complex and difficult to understand as
computing penetrates a wide range of applications. Many critical industrial
and military real-time systems are controlled by software. In these application areas imprecisely worded requirements can lead to extremely
dangerous and costly consequences. Formal specifications, it is argued, are
at least necessary in embedded real-time systems, and will become common
in a wide range of applications in the future as their value becomes
apparent. To appreciate the value of formal specifications, however, it is
not necessary to consider only critical systems. Even small, innocuous and
apparently well-understood program specifications may hide all kinds of
traps for the unwary when expressed in natural language which become
glaringly obvious when formal specification techniques are adopted. Meyer
(1985) gives an example of the evolution of a formal specification of a simple text processing program from an original apparently satisfactory, but in
reality highly flawed, natural language description.

3.1 Advantages and Pitfalls of Formal Specifications

Formal methods are still a subject of active research and have not reached the maturity that is desirable in a technology that can be applied to large practical problems. As a result they have been applied on only a few industrial software development projects, mainly for specifying system software. For example, Björner and Jones (1983) present some case studies in which language processors and DBMS software are specified in VDM, and Hayes (1985) provides a partial specification of CICS in Z. There have been few large-scale exercises in formally specifying application software, and even here the applications chosen are mainly from worlds such as telecommunications in which practitioners are used to mathematical rigour. Thus the use of formal specifications in communicating with clients has been neglected.

Many of the pitfalls associated with adopting formal specification techniques in industry are discussed by Cunningham, Finkelstein, Goldsack, Maibaum and Potts (1985). Few relate to formal matters, most are concerned with the human side of software engineering. For example, some formal systems (e.g. first order predicate logic) are unnatural. Their primitive categories are unsuitable to most application domains or are insufficiently rich to express problems with clarity. A specification may be contorted beyond all recognition when coerced into the confines of such a formal system. When this happens, the practitioner may frequently respond that because the problem cannot be expressed easily the problem must be at fault. Real life is unfortunately not always so pliant!

Another problem with formal specifications, and this forms the basis of the most commonly heard objections, is that they are so incomprehensible to most people (including the vast majority of software professionals, let alone the clients with whom they must work) that formal methods are unworkable in practice. There is a fair amount of evidence to support this opinion, and formal methods theorists cannot be accused of populism. Many formal specification languages are very terse and employ daunting symbols from logic and discrete mathematics. Furthermore many languages have been subject to incremental and undocumented change, and even idiolectic variants. Specifications written at different times or by different practitioners may employ such different subsets of the language's constructs or are written in such different styles that one cannot see the resemblance.

Although applying a formal method requires considerable technical competence, it should be achievable by all intelligent and analytically minded people - perhaps the same population that can cope with programming. If a prerequisite of learning a formal method is that the practitioner be a creative mathematician it is unlikely that such a method will become widely used.

Certainly, such a requirement would make communication with the client almost impossible. One can imagine the difficulties an organisation would have trying to recruit analysts of the requisite technical calibre who also possessed good interpersonal communication skills. Failure to meet this requirement accounts for the resistance often encountered by software engineers: they have a gut reaction against the imposition of new skills that they may not be able to master. It is important, however, not to confuse the precision and unambiguity that gives formality its power with the use of unfamiliar and daunting notations. The frightening appearance of formal specifications may be a minor blemisch in the lab, but considered ugly in the practical world of system procurement. But it is only a blemish, and the development of formal notations - possibly application-specific - along principled lines may permit formal specification techniques to be applied increasingly in the future.

3.2 Example: VDM at IDEC

So much for the supposed potential of formal specification methods; what specific advantages and problems have been observed when they have been introduced in practice? To answer this, it is best to consider in detail the findings of one such exercise, the introduction of the specification language VDM by the UK company STC IDEC, as discussed by Shaw, Hudson and Davies (1984). This initiative was instigated when IDEC became involved in the development of packaged office automation (OA) software. Shaw et al. report candidly that the organisation had failed in the past to identify product requirements as well as it might and the decision was made to use a formal method in the specification of the OA product.

VDM was chosen for reasons that may surprise because they do not relate to the superiority of its formal basis over that of other formal systems. It was chosen instead because its model-based approach was thought to be likely to appeal to designers, because other organisations - notably IBM - had polished the process of training staff in VDM, and because an excellent textbook (Jones, 1980) was widely available. In other words, VDM was selected for informal psychological and organisational reasons: it was believed that its conceptual approach would accord most closely with the way software designers think, and because it was well-suited to the organisation's educational programme.

VDM was introduced first to a small team of analysts and only later to the OA team of designers. The analysts produced a detailed formal specification of the OA system functionality which it was intended should form the first representation in an integrated specification and design method. Although a high-level design was produced, no further design work was carried out in VDM for economic reasons, so it is not possible to say how effective the specification would have been as a starting point for a coherent design and implementation process.

Shaw et al. conclude that VDM provides very powerful thinking tools, particularly the notion of "state" which was very effective as a source of brainstorming and greatly enhanced the analytical potential of the analysts. VDM also enabled the developers to distinguish more closely between specification and design. Perhaps the frequent blurring of this distinction in practice referred to earlier results from the use of blunt specification tools. Practitioners sometimes object to the imposition of formal specification techniques on the grounds that they are inapplicable in situations where specification decisions are made throughout the design and implementation effort. But it is precisely these types of decisions which must be made - by people qualified to make them - as early as possible. Shaw et al. report that the need to make many such decisions was recognised at the appropriate time, thus vindicating the claim that formality permits crucial concerns to be identified as early as possible, rather than later when the latitude for choice has been narrowed.

Another advantage of VDM claimed by Shaw et al. is that it need not be applied fully formally. Just as mathematicians can and frequently do insert into proofs assertions of the kind "it can be shown that" without spelling out the intermediate steps, so a VDM analyst need not rely on the proof rules of VDM. Their experience as analysts and the extra rigour and precision encouraged by VDM enabled them to feel far more confident that the specification was consistent and captured all the desired requirements.

Several shortcomings of VDM were noted but these were all of a technical nature relating to its expressive power (e.g. the lack of support for concurrency and unsuitability for specifying communication protocols or user interface layouts) rather than its ease of use or ease of introduction. It might have been a very different story had VDM been adopted on a project where there was an existing external client with whom the evolving specification had to be communicated.

Turning to the educational programme, Shaw et al. report that previous experience with VDM had suggested that training should be based on in-house expertise developed initially with the help of an external consultant. Trainees should cut their teeth by specifying familiar software, ideally software from their current project. Both of these recommendations are designed to avoid the common fault of imposing wisdom from outside the organisation. There is an acute danger of rejection of formal specification techniques if the people concerned feel threatened and uninvolved. The use of locally cultivated expertise also means that the organisation has a commitment to the techniques, whereas external training courses can always be stopped.

This approach appears to have worked at IDEC because most of the students, originally dubious, became convinced of VDM's power and value. However, some students with a weak background in discrete mathematics fell behind and found the course difficult. This was ameliorated to some extent in later courses by preceding the VDM course itself by a short introductory course in discrete mathematics.

As to the objections to formal notations, Shaw et al. report no training difficulties with the standard VDM notation, META-IV but the decision was made nevertheless to use a different, less mathematical notation in the design stages. SLAN-4 (Beichter, Herzog and Petzsch, 1984) was chosen as it is a block-structured specification language which includes a procedural pseudo-code that is compatible with most implementation languages, and supports the structuring of specifications rather more clearly than META-IV. Other attempts to modify mathematical notations used for specifying software have been made, but it appears that practitioners soon tire of long-winded notations and, if possible, migrate back to the more succinct, if more impenetrable notation.

Thus any difficulties there may be with formal methods as communication aids between analysts and designers appear to be deeper than at the level of interpreting notation. The selection of notations clearly becomes far more critical for communicating specifications with the clients, but at the time of writing nothing is known about language design for this purpose.

In conclusion, the STC IDEC experiment demonstrates that formal methods can be introduced effectively into a practical software engineering environment. The success of this experiment seems to stem from several factors, notably the inculcation of commitment at the organisational and individual levels by rapidly developing in-house expertise and commitment, and teaching that method in the context of relevant examples, and by selecting a method that appeared on the face of it to suit the designers' observed problem solving habits. However the experiment was not pursued far into the design stage and there is no quantitative evidence that it has enhanced the productivity of the development team or the quality of the product. It is also an experiment with a sample of one, so caution must be exercised in extrapolating the experience to other organisations, applications or formal methods.

4 FORMATTED AND DIAGRAMMATIC SPECIFICATIONS

Between the two extremes of the ad hoc, and now largely discredited, use of unsupported natural language and the adoption of formal methods there is a spectrum of more or less rigorous and disciplined methods. These 'formatted' methods all utilise various diagrammatic and formatted notations as tools for thought. These, it is argued, are easier to understand and manipulate than large natural language specifications, impose a discipline on the specification process, and highlight some problems with an evolving specification which are submerged in large texts, such as some forms of inconsistency. Yet they do not penalise the practitioner with the large learning overhead of formal methods, many such methods are tried and tested on significant industrial applications, and the notations employed afford a convenient means of communication with the client.

4.1 Data Flow Representations

To illustrate the potential and practical limitations of formatted methods in general, the largest and most popular class of such methods, data flow methods, will be discussed in some detail. The most commonly used data flow methods are SADT (Ross 1977, 1980, 1985; Ross and Schoman 1977), and structured analysis (De Marco 1978; Gane and Sarson 1977). In the United Kingdom two other data flow methods have become widely used - CORE (Mullery 1976) and SSADM/LSDM (the method selected by the UK Civil Service technical procurement body, the CCTA for requirments analysis on all new government funded civil computing systems).

The simplest and most typical of these methods is structured analysis. Any system, whether it is an existing enterprise, a proposed computer system, or a description of a system embedded in its operational environment can be represented in structured analysis as a data flow diagram (DFD).

Some of the functions in a DFD may be regarded as primitive, while others are so complex as to be best considered as sub-systems represented by their own DFDs. Thus the 'functional architecture' of the system is described by the hierarchical decomposition of a set of DFDs. This clearly supports the management of complexity. A specification which would be huge and unwieldy in natural language and difficult to structure cleanly can be organised with clarity in terms of a hierarchy of DFDs. Moreover, psychologists may be interested to note that there is a good cognitive ergonomic rationale for layering DFD hierarchies in the way prescribed in structured analysis - Miller (1956), no less.

Data flow methods differ in the way they handle the definition of primitive functions (i.e., those which are not themselves represented by lower level DFDs). SADT, CORE and SSADM provide no recommendations except that the primitive functions should be mnemonically and unambiguously named, or annotated by a natural language description. De Marco (1978) advocates the use of a variety of notations for defining primitive functions which seem most applicable in the specification of commercial data processing systems: decision tables, decision trees and "mini-specs" (algorithmic definitions of the functions in an informal program design language called "Structured English").

These various approaches have strengths and weaknesses in practice. Using natural language implies that a DFD-oriented specification is essentially a natural language specification supported by a diagrammatic notation to describe its organisation. The syntax of the diagrams and the structure they impose upon the total set of requirements greatly eases navigation around the specification and understanding of its macro-structure. It also means that any misunderstandings that do occur about the nature of specified functions, because of the imprecision and ambiguity of natural language, can at least be precisely localised and are therefore easier to detect and correct. Nevertheless, where communication between client and analyst is at a premium, the definition of primitive functions in natural language is an impediment to mutual understanding. In many cases, particularly where the application is novel, it is difficult to name and describe functions in a way that is effectively unambiguous.

De Marco's suggestions are also not without their problems. Decision tables and decision trees can become extremely unwieldy if the input contingencies modelled by the function are at all complex. They also cannot adequately model the repetitive processing of a stream of inputs along one data flow for single inputs along another. Mini-specs, on the other hand, are inappropriately imperative and may freeze premature implementation decisions. Few clients are sufficiently familiar with high-level block-structured programming languages - upon which Structured English and its ilk are based - for them easily to validate that the specification of a function really reflects what they think it should do. The more complex the function, the more difficult and error-prone is this validation decision.

Although data flow representations depend centrally on the notion of function, the glue that holds the functional architecture together is the definition of data flows between functions. This is typically done at the syntactic level using structure diagrams (Jackson, 1975) and BNF.

The advantages adduced in favour of data flow methods for representing functional architecture are twofold. First, concentrating on data flow as the structure glue focuses attention away from implementation issues such as flow of control. The ordering of function execution arises out of the data flow dependencies; if one function produces data that are consumed by another then the production must temporally precede the consumption. Specifying other arbitrary orderings is prohibited as this is an implementation issue and does not help clarify the problem being specified.

Secondly, the top-down decomposition of DFDs allows the abstraction of key features without them being lost in a mass of detail. The detail is available, and because of the diagrammatic syntax and the data decomposition it can be localised relatively easily.

These are undoubtedly real advantages, but there are problems with data flow methods, problems that are representative of all formatted methods. In common with natural language specifications, the imprecision of formatted specifications can lead to misunderstandings. For example, what does it mean for a data flow to split? If data flow D splits into two data flows E and F, each flowing to different destination functions, does this mean that E and F are parts of D and each of the destination functions get bits of D to work on independently? Or does it mean that sometimes an E flows and sometimes an F (for example, a standard report and an exception)? Sometimes there is no need to disambiguate between these alternatives, but sometimes there is. Likewise, does every packet of data flowing into a function have to be consumed or not? A simple data flow notation is silent on this. The destination function may ignore the incoming data flows or not as the case may be; the only way to tell is to analyse the definition of the consuming function to see what it does.

This brings up the informality of mnemonic function names, natural language descriptions or even Structured English. Some functions, such as a payroll computation, may be relatively easy to define and understand because essentially they manage information. Their complexity arises from the quantity of data they process and not from any intrinsic factors. On the other hand, there are functions - such as aircraft navigation - which are primitive in the sense that it is difficult to decompose them into lower level DFDs without making arbitrary design decisions but which are highly complex and difficult to define. But if the analyst is not a navigation expert and the client, who is, cannot understand the specification of that function, or the analyst's and client's understandings are different without their realising it, there are clearly great opportunities for misunderstandings.

Another problem with data flow methods, also in common with natural language, are their seductive aura of familiarity. Unfortunately many clients in practice misread data flows as control flows. Similarly, ambiguous constructs such as splitting and merging data flows can be interpreted differently by the two parties.

DFDs are difficult to write and edit because of the graphical component of the notation. Analysts can be reluctant to make minor modifications to the specification if this means radical redoing of their artwork. This is especially acute when the DFD hierarchy requires a restructuring that affects several diagrams at different levels. This means that, in spite of the noble intentions of most practitioners, formatted methods that rely heavily on graphics are not used as systematically in practice as they should be and specifications created using these methods are seldom kept up to date when requirements change frequently.

The most serious practical criticism of the majority of formatted methods, however, is that they are not methods at all. A method should be prescriptive: it should tell the practitioner what to do next to make progress toward a satisfactory solution to a problem. Simply being able to characterise a good solution once one has got one is not good enough. It may be better that no guidance at all, but it is still not good enough.

To illustrate this point, consider structured analysis. As has already been stressed, a structured analysis specification is hierarchically structured in terms of the levels of abstraction of the functions in each layer of DFDs, and this undoubtedly is an aid to understanding. But where does such an elegant structured solution to the problem of specifying a set of requirements come from? What should happen is that the analyst talks a lot to the client and interviews other concerned parties, such as end users and potential recipients of reports, and then proceeds to develop understanding of the problem by top-down stepwise refinement.

This is a myth. Only well-structured problems can be decomposed in this way. What makes requirements analysis so difficult is that it is concerned with elucidating the structure of the problem in the first place. When one is not an expert in the application domain, one's first attempts at structuring a problem are inevitably inappropriate.

These negative comments are by no means fundamental criticisms of formatted methods, but they demonstrate the need for three kinds of development; new ways of depicting function, tool support for specification housekeeping and modification, and the application of genuinely prescriptive methods.

One approach to the depiction of function is the axiomatic specification of functions either as recursion equations or as actions with defined preconditions and post-conditions. This hardly assists in the validation of function by clients but it is feasible to animate such formal definitions so that the analyst or client is confronted by the result of executing the function. Execution of specification is a hot topic, which deserves a section to itself (see Section 5 below). The other two developments will now be dealt with.

4.2 A Real Method: CORE

CORE (Downes and Goldsack, 1982; McDermid and Ripken, 1983; Mullery, 1976) is a prescriptive formatted method, not just a notation. The public domain information on CORE is very scanty, and the following account is based on Mullery (personal communication). It is illustrated by examples from an on-line patient monitoring system formulated by Steve Knight of Hewlett-Packard and the author (see Finkelstein and Potts, 1985). There are several phases to CORE:

    Start-up;
    Tabular collection;
    Data structuring;
    Action structuring (isolated);
    Action structuring (combined);
    Reliability and availability analysis;
    Completion.

The phases from tabular collection to reliability and availability analysis are applied repeatedly in a process known as 'viewpoint decomposition'. One of these, reliability and availability analysis, is not pertinent to the present discusson and will be passed over.

Each phase is associated with strategy (global objectives) and tactics (local hints). These suggest what the analyst should do next: what questions need asking, what analyses might be performed, what information must be looked out for, etc. They do not guarantee a successful analysis, of course, but are useful heuristics. The major phases are described below with their principal strategies and sample tactics to illustrate the prescriptive nature of CORE.

a. Start-up
Strategy:

The strategic objective of the start-up phase is the establishment of the scope of information that is needed about the application domain. This produces a list of those people, organisational roles or functions affected by or affecting the systems. These are called "viewpoints". Secondly, structural relationships between the viewpoints must be ascertained. This produces a *viewpoint hierarchy* (Figure 1).

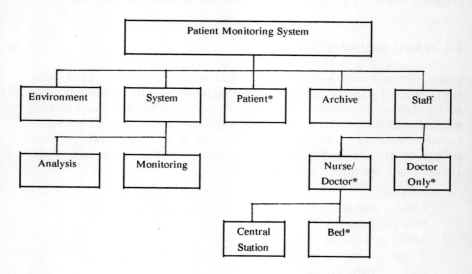

Figure 1.   Patient monitoring system viewpoint hierarchy

The nature of the application domain dictates whether the *viewpoint* hierarchy should be based on *organisational* viewpoints, or *functional* viewpoints. Organisational analysis is most appropriate when the system is providing a service for many people, or is embedded in an organisation context. If it is an "embedded" system - that is, its main interactions are with hardware devices and people are only indirectly involved (e.g. telephone exchanges, burglar alarm monitoring systems), then it is best to analyse the viewpoints functionally. This is always more difficult, because it is not always apparent what the viewpoints are, and there is no one person to interview for each functional viewpoint. On the other hand, functional viewpoint analysis can usually rely on a large amount of written material about the application domain and procedures (e.g. think of air traffic control), whereas organisations are not usually documented with the same precision.

Tactics:

The following tactics should give an idea of the type of heuristics available to the analyst during the start-up phase. To identify a viewpoint, check for anything that hints at viewpoints in the client's description, such as job titles, proper names, global functions (e.g. 'navigation'). Having identified a potential viewpoint, ask whether it is relevant to the target system. To be relevant it need not interact directly with the system, but may do so indirectly. Look for structural relationships between viewpoints - particularly containment (i.e., reporting, or membership). This is where the viewpoint hierarchy comes from. Check membership of more than one viewpoint. This may be opportunity for organisation redesign. Check whether one person could fulfil more than one viewpoint. These are called 'roles' and have privacy and security implications (e.g. a person may be a tax inspector and a tax payer simultaneously). Identify those viewpoints that are difficult to analyse further (e.g. the patient in a patient monitoring system). Obviously the analyst cannot usually interview such people, but it is important to take them into account, and there is often another source of relevant information (in the case of the Patient viewpoint it would be a Doctor).

b. Viewpoint decomposition
The middle phases (tabular collection, data structuring, isolated and combined action structuring and reliability and availability analysis) are performed on each viewpoint from the top of the hierarchy downwards.

After a viewpoint has been decomposed it is compared with the analysis of its parent viewpoint. The analyst must go back to the clients to resolve any conflict between parent/child viewpoints. Generally the superordinate viewpoint is represented by a more senior person, but the subordinate viewpoint is represented by someone who really understands what he or she does. Resolving such conflicts therefore is an inter-personal rather than a technical skill and requires some tact. If possible, what the subordinate viewpoint says should be taken as accurate, because the person interviewed will have a better knowledge of day-to-day operations.

Now for the main phases in turn:

c. Tabular collection
The objective is to obtain an action table for the current viewpoint. An action table enumerates the functions or actions performed by the current viewpoint, the inputs (data flows) to those actions, their outputs (also data flows), the sources of the inputs (i.e. viewpoints) and the destinations of the outputs (also viewpoints).

The action table for the System viewpoint of the Patient Monitoring System is represented in Figure 2.

—   Action tables provide an instant source of consistency checks: every mentioned source viewpoint must produce some input to the current viewpoint;

—   every mentioned input data flow must come from somewhere (its source viewpoint) and be used by a named action in the current viewpoint;

—   conversely, every mentioned output data flow must go somewhere (its destination viewpoint) and be derived by a named action;

—   (almost) every mentioned action must have some input data flow(s) and some output data flow(s);

—   and every mentioned destination viewpoint must receive an output data flow from the viewpoint.

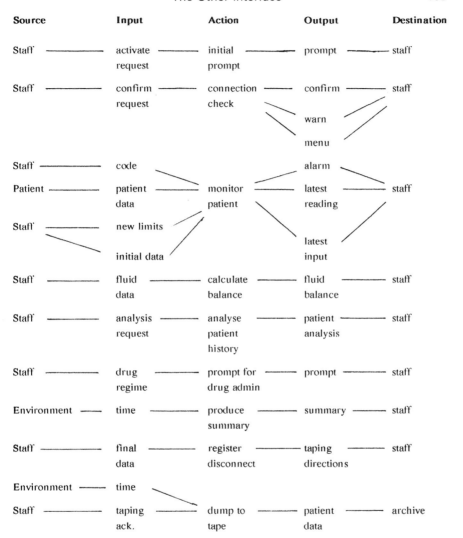

Source	Input	Action	Output	Destination
Staff	activate request	initial prompt	prompt	staff
Staff	confirm request	connection check	confirm	staff
			warn	
			menu	
Staff	code		alarm	
Patient	patient data	monitor patient	latest reading	staff
Staff	new limits			
	initial data		latest input	
Staff	fluid data	calculate balance	fluid balance	staff
Staff	analysis request	analyse patient history	patient analysis	staff
Staff	drug regime	prompt for drug admin	prompt	staff
Environment	time	produce summary	summary	staff
Staff	final data	register disconnect	taping directions	staff
Environment	time			
Staff	taping ack.	dump to tape	patient data	archive

Figure 2.   Action table for system viewpoint of the patient monitoring system

d. Data Structuring
The objective is to derive a grammar (Jackson, 1975) for all named data flows.

Checks should be performed for consistency of external data flows between viewpoints. For example, in the Patient Monitoring System is the definition of the patient analysis supposedly received by the Staff viewpoint the same as that supposedly sent from the System? This is a very common source of misunderstanding. The data decomposition for the Patient Analysis data flow is shown in Figure 3.

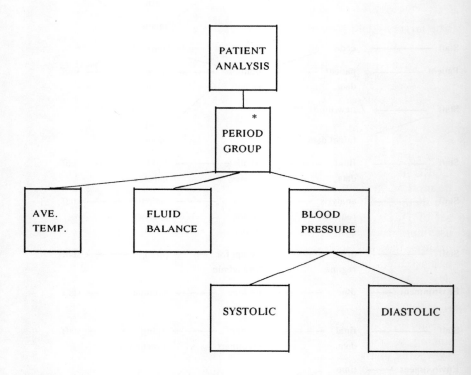

Figure 3.   Data structure diagram for "patient analysis" data flow

e. Action Structuring

The objective of isolated action structuring is to derive a DFD for the current viewpoint from the action table. In combined action structuring, interesting 'threads' of actions of different viewpoints are represented in single DFDs.

The analyst should check that there are no circular dependencies between actions unless there is genuine feedback in the problem being specified.

f. Completion

A CORE analysis is complete if the following checks have been performed:

— Viewpoint decomposition has been performed on the entire viewpoint hierarchy from level two downwards;

— Inconsistencies between sister viewpoints have been resolved;

— Inconsistencies between parent/child viewpoints have been resolved (usually in favour of the child).

The target system is developed from part of the CORE specification:

— If the client had a good idea of what the system would do in advance (this is usually true of embedded systems) then one viewpoint will usually be regarded as the "system";

— if the client did not (this is more often the case in DP) then the system will assist a subset of actions cutting across several viewpoints.

g. CORE: Discussion

CORE has been described in detail for several reasons. First, it deserves to be more widely known than it is. Secondly, only a detailed consideration of the method can show the kinds of heuristics that result in a well-structured set of DFDs. CORE tactics continually force the analyst to question his assumptions about the application domain. The centrality of 'viewpoints' ensures that the analyst will ask the right person any questions that arise and ask them in terms with which that person will be familiar.

CORE is becoming increasingly widely used in the UK for specifying many types of computer systems, including embedded real-time systems, data processing systems and programming support environments. As well as producing several representations that aid client/analyst communication (the viewpoint hierarchy, action tables, DFDs and data structure diagrams) it appears very suitable as an interface to subsequent design representations in MASCOT (DoI, 1981), A7 (McDermid and Ripken, 1983) and the CCITT telecommunications system design language SDL (Vefsnmo, 1985).

4.3 Tools for Specification Housekeeping

The chore of creating and modifying formatted specifications for big systems can be largely ameliorated by the provision of software tools. First, management of the size and complexity of large specifications can be assisted by special-purpose database management systems. For example PSL/PSA (Teichroe and Hershey, 1977) and SREM/REVS (Alford, 1977,

1985; Bell, Bixler and Dyer, 1977) incorporate database management, consistency checking and report generation software. Both have been used for the management of specifications of many large systems. They are now widely regarded as software engineering classics but are limited by their user interfaces which are based on database input and query languages.

Although PSL/PSA has been widely used relative to most software tools (say a few thousand projects in a decade), it certainly has not been widely used by any abosolute criteria. REVS is even more restricted, having been unused outside the US defence sector. In an interesting survey of the practical use of SREM/REVS, Scheffer, Stone and Rzepka (1985) observe that even skilled SREM analysts only "code" an average of 19 lines of the RSL specification language a day, a low productivity rate which must be due in part to the shortage of modern direct manipulation tools in the REVS environment and the necessity to specify in RSL information that could be better represented diagrammatically.

In contrast to PSL/PSA and REVS, there has been a crop of recent software tools based on personal workstations which support the graphical presentation and direct manipulation of formated specifications in addition to the data management and consistency checking support provided by the older style of tool. Most of these tools are little more than special-purpose graphics editors with the capacity for some syntactic consistency checking. Where the method is based on a set of strategies and heuristics, as with CORE, however, there is far greater potential for intelligent assistance (e.g. Stephens and Whitehead, 1985).

The development of the new generation of support tools suggests that the penetration throughout industry of support tools for formatted methods, and therefore of formatted methods themselves, is about to begin. It is too early to say whether such tools will aid the production of high quality and readable formatted specifications in practice, but the clearest indication that this will be so comes from informal evidence that analysts find using such tools fun and are prepared to experiment with ideas. Far from encouraging sloppy thinking, such tools enable requirements analysts to reformulate specifications without the tedium of redrawing a large number of diagrams and manually rechecking the consistency of the new specification. Furthermore, the use of rule-based programming techniques in the implementation of such tools opens new avenues. First, a generic tool can be instantiated for a set of different formatted methods with different strategies and tactics, and skilled users should be able to customise such methods by adding their own rules. Secondly, as well as checking for absolute inconsistencies, it is possible for a less experienced analyst to be given advice and warnings about the "style" of his specification.

Furthermore, such techniques permit the manifestation of a variety of views of a specification represented in an unstructured underlying database (Potts, 1984). Consider the structuring of a CORE specification in terms of viewpoints. This may provide a suitable structuring for elucidating some properties but not for others, for which other orthogonal patterns, such as threads of actions from different viewpoints, could equally well be defined. When the specification has a static structure, such view generation is not feasible, but it can be done given suitable tool support.

This shifts attention away from the idea of specifications as documentation to that of specifications as databases from which documentation may be derived. There is a prevalent opinion that specifications are indeed documents - in some sense "like" programs. Just as programmers spend much of their time poring over program listings, so analysts of the future will spend much of their time (presumably in the company of clients) poring over PSL or RSL listings. This is an inaccurate metaphor that has outlived its usefulness. It seems more appropriate to view a specification as a database which can be scrutinised from a variety of orthogonal views. Thus a specification need not have one single structure, but the perceived structure will reflect the question being asked by the tool user. Incidentally, this notion of specification as database applies equally to object-based programming languages, and has been applied to great effect by Fischer and Schneider (1984) in an experimental programming environment in which object-oriented Lisp programs are never 'listed' but are viewed through user-defined filters that let through desired information and filter out everything else.

5. RAPID PROTOTYPES AND EXECUTABLE SPECIFICATIONS

Disciplining the specification process by the use of formal or formatted methods helps to overcome the difficulty of visualising a planned system from a large and intractable textual specification. An alternative approach is to use executable models as the means of visualising the planned system and to treat the specification as a definitive reference.

5.1 Rapid Prototyping

The idea of a model is familiar from many other constructive disciplines, for example architecture. The scale model or artist's impression of the new shopping centre that is on display in the local council office is a reasonable vehicle for allowing non-technical people who are to be affected by the planned building to visualise what their town will be like if it is built. But in no sense is this model a "specification" of the building. It will not be used by the builders as a source of information when they come to dig foundations. Nor is it of much use as a contractual agreement between the architect and the client. In computer systems which, unlike buildings, exhibit behaviour, the analogue of the architect's scale model or sketch is the executable model or prototype. Here a user or client representative can sit in the cockpit, so to speak, and drive a sub-functional and inefficient implementation of the planned system. If he crashes it no one gets hurt.

Very often clients do not know precisely what they need. Looking at a rapid prototype that is ostensibly derived from a first cut requirements statement concentrates the mind wonderfully. Rapid prototyping is therefore a potentially powerful method for helping the client to articulate the requirements.

Rapid prototypes suffer from several serious inadequacies, however. They are usually derived informally, so their portrayal of the behaviour of the proposed system is not guaranteed to be reliable. There is no controlled way of feeding back conclusions about the behaviour of the prototype to the specification to make appropriate modifications. Some attempts have been made to mitigate this problem. For example, Shaw et al. (1984) report the derivation of a C prototype of the user interface of the OA system from the VDM specification by using the rigorous VDM design method, and Potts, Bartlett, Cherrie and MacLean, (1985) likewise derived an Ada discrete event simulation program to model the performance of a lift system specified in JSD (Jackson, 1983).

It is also tempting to encourage the client (who is often not an end user) to play with the prototype, rather than experiment carefully. Indeed, a prototyping effort can easily become a public relations exercise. Officials from the client organisation are invited to the demonstration of the prototype, a lot of wasted effort is put into making it look nice, they make ill-considered and superficial comments, and the developers - having invested much effort in what has now become not such a "rapid" prototype after all - come under pressure from their management not to throw away their untidy code and hastily conceived design ideas. To avoid this temptation, languages such as Lisp, APL and Prolog can be used which have interpreters that are not of industrial production quality. To ensure the genuine rapidity of prototyping, an interpreted language is not enough. Instead, a rapid prototyping environment like USE should be used (Wasserman and Shewmake, 1982).

Finally, and this is not really an inadequacy, rapid prototypes are mainly judged in terms of their usability. This restricts the suitability of rapid prototypes as a communication medium between analysts and clients to those systems or parts of systems which involve a high degree of human-computer interaction. Since these are kinds of systems which tend to be the least rigorously specified, and the requirements for which are the most fluid, rapid prototyping is very useful. It is essential, though, for the prototype to be assessed by genuine users of the proposed system, as the well-intentioned assessments of other people from the client organisation can be based on ignorance of what the end users' job really is, and how they do it. It is also advisable, wherever possible, for prototypes to be evaluated for some time so that user performance can be observed and analysed objectively rather than impressionistically.

5.2 Animation of Specifications

Alternatively, with tool support the client can be "walked through" parts of a specification using real or symbolic input data and view the animation or simulation of the specification not as the end user of a prototype but from a "God's eye" view. Specification animation can be regarded as making dynamic - and therefore more immediate and compelling - the dynamic properties of the system being specified. Computer-aided walkthroughs of this nature show great promise in elucidating the properties of a proposed system. They illustrate the power of computer-aided assistance, not just to supplement human thought, but to clarify complex system properties that could not possibly be made intelligible by manual techniques.

That, at least, is the theory. As yet there is only limited experience with such animation techniques, so one must be cautious in expecting too much in the immediate future. The author is currently involved in an effort to enhance the capabilities of the CORE Analyst workstation (Stephens and Whitehead, 1985) to support animation and assess its effectiveness in use.

5.3 Executable Specifications

Instead of relying upon extraneous animation tools, it would be more economical if the specification could simply be executed in the same way as a program, albeit less efficiently.

General purpose logic programming languages (e.g. Prolog) and functional programming languages (e.g. Hope) can be used for this purpose, as can special-purpose operational specification languages for which interpreters or symbolic evaluators have been implemented - e.g. Paisley (Zave 1982), Gist (Balzer, Goldman and Wile, 1982; Cohen, 1983) or OBJ (Gallimore and Coleman, 1985).

Executing a specification may appear to be a very good way of "debugging" it. However, there are shortcomings with this method. First of all, there are fundamental computational limits which make the execution of some functions either impractical or non-terminating. This unfortunately can lead to specification "hacking"; the specification is written in such a way as to permit execution, even though premature implementation decisions may have had to be made. Secondly, executable specifications are not for amateurs; to make sense of an unexpected result it is usually necessary to have some understanding of the formal system on which the language is based. Finally, executable specifications have not yet been used on the specification of large systems. Thus executable specifications do not appear to be capable of helping a client and an analyst communicate better.

5.4 Iterative Development

A final, and ultimately radical approach is to do away with specification altogether and just let the system evolve as a series of increasingly more satisfactory prototypes.

This approach inherits all the problems of rapid prototyping. Genuine and frequent communication between end users and developers is necessary. Rapidity of productivity is essential. To accomplish this and to raise iterative development above the level of hacking, special-purpose application development support tools should be used.

Iterative development is applicable when the reliability and real-time performance of the system is not critical and where the requirements are likely to change faster than they can be specified. Such conditions occur in research environments (many of our interactive programming environments started life this way), and in business organisations where certain applications are required for short periods before being thrown away. Large business organisations commonly have long software development backlogs. More conventional development techniques therefore cannot be used for experimental systems in these circumstances.

6. CONCLUSIONS

So, there is a lot of hot air in software engineering, and not many hard facts. Far more attention has been paid to the development of software engineering techniques for specifying and visualising systems than in assessing such techniques. What we do know is very subjective. Everyone can tell a tale.

There has been little research into the cognitive ergonomics of software specification. This is regrettable for two reasons. First, specifications are nothing other than descriptions of the world, and the comprehension of complex descriptions is an intrinsically fascinating topic. A specification, in common with any complex information repository, must be viewed from different angles to achieve a full understanding. The technology now exists to support such view generation dynamically. Careful assessment is necessary and would be valuable in the computer-aided presentation of complex information in general.

Secondly, the development of tools and notations to assist in the specification of software must be based on cognitive principles as well as on practical and theoretical software engineering requirements. The design of specification methods and languages has proceeded as if no human factors concerns deserved consideration. Yet the only reason that specifications are written is that they form an agreement between people: there are human beings on each side of the procurement interface. Aside from any other considerations, the need for knowledge in this area should be evident simply because of the frequent and disastrous consequences in practice of failures of communication across this interface.

At a more pragmatic level, we need to know a great deal more about how to present formal specifications in an intelligible, or at least explicable, form. What kind of static graphical symbols can best depict dynamic interaction?

How should the animation of a specification be depicted? It is no use "executing" a specification only to watch it wobble bewilderingly; the behaviour of the specified system must be explained in terms of application-specific constructs with which the client is familiar. This presents a significant challenge in the construction of intelligent tool support. Turning from the client to the analyst, there is an urgent need for training techniques for methods in general, not just formal ones. We know something about how to go about training analysts and designers, thanks to the work of people such as Shaw et al. (1984), but this is hardly sufficient.

However, one cannot develop detailed training requirements without knowing what is being taught. And this brings us to the most important requirement of all: we need methods, not data flow diagrams or formal systems, but real methods, methods that assist in the elicitation of expert domain knowledge and consolidation of knowledge from different sources, methods that bristle with heuristics to check the consistency, quality and appropriateness of the specification, methods which define the viewpoints from which one can inspect the specification, methods which produce specifications that can be used in their different ways by clients, lawyers, requirements analysts, project managers, quality assurance auditors, hardware interface engineers, and software developers. These people are people. With so many of them involved it is time software engineers started paying more serious attention to the human factors of specification methods.

REFERENCES

Alford, M. (1977). A requirements engineering methodology for real time processing requirements. *IEEE Trans. Software Eng.*, SE-3, pp. 60-69.

Alford, M. (1985). SREM at the age of eight: the distributed computing design system. *IEEE Computer* 18(4), pp. 36-46.

Balzer, R., Goldman, N. and Wile, D. (1982). Operational specification as the basis for rapid prototyping. *Proc. ACM SIGSOFT* Symp. Rapid Prototyping.

Beichter, F.W., Herzog, O. and Petzsch, H. (1984). SLAN-4 - A software specification and design language. *IEEE Trans. Software Eng.*, SE-10, pp. 155-162.

Bell, T.E., Bixler, D.C. and Dyer, M.E. (1977). An extendable approach to computer aided software requirements engineering. *IEEE Trans. Software Eng.*, SE-3, pp. 49-60.

Björner, D. and Jones, C.B. (1983). Formal Specification and Software Development. Englewood Cliffs, N.J.: Prentice-Hall.

Cohen, D. (1983). Symbolic execution of the Gist specification language *Proc. IJCAI83*.

Cunningham, R.J., Finkelstein, A.C.W., Goldsack, S.J., Maibaum, T.S.E and Potts, C. (1985). Formal requirements specification - the FOREST project. *Proc. 3rd Int. Workshop Software Specification and Design*, IEEE Comp. Soc. Press.

De Marco, T. (1978). Structured Analysis and System Specification. New York: Yourdon Press.

DoI. (1981). Report on the Study of an Ada-based System Development Methodology. Dept. of Industry.

Downes, V.A. and Goldsack, S. J. (1982). Programming Embedded Systems with Ada. Englewood Cliffs, N.J.: Prentice-Hall.

Finkelstein, A.C.W and Potts, C. (1985). Evaluation of Existing Requirement Extraction Strategies. FOREST Project Report 1, GEC Research.

Fischer, G. and Schneider, M. (1984). Knowledge-based communication processes in software engineering. *Proc. 7th Int. Conf. Software Eng.*, IEEE Comp. Soc. Press.

Gallimore, R.M. and Coleman, D. (1985). Algebra in software engineering. *Proc. 3rd Int. Workshop Software Specification and Design*, IEEE Comp. Soc. Press.

Gane, C. and Sarson, T. (1977). Structured systems analysis: tools and techniques. Improved System Technologies Inc.

Hayes, I.J. (1985). Applying formal specification to software development in industry. *IEEE Trans. Software Eng.*, SE-11, pp. 169-178.

Holley, C.D. and Dansereau, D.F. eds. (1984). Spatial Learning Strategies: Techniques, Applications and Related Issues. London: Academic Press.

Jackson, M.A. (1975). Principles of Program Design. London: Academic Press.

Jackson, M.A. (1983). System Development. Englewood Cliffs, N.J.: Prentice-Hall.

Jones, C.B. (1980). Software Development: A rigorous approach. Englewood Cliffs, N.J.: Prentice-Hall.

Lehman, M.M., Stenning, V. and Turski, W.M. (1984). Another look at software design methodology. *ACM SIGSOFT* Software Eng. Notes.

McDermid, J. and Ripken, K. (1983). Life cycle support in the Ada environment. Cambridge Univ. Press.

Meyer, B. (1985). On formalism in specifications. *IEEE Software* 2(1), pp. 6-26.

Miller, G.A. (1956). The magical number seven, plus or minus two: some limits on our capacity for processing information. *Psych. Rev.* 63, pp. 81-97.

Mullery, G. (1976). CORE - A method for controlled requirements expression. *Proc. 4th Int. Conf. Software Eng.*, IEEE Comp. Soc. Press.

Myers, G. (1975). Reliable Software through Composite Design. Van Nostrand Reinhold.

Potts, C. (1984). Understanding complex descriptions. *In: Cognitive Ergonomics: Mind and Computers.* G.C. van der Veer, M.J. Tauber, T.R.G. Green and P. Gorny (eds.). Heidelberg: Springer-Verlag.

Potts, C., Bartlett, A.J., Cherrie, B.H. and MacLean, R.I. (1985). Discrete event simulation as a means of validating JSD design specification. *Proc. 8th Int. Conf. Software Eng.*, IEEE Comp. Soc. Press.

Ross, D.T. (1977). Structured analysis (SA): a language for communicating ideas. *IEEE Trans. Software Eng.*, SE-3, pp. 16-34.

Ross, D.T. (1980). Removing the limitations of natural language (with principles behind the RSA language). *In: Software Engineering.* H. Freeman and P.M. Lewis (eds.). London: Academic Press.

Ross, D.T. (1985). Applications and extensions of SADT. *IEEE Computer* 18(4), pp. 25-34.

Ross, D.T. and Schoman, K.E. (1977). Structured analysis for requirements definition. *IEEE Trans. Software Eng.*, SE-3, pp. 6-15.

Scheffer, P.A., Stone, A.H. and Rzepka, W.E. (1985). A case study of SREM. *IEEE Computer* 18(4), pp. 47-55.

Shaw, R.C. Hudson, P.N. and Davies, N.W. (1984). Introduction of a formal technique into a software development environment (early observations). *ACM SIGSOFT* Software Eng. Notes 9(2), pp. 54-79.

Stephens, M. and Whitehead, K. (1985). The Analyst - a workstation for analysis and design. *Proc. 8th Int. Conf. Software Eng.*, IEEE Comp. Soc. Press.

Teichroew, D. and Hershey, E.A. (1977). PSL/PSA: a computer-aided technique for structured documentation and analysis of information systems. *IEEE Trans. Software Eng.*, SE-3, pp. 41-48.

Vefsnmo, E.A.M. (1985). DASOM - A software engineering tool for communication applications, increasing productivity and software quality. *Proc. 8th Int. Conf. Software Eng.*, IEEE Comp. Soc. Press.

Wasserman, A.I. and Shewmake, D.T. (1982). Rapid prototyping of interactive information systems. *Proc. ACM SIGSOFT Symp. Rapid Prototyping.*

Zave, P. (1982). An operational approach to requirements specification for embedded systems. *IEEE Trans. Software Eng.*, SE-8, pp. 250-269.

INTERVENING INTO SYSTEM DEVELOPMENT AREA PROJECTS: TOOLS FOR MAPPING SITUATIONS

Giovan Francesco LANZARA
*Lars MATHIASSEN

University of Bari
Italy

*University of Aarhus
Denmark

Abstract

In this chapter we propose some new tools for mapping system development projects. Maps - as we propose them - contain descriptions and interpretations of project situations: they are helpful in collecting and organising relevant, often neglected knowledge and experience. Maps are cognitive constructs containing pictures that actors make of the situation in which they are involved. They are typically made within the situation or transposed from similar situations and are used by the actors themselves as tools for exploring, for learning, for increasing awareness, for inventing solutions to problems, and for undertaking action.

> *Where is the wisdom we have lost in knowledge?*
> *Where is the knowledge we have lost in information?*
> "Choruses from the Rock"
> T.S. Eliot

1 INTRODUCTION

There is a growing awareness in the field of system development that the problems and failures exhibited by the implementation and the overall performance of systems are closely connected to the features of the methods and techniques employed, and ultimately to the ways in which activities within projects are carried out and evaluated.

It is puzzling and sometimes painful for the actors engaged in a system development project - be they designers, managers, or users - to be confronted with problems and events which arise unexpectedly in the course of a project. In such situations deviations from current project practices are required, or even - in some cases - a more radical restructuring of those practices. It is generally accepted that it is difficult for system development projects to be carried out on the basis of guidelines which are fixed from the outset (Mathiassen, 1981; Ciborra, 1984). But on the other hand, an effective project management requires a capacity for learning and acting which is far beyond what current techniques for updating descriptions and assessments can offer. The tools and techniques applied today to gain insight into the situation of a project all focus one-sidedly on the products or subproducts. The most well-known of them are reinspections, structured walk-throughs, and reviews (Weinberg and Freedman, 1982).

What seems to be a crucial point related to the actors' learning skills and to their ability to identify and solve problems is how to get relevant information in a project situation. Selecting relevant information has to do with how project members describe the situation in which they are involved, with what they *know* about the situation. However, as some social scientists and organisational practitioners have remarked, current design and evaluation techniques tend to obscure much valuable insight from members of organisations, which therefore goes unrecorded and is lost most of the time (Argyris and Schon, 1978; Wynn, 1983).

In this paper we intend to bring this knowledge to the foreground of our attention, and to develop some tools and techniques to help the actors themselves to bring it to the surface. The approach has been developed in connection with a field research project on methods for systems development (MARS, 1984). This research project has studied eight projects in four different organisations employing the techniques and tools which will be presented later in this chapter. These tools have a basically two-fold application: either they may be used by researchers in the analysis of system development projects, or they may be helpful to the project members themselves to map their own project situations and to intervene into them. In the second case "mapping situations" is seen as a relevant activity in practical systems development, that may offer insight into the problems and conflicts connected to both processes and products.

Our suggestions should also be seen as an attempt at designing a new conceptual framework for thinking about the development and the use of computer technology within organisations. We emphasise the cognitive and learning aspects of system development, in some ways taking a step away from the current literature on system development methods, which mainly focus on technical matters (Hice et al., 1978; DeMarco, 1979; Jackson, 1983; Yourdon, 1982).

Within our framework system development is seen as a process of intervention into an organisational setting with the purpose of transforming work processes and methods, and ultimately human behaviour and knowledge at the place of work (Lanzara, 1983). Looked at in this perspective, mapping becomes a means for intervening into the system development process, which in turn is an intervention itself when seen with respect to other organisational relations. The relevant question to put here is: will mapping - as a strategy for understanding and changing work processes and organisational practices - have a positive impact on how people in projects and organisations think about current system development methods and techniques and how they operate with them?

We feel that this paper is somehow the tentative result of the merging of two different disciplinary domains and research interests, one focusing on organisations and human behaviour, the other on information systems and system development methods. Independently of whether we have succeeded or not in this endeavour, we strongly believe that the marriage between the behavioural studies and the information sciences should generate new insights into both areas, and therefore it is devoutly to be wished for.

We will present our viewpoints in the following way: Part 2 will contain a more detailed definition of maps and mapping. Part 3 will contain a case of intervention into a system development project. The intervention proved to have a limited effect, and on this background we will present a critique of the approach which was applied. In part 4 we will present our suggestions for tools and techniques for mapping project situations in the form of diagnostic, ecological, virtual, and historical maps. Each map will be presented and illustrated, and then - in part 5 - we will present a second case of intervention where the idea of mapping is used in a real-life situation. Finally, in part 6 we will discuss how mapping may be seen as a first step towards a practical theory of intervention.

2 MAPS AND MAP-MAKING

Our interest in drawing maps of project situations only in part originates from the goal of analysing a project. We are also interested in identifying characteristic and recurrent patterns and relations in project situations. A better understanding of these patterns and relations will hopefully enable people to improve the way in which a project is carried out or an organisation works. Our intention is in other words to help people (including ourselves) to describe what are the relevant features of a project situation, to see what are the problems at hand, and to change patterns of action according to the requirements of the situation. Maps should help people to develop an awareness of where they stand in the situation and to interact in a more direct, articulate and creative way.

2.1 What are Maps?

A *map* is an interpretive description of a situation which provides insight into possible ways of acting on that situation or on similar situations. Maps are, like all descriptions, incomplete, but they contain some knowledge about the situation which might be useful for understanding and undertaking action. By drawing a map we choose to select and to attach meaning to some elements or events instead of others.

We always construct and use some sort of map in situations of action: *mapping* is a cognitive activity and, in a way, a form of action in itself. We construct our maps individually by interacting and communicating with other people. We often build up on other maps which we take for granted. We also test the consistency and relevance of our maps in our interaction with others.

Maps are cognitive phenomena in two senses: they reflect our cognitive processes - the way we look at reality - and they allow us to build up further knowledge of our reality as we use them. As we have said earlier, maps are tools for undertaking action. We do indeed perform our maps in our behaviour (McCaskey, 1981).

Hence an actor's interpretation of a situation includes an understanding of where and how he or she can act to change (or maintain) that situation. We can call the set of perceived constraints and opportunities, defining somehow the boundaries of what the actor sees as feasible or infeasible, the *domain of action* addressed by the map.

Each type of map presented in this paper provides a specific way of describing a situation, along various organising principles; it suggests which aspects of the situation one should focus on and how these aspects relate to one another. These tools are, however, incomplete as guidelines for action and need to be completed by concrete action and choice. The maps produced address both product and process issues, they reflect daily life thinking, and are typically formulated in natural language.

It is possible to distinguish among different kinds of maps. For instance, maps are said to be *formal* or *informal* depending on to what extent they rely on or reflect codified rules of language or behaviour; they are said to be *individual* or *collective*, depending on whether they belong to a single actor's or to a group's memory or cognitive equipment; they may also be distinguished between *private* and *public*, depending on to what extent they are socially shared. Thus maps may contain information which everybody knows and tells explicitly, or else which everybody knows but would not tell openly in public. Private individual maps may contain information which only one person knows and keeps to himself even if requested, or that the person would share if requested, thus making it public.

Maps need not be explicit. That can happen for a variety of reasons: because we find it convenient to keep them as private maps, because we are so familiar with them that we store them in the back of our conscious cognitive activity, or because we may find it difficult or sometimes impossible to put our interpretation of a situation into words or diagrams even if we wanted to. We often use maps which are *tacitly* embedded in our cognitive skills, and these maps may be very important in helping us perform complex mental and manual tasks.

As they are presented here, maps should be used as tools to develop public and collectively shared knowledge within a project group, eventually starting from individual maps. In order to expect that, we assume that some minimal requirements are fulfilled at the outset of the mapping process, namely that all actors involved in a project situation share an interest in understanding and in taking action. We need not make assumptions about the identity or convergence of interests and about the absence of conflicts within a situation: in fact different or conflicting viewpoints may emerge even in a highly socialised project group. What we assume instead is that, irrespective of their views, actors share an interest in expressing those views and in undertaking some sort of actions, be it for public or private purposes. The proposed approach might lead to an improved shared understanding of what the project members actually do and think or, alternatively to the surfacing of the conflicting interpretations and interests that they may have.

2.2 Mapping Systems Development Projects

Traditionally the issue of collecting and structuring information within a system development project has been approached with a bias for formal maps of products and subproducts. Nearly all descriptions made during a system development project deal with the intended product, i.e., what is normally called "the system", and these descriptions are typically built up with artificial language elements. This emphasis can be partly explained with reference to the technical environment of these projects and with the dominant technical skills of the system analysts. However, many practical projects fail in meeting requirements and deadlines (MARS, 1984) partly because formal descriptions have shown serious shortcomings (Briefs, 1983; Budde, 1984), and partly because the projects are managed without any thorough and up-to-date insight into the actual state of development.

Whenever a person steps in to an organisational setting for the purpose of changing it, she may choose different perspectives of looking at the situations she is exploring. Depending on this basic choice of perspective, she will be likely to construct very different maps. Choosing one perspective she might put systems in the foreground and keep people in the background. Choosing another perspective she might put people in the foreground - as actors on a stage - and push the systems in the background of the action scene. Or she may even try to use both perspectives to produce a more complete description of what is going on in the organisation.

If we take office work as an example, one familiar way of looking at it is to see it as a set of procedures and tasks which are executed by employees across a hierarchy of levels. Within this perspective we put into focus the system of functional components, while people in the office are just attending to the information-flows and procedures (Hammer & Ziesman, 1979). But taking a different view, one might see the office as a network of transactions and conversations among people (Wynn, 1979; Flores & Ludlow, 1979). Employees carry out activities such as researching, constructing, bargaining, deciding, making commitments, and these activities require a remarkable amount of problem-setting and problem-solving skills. Work procedures are, in this view, programs that employees apply to solve problems and change situations: they belong to the actor's cognitive equipment and are adapted to every varying situation (Lanzara, 1983).

We look at the activity of system development and, more generally, at the whole field of organisational design, as related to professional practice in real-life situations. Hence our approach leans to the second perspective mentioned above; it attempts to map the real-life behaviour of the actors involved in organisational situations. In situations of practice, however, our approach can well be supplemented with more technical and systems-oriented approaches.

It is our intention that a more reflective process of mapping should support all actors involved in a project in learning from their own experience as the project is being carried out. In other words, maps should ideally help the project members in performing on-the-spot diagnoses of what is happening. Maps could be helpful tools to improve the understanding of situations, to increase the capacity of inventing and producing alternative practices, and to provide a more effective dynamic regulation of ongoing projects.

In the actual practice of system development projects, maps can be made by observing and recording which activities actors carry out throughout the project, or by recording what actors say they are doing, or should be doing. In this case maps are detailed descriptive accounts of specific situations made by the actors themselves in an interpretive analysis, which we prefer to call *evaluation* or *appreciation*. Maps are pictures of a situation, with some order in them, relating the main features and themes of a project situation at some level of generality.

3 FIRST CASE OF INTERVENTION

Mapping, as we propose it, is an essential activity in the behaviour of systems-oriented professionals and analysts. To emphasize this point we proceed by presenting and analysing a real-life situation where a university-based research group has intervened into an on-going system development project which is being undertaken within the JCN company (MARS, 1984). As we shall see more extensively in the following, the main issue of the intervention is the review of a project report conducted by both the project group itself and the research-based group. The intervention brings out a mismatch between the official evaluation of the report by management and the pitfalls and problems that surfaced in the course of the discussion.

3.1 The Organisational Context

JCN is a software house owned by several, mutually competing savings banks. The purpose of the project in question is to develop a computer based system which can be used in savings banks in the budgeting and accounting services for private customers. At present a large part of this service is performed manually, although with the aid of the general computer based account system of the savings banks.

During the period under consideration the savings banks are converting their existing computer based account system to new equipment. This conversion project is carried out by JCN, and has the following characteristics:

—   it is by far the largest activity undertaken by JCN during the past five years;

—   it gives the local savings banks more computer resources, hence the technical possibilities of new applications (that was the major reason for the conversion);

—   there are technical problems in converting. Some savings banks, some individuals, and trade unions are developing a negative attitude towards the project - and consequently towards JCN.

The management of JCN wants the budget project to be a success to stop mounting negative attitudes and re-establish positive attitudes towards JCN.

The budget project team has been asked to follow the new JCN project model which only slightly resembles the old one. The project team is directly responsible to a steering committee which evaluates and accepts each phase of the budget project. Around the project there is an organisation which connects the project to JCN and to the savings banks. It is difficult for the project team members - because of institutional arrangements - to have direct contact with the local savings banks and the bank employees. The information they can get is filtered by bank representatives, who are acquainted with formal procedures, but not with the actual operations and needs of the local savings banks, nor with the existing computer system of the savings banks. The representatives, however, are in charge of the decision about what should be done in designing the system.

The purpose of the project team - though it may seem superfluous to say that - is to get the project completed at deadline and accepted by the steering committee. They are requested to produce reports to the steering committee at the completion of each phase of the project.

The budget team meets regularly every fortnight with the university-based research group, the MARS group, to discuss reports and problems. The objective of the MARS group may, in relation to the budget project, be summed up as follows:

—   they want to do field research to gain insight into how system development projects are carried out in real life;

—   they want to play an advisory role: giving advice on alternative actions;

—   they want to help highlight project problems;

—   they want to support the budget project team in the completion of
     their work.

The MARS group consists of two researchers from the university together
with five practitioners from JCN.

3.2 The Intervention Situation

One of the meetings is dedicated to the discussion of a report from the
budget project team to the steering committee. The report is accepted by
the steering committee and is then read beforehand by all members of the
MARS group. The situation with which we are concerned here is the discussion of the report which lasted about two hours. Each actor participating in the meeting expresses his or her view on the report in turn; then an
open discussion takes place. Criticism is raised by the MARS group
members in the course of the discussion. The budget project team reacts
with some passivity and defensiveness to this criticism and to the comments, though some find the discussion interesting. In the following we
present a summary of the main critical points of the report as they are
raised in the discussion.

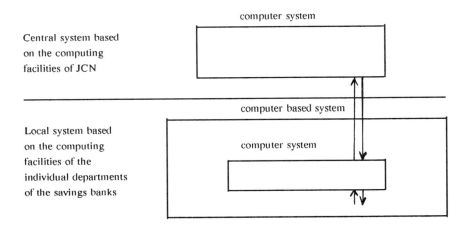

Figure 1.   Relationship between local and central systems

Inappropriate frame for describing local computer system: the relationship between the local and the central systems may be illustrated as shown in Figure 1. Both the local and the central systems are described with a flow oriented system description tool (DeMarco, 1979). The central computer system is structured in a way which makes such a flow oriented frame of description appropriate.

The future local computer based system, (i.e., the local computer system and the functionally related parts of the individual savings banks) however, is not basically structured as a flow; it includes a very important element - the clerk/customer dialogue on budgeting. Hence, by choosing a flow oriented description of the local computer system, it becomes very difficult to relate this to a structured description of the computer based system.

The report lacks coherence: the various descriptions of the future local computer system within the individual departments of the savings banks and the description of local events related to budgeting do not relate to each other in any clear and understandable way. This relates to the first point mentioned.

Structured description of the local computer system: the future local computer system is described by: data flow diagrams, mini-specs, and examples of outputs (paper, screen images). From a technical point of view these descriptions are fine, except for one very important pitfall: there is no description of the data dictionary (as there should be according to the applied method). This means that it is difficult to get a clear understanding of what information is available from the system and of the means by which this information is structured.

Unstructured description of local computer based system: the only description of the future local computer based system, apart from the technical description of the existing local computer system, is a list of events related to budgeting within a savings bank. There is one list of events initiated by customers and one list of events initiated by the bank employees.

The report is not suitable as a basis for decision making: the above-mentioned criticism implies that it is not possible to evaluate the product (a new tool for budgeting). Furthermore, the report offers no information on the present status of the project, nor any plans for future development. One fundamental problem is that the report does not deal with the distance between the situation now (within the savings banks, within JCN), and the situation after the implementation of the new system. For these reasons the report is not suitable as a basis for a steering committee decision on the project's future development.

3.3 Diagnosing the Project Situation

The report seems to show two basic weaknesses which are perceived as problems by most of the people involved in the situation.

Firstly, there are incoherent descriptions of the system which prevent a clear understanding of the functionality of the system once it is implemented. Each description is incomplete in itself: the flow oriented description of the computer system lacks the data dictionary, and the description of clerk/customer events does not take account of the structure and frequency of dialogues. The description of events is a simple checklist of possible questions and answers, and is of little relevance. The incoherence between the descriptions is not simply a technical matter, but has to do with how analysts frame the reality of the problem. The two descriptions pertain to two different levels of reality. From the descriptions contained in the report it is difficult to infer what the situation will be, and that also makes it difficult to establish criteria for evaluating the computer system. This point is concerned with method of analysis and quality of the product.

Secondly, the report is weak in the planning and evaluation of functions, and it is not good as a basis for future decisions. This makes it difficult to have an efficient, dynamic regulation of the project. How will the steering committee make decisions on project development? The report does not contain the clues and statements relating the project's present situation to the initial situation and to the envisioned final situation. This point has to do with organisation of the project and quality of process.

There are, of course, underlying behavioural dynamics taking place in this situation: There are people from the university and the MARS group, people from JCN and MARS group, and members of the budget project team.

All these different affiliations make the dynamics rather complex. One clear pattern, however, emerges. Most of the criticism comes from the JCN employees not participating in the budget project. Project members, on the other hand, are rather passive: they find the discussion interesting - except the project leader who takes a defensive stance, advocating the achievements of the project.

One major reason for this pattern to emerge is the following: Project team members identify the problems and the defects of the report and of the project, but they fail in searching for an explanation for them, in relating them to their own actions and choices and to the existing conditions. The budget project members in particular, who should account for their own behaviour and choices, do not express their views explicitly.

Only one participant in the meeting tries to identify causes. He picks up two relevant points for diagnosis, but he fails to connect problems and defects in the project to observable human actions. The actor - who is not a member of the budget project team - on one hand makes an effort to provide a more articulate diagnosis, but on the other uses conditions as explanatory causes for the project outcomes and problems. But conditions do not explain in themselves why some specific actions have been undertaken, and why some have not. His account of the problems considers other domains of action than the one defined by the actual situation. In fact, by not invoking human actions but only external conditions as a source of problems, he does not assume or attribute responsibilities for the events, thus protecting himself and others from possible negative consequences of such events. A consequence of this mode of reasoning and behaving is the almost self-fulfilling conclusion that *if* the conditions are such and such (i.e., if the causes are somewhere else and out of reach), *then* there is nothing that we can do (or nothing different that could have been done).

According to this actor's map the project is poorly carried out, but defects can be traced back to causes out of reach of the project members' action: the "typical" dynamics of a project explain delays, incompleteness, and lack of evaluation and control; the environmental relationships explain the lack of commitment and communication. But then - where do human action and responsibility come into the picture?

One other major actor - namely the budget project leader - tends, in our view, to take contradictory stances towards the project: on one hand he states that he agrees with most of the points made (hence admitting that the project has defects, and the criticisms are right), on the other he emphasises the project team's and his own competence. The arguments he puts forward are:

—   project model prescription was correctly followed;

—   the steering committee accepted the report;

—   they worked under time pressure.

In the project leader's explanation, formal, objective evaluation criteria, where no explicit human actions are involved, are used to advocate the project. This is clearly a symptom of lack of commitment: this actor does not seem to consider himself as part of the situation in which he is involved, and which he helped produce. He does not seem to share a feeling of personal causation and responsibility with the situation.

Other actors show a good sense for the problem at hand - criticism is sharp and articulate - but they only perform *limited inquiry* into the problems: they are identified, but not accounted for. The discussion stops where it should have started: asking why specific defects and failures of the project report are there, what makes them be there, what are the consequences of those pitfalls and features for the success of the project, what can be done about the situation, how could the situation be reshaped.

It is the joint surfacing and discussion of the causal or conditional loops connnecting assumptions to actions and to outcomes, and these in turn to alternative options and assumptions that is missing here. People involved fail to make their private maps public, to surface and concert information, to discuss dilemmas and conflicts, etc. But only by performing this joint diagnostic activity, may one hope to proceed to new interventions later on. It is only by becoming aware of *what happened* and *why*, that one can be in a better position to see other options ahead, or at least to see what could have been done instead.

3.4 Some Consequences of Limited Inquiry

Limited inquiry into the problem leads to poor awareness, and this, in turn, to reduced competence at reframing. But limited inquiry into each other's perspective also leads to mistrust and defensiveness, and these, in turn, to reduced commitment at correcting defects and at reframing.

There is, in a few words, no joint construction of a collectively shared perception of reality, of a common awareness of the problem, and of a joint commitment to action. No collective map of the situation has surfaced for which people can take joint responsibility.

A limited inquiry and the particular behavioural dynamics at work also prevent the actors from being able to reformulate the problem and to connect it to other relationships in the organisation. If we, as an example, take the issue of "system description", this is defined by the actors as a matter of inaccuracy, incoherence, incompleteness: they see it as a technical problem which can and should be faced and solved within the technical or instrumental domain. Actors do not seem to appreciate that the flow-oriented description (procedures) and the actor-oriented descriptions (dialogues, conversations) are embedded in two different frames of organising reality, frames which discriminate what is relevant, and what is irrelevant, what is in the foreground of attention, and what is in the background, what is to be modelled and described, and what is not.

Describing a system of flows means to be more concerned with the internal efficiency of the computer system; describing a set of dialogues means to be more concerned with the effectiveness of the banking service, with what really happens in the real-life clerk/customer interaction. Actors are caught in this dilemma between system efficiency and service awareness and it is not discussed by the actors.

Making this dilemma explicit through inquiry into the technical problems of descriptions would presumably help the actors to relate the description issue to such other problems as users' participation or communication with users and, in turn, to the institutional setting, and to the system of values and norms regulating the interorganisational relationships.

It would also help the actors to inquire into the adequacy of the project model, and into JCN's project-policy. An attempt at reframing project-policy could, for instance, start by asking this question: is the new project model really adequate for our purposes? Does it need to be adapted or changed? How can we enact an organisational situation which is appropriate to the issue? Proceeding through these questions and answers requires not only skill at correcting errors, but also competence in relating to current frames and norms for action, to evaluate whether they are appropriate or not, and eventually to change them. Finally, inquiry into one's own and other's behaviours and assumptions would help actors to relate positive and negative consequences to personal actions and to take responsibility for the occurrences - be they positive or negative.

4 TOOLS AND TECHNIQUES FOR MAPPING

We present here some basic types of maps which we believe useful for project analysis and evaluation in the course of intervention. Each type of map focuses on a specific dimension of reality and is of course appropriate for particular purposes. However, comprehensive intervention should be able to produce all types of maps. We have distinguished between:

— Diagnostic maps
— Ecological maps
— Virtual maps
— Historical maps

In the subsequent sections we will describe the basic pattern of each of these types of maps. These patterns describe ideal types of maps and they represent possible mapping behaviours. They are not procedures to be followed. On the contrary, they have been designed on the basis of our own experiences with the intention of communicating the idea of intervention and with the expectation that the suggested patterns would be picked up, eventually adapted, or even changed in practical use.

4.1 Diagnostic Maps

The purpose of diagnostic maps is to relate project situations specifically perceived as problems (anomalies, failures) to sources and to more general organisational or behavioural features. Diagnostic maps locate and describe existing problems and disfunctional responses in the project or the organisation as they are perceived and accounted for by the actors. The basic pattern of a diagnostic map is shown in Figure 2.

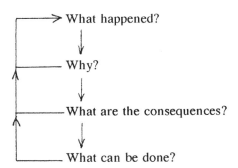

Figure 2.   Basic pattern of diagnostic map

The questions the interventionist may start asking when he or she intervenes into a project situation that needs to be diagnosed are:

What happened? Actors identify problems, failures or anomalies. They see the situation as problematic and attempt to define what the problem is. A key feature of the diagnostic map is in fact that the actors are forced to see the situation in a specific, simplified way - as a problem. The problem might be reformulated several times, even on the basis of the other questions. However, the interpretation of the situation expressed through the problem should be seen as the focus of the analysis to which possible causes, consequences and alternatives are then related.

Why? Actors formulate general or specific theories about what happened in the project situation. The inquire about possible causes and provide their explanations. Actors may:

— list acknowledged or perceived causes or actions that might have been sources of the problem;

— check and assess to what extent a perceived cause or action is relevant to the problem;

— check for incoherence or inconsistency between different sources;

— provide evidence for what they account for as a source of the problem.

In this process actors produce their own explanations, they might expose individual maps, and this in turn might bring to the actor's awareness conflicts and dilemmas embedded in contradictory explanations.

What are the consequences? Actors assess the consequences of the problem, that may be actually observable in the situation at hand or may occur in the future. This is a way of evaluating the chosen interpretation of the situation: Is it a serious problem? For whom is it a problem? One possible outcome of this process is to drop the chosen problem and return to a new interpretation of the situation. Evaluating the importance of the problem this way is a valuable step before undertaking any correcting and restructuring action.

What can be done? Actors attempt to restructure the situation by designing options for action. They project the existing situation into a desired one; they go from evaluation of consequences of existing problems to positive statements about a possible future. The process starts with the conditions and possibilities within the actor's domain of action, and addresses the desired goals and future states that can be achieved through active intervention on the situation.

What happened?	Why?	What are the consequences?	What can be done?
the various system descriptions are incoherent	meeting deadlines is given high priority	new activities are initiated on a defective basis	quality control should be improved during the early activities
it is not possible to obtain detailed knowledge about the new system from the descriptions	time schedule produced before anything is known about the degree of change involved	at some point of development deadlines can no longer be met	reviews should be performed with the participation of both programmers and direct users
the descriptions are unfinished and defective	new methods are applied, but no time for experimenting with them is allowed for	the savings banks know too little about what they will get. A number of changes can be expected after implementation	time schedules should be based on descriptions of the degree of change involved
	the description tools are inappropriate for describing dialogues	project members are often frustrated and unmotivated	time schedules should be changed as soon as the conditions on which they are based change
	no reviews have been performed	difficult for new project memebrs to work efficiently	versioning should have been applied as the basic strategy of the project
	many replacements of project members		different types of descriptions addressing different target groups should have been developed during the early stages of the project
	no baselines are set up to indicate sub-products and criteria for evaluation of sub-products		there should be time for experiments when new methods are taken into use

Figure 3.   An example of a diagnostic map - the JCN case

Figure 3 summarises an instance of a diagnostic map. This map has been developed by the JCN members of the MARS group on the basis of the situation discussed in section 3. The map illustrates how a diagnostic analysis could have been performed in the situation in question with the purpose of developing both a collectively shared awareness of what the problem is, and a joint commitment to action. As the figure illustrated, the situation is interpreted as problematic very much along the lines of section 3.2. However, this map provides explanations for the shortcomings of the descriptions. The problem is now related to the actions and choices of the project group (e.g. no baselines are set, no reviews are performed) and to the existing conditions (e.g. meeting deadlines is given high priority, new methods are applied). Moreover the chosen interpretation of the situation is evaluated by clarifying the consequences for the project group (e.g. project group members are often frustrated and unmotivated, difficult for new project members to work efficiently) and the consequences for its environment (e.g. the savings banks know too little about what they will get). If this analysis had been carried out within the situation, the actors could have developed an understanding of what could have been done about the situation (e.g. performing reviews and quality control, demanding time for experiments within projects using new methods). By performing this joint diagnostic activity, they might eventually come to share a common understanding of the situation and of possible actions, and on that basis they might proceed to new interventions later on.

---

take one problem at a time and stick to it;

dig deeply into the situation and try to surface as much information as you can;

be confident that you will go a long way; problems are all nested together in organisations;

go back in loops and test previous formulations;

search for new evidence;

take another problem ... and repeat.

Figure 4.   Practical hints for diagnostic mapping

The strength as well as the weakness of the diagnostic map is very much related to its idea of causation: causes (why?) lead to problems (what happened?) which in turn lead to consequences (what are the consequences?). On the one hand this strictly sequential idea of causation is very simple, and in fact it cannot be difficult to distinguish causes, problems, and consequences. On the other, diagnostic maps force you to see a given situation as a specific problem, and hence it provides you with the means for surfacing and structuring information about the situation - relative to the problem. This problem then could in turn be seen as the cause or the consequence of other problems within the framework of other maps. To put it another way, diagnostic maps are practical because they provide you with criteria for relevance and with means of structuring information. Diagnostic maps are, however, simple, and they should be complemented with other maps of the same situation. Figure 4 contains practical hints for developing diagnostic maps.

4.2 Ecological Maps

These maps describe what we refer to as the ecology of a given situation of intervention. They connect the situation to the overall organisation. They show in a time-independent manner the relationships between relevant domains of action. Ecological maps describe how perceived problems of issues in the situation can be connected to conditions in the landscape we are exploring. The basic pattern of an ecological map is shown in Figure 5.

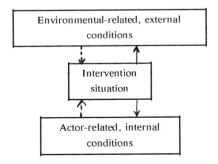

Figure 5.   Basic pattern of ecological map

The ecological maps are strictly relative to the situation we are actually intervening into. If we intervened into another area of the organisational setting, or in a changed situation, the resulting maps would also be modified, e.g. what was once perceived as external could become internal, or vice-versa.

Internal conditions refer to the behavioural world of the actors involved in the situation. They are characteristics of the situation that are primarily produced and reproduced through the behaviour of the actors. *External conditions*, on the other hand, refer to environment-related characteristics of the situation, i.e., to characteristics that are primarily produced and reproduced through processes in which the actors of the situation are not engaged.

The arrows in Figure 5 indicate how the conditions shape and restrict what happens or what can happen in the given situation, and how the behaviour of the actors can have consequences for the intervention situation. Internal and external conditions, as perceived in ecological maps, have influence on the performance of a project and they are in turn influenced by actions undertaken within the project. Ecological maps allow an understanding of how problems relate to conditions, and a reflection on which are the relevant domains of action and on which relations hold between two or more domains of action.

Figure 6 summarises an instance of an ecological map. Again this map has been developed by the JCN members of the MARS group on the basis of the situation discussed in section 3. The headlines, i.e., the general types of conditions, have been developed on the basis of several diagnostic and ecological maps produced by the group.

There is a close relationship between diagnostic and ecological maps. Typically, one can describe conditions in ecological maps on the basis of causes and consequences in diagnostic maps. In fact this is the way the ecological map of Figure 6 was developed by the MARS group. When intervening into a system development project one should begin with developing diagnostic maps which interpret the situation in various ways. On that basis ecological maps may be developed quite easily with the purpose of producing an overview of the situation. Diagnostic mapping leads to an awareness and understanding of single problems, whereas ecological mapping, fostering an awareness of the whole setting, leads to a clearer perception of the bridges and gaps between individual problems and relevant domains of action. Figure 7 contains practical hints for developing ecological maps.

External Conditions

Relations to savings banks

    difficult to get access to internal savings bank routines

    JCN management wants the project to be a success

    no savings bank representatives within the project

Project practices at JCN

    maintenance assignments are given higher priority than projects

    little continuity of participants during project activities

    during the early activities participants have to finish other assignments

    JCN has no tradition concerning quality control

Guidelines for project work

    new methods are applied

    few guidelines for quality control

Existing equipment and system

    project based on new equipment

    new systems strongly depend on existing systems

Special conditions

    time schedule and requirements specified in advance

    none of the participants took part in specifying time schedule and requirements

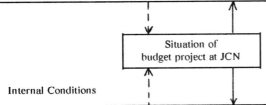

Situation of
budget project at JCN

Internal Conditions

Vaules and norms

    participants do not acknowledge the necessity to experiment when using new methods

    disagreement to what extent the system should be based on existing programs

    quality of products is identified with steering committee acceptance

Working practice

    one-shot strategt....

    mainly formal contacts with savings banks

    defective short term management

Figure 6.   Example of ecological map

begin with the intervention situation and stick to;

build bridges and establish linkages between the problems at hand and the surrounding domains of action;

bring to the surface external and internal conditions relative to the intervention situation;

develop a couple of diagnostic maps before proceeding to ecological mapping;

use causes and consequences from diagnostic maps as sources of inspiration;

attempt to categorise the various conditions with the purpose of clarifying relevant domains of action.

Figure 7.   Practical hints for ecological mapping

4.3 Virtual Maps

Virtual maps represent future situations which are possible or desirable. Virtual maps are pictures constructed to represent actions which we can simulate and test, and eventually choose to enact later on. Virtual maps help us in assessing the consequences of our actions and choices and may be useful as projective tools in intervening and producing intervention that would change the present conditions. These maps allow us to compare and test different assumptions and hypotheses about a future situation. By drawing virtual maps we perform what could be called the invention leap, a project transformation of a situation into a desirable one: "how do we go from here to there?", or: "how would it feel being there?"

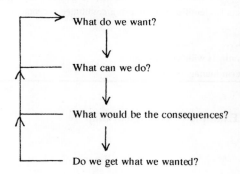

Figure 8.   Basic pattern of virtual map

It is worthwhile to remark that analysts have dedicated very little time and attention to the issue of what consequences will be generated by their own actions and by other people's actions. Virtual maps contain images of ourselves and our own actions. They state: "If we do such and such, we shall be likely to obtain such and such", or: "What would happen if we did such and such?" A basic pattern for developing a virtual map is illustrated in Figure 8. The questions the interventionist may start asking to construct virtual maps are:

What do we want ?
Actors envision future situations or worlds. They start out with the problems and conditions they perceive as related to the situation in question, and from there they attempt to envision how it could be different. In constructing possible future situations actors do not start from scratch. Usually they transpose and rearrange features and themes of actual or experienced situations in a new pattern. Most of the time inventing consists of being able to see old things in a new way.

What can we do ?
Actors formulate actions to be undertaken to realise what they want. They investigate how they can go from present situations to the desired ones. In these two first activities actors invent and explore possible worlds and actions to realise them, for instance by removing or releasing conditions, or by designing new sets of conditions and opportunities.

What would be the consequences ?
Actors assess the likely consequences and impacts of undertaking the envisioned actions. They evaluate what would happen if they did such and such. From the envisioned actions they generate possible new sequences of processes and outcomes, e.g. what would the impacts and counter effects be, and what would one face trying to act as envisioned.

Do we get what we wanted ?
On this basis the actors then evaluate whether the suggested actions really lead to the desired situation, and whether the strategy represented by the suggested actions would have any reasonable chance of realising what was desired. The insight gained into possible actions and consequences is used to evaluate how it would feel to be in the projected situation.

Diagnostic and ecological maps can be applied when developing virtual maps. The appreciation of specific problems and conditions related to the intervention situation should be used as the basis for envisioning alternatives. In the JCN case one might envision a situation where descriptions are developed in close cooperation with savings bank employees who have practical insight into the routines, traditions, and problems related to savings bank practices. In this situation savings bank employees should play an active role in analysing the existing situation and in evaluating proposals of new systems.

Furthermore both the actions suggested in diagnostic maps as well as the possible domains of action described in the ecological maps are useful sources for exploring how one can go from the present situation to the desired one. On the basis of the diagnostic map in Figure 3 one might ask: should different types of descriptions be developed addressing the same subject from various viewpoints? Should versioning be applied to support the cooperation with savings bank employees? How and when could savings bank employees review and influence proposals for new systems? And on the basis of the ecological map in Figure 6 one might explore which conditions for systems development projects would have to be changed in order to obtain the desired situation. Figure 9 contains practical hints for developing virtual maps.

---

pick up one or more points which you think are central, and try to restructure them;

in restructuring go forward from the old to the new situation, and backwards from the new to the old, in loops;

look at the new situation in terms of the old one, and then at the old in terms of the new;

test: if what we had was bad, is what we get good enough? or, is something missing?

as you proceed in restructuring and reframing, check if secondary or peripheral themes and features fit into the new picture.

Figure 9.   Practical hints for virtual mapping

4.4 Historical Maps

We need maps which allow us to trace the project's history from a starting point to a terminating point. These maps have time as their main dimension, divided into units depending on how detailed a descriptive account we want. These maps should not only record events or issues, but also actions, and conditions perceived as yielding events and problems in specific situations.

System development handbooks are full of prescriptive schemes and diagrams on how a project should be carried out. What system development projects lack, however, is a kind of historiography which should allow people to track the development of the project - as it is actually taking place. We need to reflect and discuss what happened in the past at different points of time, and to learn from there what might be important for future activities or projects.

A list of events in a time sequence without relating them to actions and conditions would be of little use for such purposes. That is why historical maps should catch the most relevant "events-actions-conditions" loops of causal or quasi-causal relationships. Historical maps should, in other words, organise past experience in a time sequence, and at the same time help one to see how events or issues are related to actions or conditions. Historical maps contain knowledge about what happened in the course of the project, and help in answering the basic questions: how were the various activities of the project actually carried out? This knowledge is essential - we believe - for effective dynamic regulation and control. The basic pattern of a historical map is shown in Figure 10. (Enderud and Borum, 1981; Mathiassen, 1981).

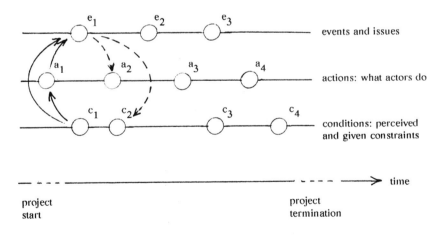

Figure 10.   Basic pattern of a historical map

A project is described on three levels. First, important events and issues are described. What is seen as important depends on the interventionist and on his or her intentions and interests with the analysis. Generally, one can distinguish between failures, i.e., events where a deviation from what was intended or planned is acknowledged in the project, and successes, i.e., events where an intended or planned situation has been successfully achieved or established. However, it is not always possible in practice - on this concrete level of description - to identify events, i.e. to date a given observation. Some observations may be expressed in more general terms as issues of the project. The specific issues might be prevailing for a shorter or longer time, and they might have surfaced many times rather than just at one particular time. They are recurrent events, or more stable characteristics of the development of the project. For instance:

—   The programming language chosen in the project under analysis is not suitable for the design of the interactive programs to be produced within the project: hence, recurrent failures tend to become a characteristic of the project.

—   The project is initiated on the basis of a contract with extremely unrealistic deadlines: hence, the project group is constantly forced to give less priority to the quality of the system in question, and at the same time they try to postpone the deadline in various ways.

Secondly, the actions in the project are discussed. Actions are what each actor involved in the project actually did, and how they are related to identified events and issues. We put under this item what originates from explicit human choices in the course of the project.

—   The use of a certain description language results in communication problems between system developers and users, and this is perceived as an important event.

—   The project is organised around a project group, a steering committee, and procedures for reporting and decision making. The project group spends a lot of effort following these procedures (action). However, they very rarely get any feedback on the quality of their reports, and they often find themselves in a situation (event) where they have to report according to procedures, although they are not ready to do so, seen in relation to the status of the project.

Finally, the conditions, as they are perceived and acknowledged by the actors involved, are described, and their relationship to actions and events are spelled out. The conditions (or the context) of a project may have decisive influence on which problems and conflict surface during the project, and on how these problems and conflict may be handled. We consider time (deadlines) to be one of these conditions, or available human and financial resources, or technical options, or existing legislation and agreements, or else the overall interorganisational relations and the structures of power and interests.

These conditions are of course not fixed. An important event may result in further processes, which again may result in a change in actions and in prevailing conditions. An action yielding undesired events can be corrected. A phase or project deadline can be postponed, and interests can be shifted. As a further example:

— The project group may acknowledge that it will find it difficult to meet deadlines (important event). Therefore they try to give less priority to the design equipment, and instead give more priority to the design of the new system (modified action). At the same time the project group tries to change the users' expectations concerning how large a part of the system should be ready at the agreed upon deadline (modified condition).

Historical maps are the most comprehensive type of maps presented. They are made and used *retrospectively* to evaluate projects either during the course of the project, or when the project has terminated and has become history. The historical maps are related in a very direct way to the ecological maps as well as the diagnostic maps. Ecological maps describing external conditions are related to the intervention situation corresponding to the third level of consideration within historical maps describing perceived and given constraints. Diagnostic maps can be seen as a vertical segment of a historical map: the perceived problem of the diagnostic map corresponds to the event and issue level of the historical map, and the causes and consequences of the diagnostic map corresponds to the action as well as to the condition level of the historical map. Hence, diagnostic and ecological maps are helpful tools in developing historical maps.

Before concluding this section, it is worthwhile to remark that historical maps, like the others which have been presented, are not rigorous in the scientific sense of the term. They have a special kind of rigour which is very much connected to their practical relevance and use. Historical maps help debating, learning, and reflecting on the most important historical and causal features of a project. They are constructed by the actors involved in the project reflecting what they think of the project, what they consider to be relevant. If properly used, historical maps give insight into projects and situations that have been lived through, an insight which can be turned into a helpful resource when preparing for future cases.

5 SECOND CASE OF INTERVENTION

The basic types of maps presented above are incomplete as guidelines for action and need to be completed by concrete action and choice. To emphasise this point, and to report on some practical experiences in mapping situations within system development projects, we proceed by presenting and analysing a real-life situation where a project group uses mapping as an intervention technique. The intervention takes place half way through the project and it addresses the overall status of the project at this time of development.

5.1 The Organisational Context

The project in question takes place in a private software house. The purpose of the project is to develop a computer based directory system a foreign telephone company. The project group consists of eight persons, and the project is estimated to last for one year.

Both the project group and management want to develop and test new working practices and organisational forms, and therefore the project is designed as an experiment. The experiment covers system description issues, several project management issues and the organisation of project meetings. Among other things the project group decides to spend one day evaluating the overall status of the project both at the end and half way through the project.

5.2 The intervention situation

The situation with which we are concerned here is the meeting taking place half way through the project. Each of the eight participants has prepared an overall evaluation of the project emphasising at least two positive and two negative statements. The first two hours of the meeting are spent presenting these evaluations, each participant giving his or her points of view, the others listening and asking questions for clarification. During the next hour the various statements are discussed and the following list of main points compiled:

Positive statements
— the process has been transparent,
— the project meetings have been well organised,
— it is fruitful to experiment with working habits,
— attempts to exercise joint management have worked well,
— the edp-based documentation system is good,
— the working climate has been stimulating.

Negative statements
— too little progress, responsibility and initiative,
— working practices outside project meetings have not changed very much,
— the product is not transparent,
— the detailed planning is insufficient,
— many decision processes have been slow.

Throughout these three hours of presentation and discussion one person is acting as referent writing down the main statements on the blackboard. From this point two negative statements are selected and starting from these, two diagnostic maps are produced. Approximately two hours are spent producing each map. In each case the blackboard is divided into four columns corresponding to the basic pattern of a diagnostic map (e.g. Figure 2). Again one person acts as referent writing down the statements, evaluations and comments in the proper column. The discussion of each of the two problems is open - except for the structure imposed by the four columns on the blackboard. After several iterations and corrections, and after two hours of intensive discussion, the first of the two maps is produced:

What happened?
Too little progress has been made. Several facts provide evidence that this is a real problem:
— reports show that less time is spend on the project than is available according to plans,
— the time spent on the project has resulted in less progress than planned,
— in long periods very few technical and organisational problems surface.

Why ?

Among the possible explanations the following are considered important:

— lack of initiative and responsibility in relation to the project;

— much of the work consists in modifying existing hardware and software modules and this type of work is not so challenging as development of new systems;

— too little attention is paid to the design and establishment of activities. Typically this task is left to the initiative of the individual participant;

— many interruptions due to external factors;

— no systematic configuration management;

— lack of responsibility in relation to joint agreements and decisions.

What are the consequences ?

Evaluating the importance of the problem the following consequences are expected:

— the contract with the foreign telephone company cannot be kept;

— due to insufficient reinforcement, the project becomes less challenging, the participants become less committed, even less progress is made, etc.;

— management demands that the participants start working overtime.

What can be done ?

The situation can be restructured along the following lines:

— the participants should change the old habit and tradition that the formal project leader is responsible for all management activities;

— a more even distribution of checkpoints will make everyone more aware of the actual status and progress of the project;

— systematic configuration management;

— joint effort on designing and establishing new activities;

— more realistic plans, also taking into account interruptions due to external factors.

In a similar way another map is produced, and then the meeting ends. All the material that has been written on the blackboard is copied and distributed to all eight participants after the meeting. At the next regular project meeting decisions are taken as to which actions to initiate.

5.3 Diagnosing the project situation

In this situation we see a project group agree a shared perception of the status of the project for which they can take joint responsibility. They use the pattern of diagnostic maps, but basically they use the idea of mapping to design their own intervention: each participant prepares negative and positive statements, these are presented to the group, a joint list of statements is compiled, etc. They complete the idea of mapping by concrete action and choice.

The project group chooses to start from individual maps and from there they try to develop public and collectively shared knowledge about the status of the project. Clearly they succeed - partly because the whole project is designed as an experiment to develop new working practices. The actors have committed themselves to understand, criticize and change established traditions. All the actors share an interest in understanding and in taking action.

At the meeting the actors identify characteristic and recurrent patterns and relations in their project. For instance they agree that too little progress is made; they agree that in this way, the project becomes less challenging, they themselves become less committed, and this in turn leads to even less progress. From the joint understanding of such patterns the actors design new ways in which the project should be carried out: joint effort on designing and establishing new activities, systematic configuration management, a more even distribution of checkpoints, etc. In this way the participants develop an awareness of where they stand in the project and they interact in a quite direct, articulate and creative way.

The project from our first case of intervention (part 3) was delayed by more than 100% in relation to the plans of the project. This last project succeeded in meeting the contract. We will not - and cannot - argue that this important difference has to do with they ways in which the two intervention situations were designed and handled. The two examples do, however, support our basic thesis that effective project management requires a capacity for learning and acting which is far beyond the established traditions of the field - and they also support our suggestion that the idea of mapping can be used to design effective interventions into system development projects.

6   TOWARDS AN INTERVENTION PERSPECTIVE ON SYSTEM DEVELOPMENT

An implicit argument which runs through this chapter is that current system development methods fall short in at least two respects: (1) they provide very few tools for evaluating the practical consequences of the proposed designs; (2) they do not deal much with the crucial issue of invention or what we have called the *invention leap*, with how one goes from the analysis of the existing system to the concept of the new one. Both weaknesses perhaps originate from an underestimation of the causal texture connecting actions and consequences in a situation of action (which a system development project actually is). Though this texture may well be loose and fuzzy, it is indeed *there*, and it plays an important role in the performance of the project. But current methods and techniques do not help people to trace consequences and outcomes back to their own actions and to existing conditions, or even to see relevant events as an unintended consequence or by-product of specific action. In the JCN case, for instance, we have noticed that project members are in trouble when requested to reveal the causal or conditional web of their project situation. Maybe that happens because they rely on method and technique as a basis to justify or explain action. A method is itself a program for action which somehow *reduces* basic inferential structures of the type "if ... then ..." to a set of instructions in a sequence: "do this, then do that, then something else, ..., finally complete with that". In this reduction, the perception of the linkages between antecedents and consequences of action is sometimes lost or weakened.

On the contrary, maps, as we have developed them, are designed to make people actively go from thinking about situations to enacting new ones. It is our intention they should improve the cognitive and learning capabilities for performing effective intervention. We claim that they help produce and convey knowledge which is not rigorous but certainly relevant. Maps reflect human constructs and interactions as they emerge in a real life project, and because of that they cannot have the same kind of rigor as formal schemes, though they might indeed have their own kind of rigor (Argyris, 1980).

Another basic argument underlying this paper is that system development can be usefully seen as a process of intervention into an organisational setting, characterised by situations of uncertainty, conflict, and change. This process yields intended and unintended changes in the information processing technology used by an organisation, in the work processes, and in the nature of work itself, in the network of economic transactions among members, in the power relationships, in the cognitive and learning modes, and in the behavioural patterns of people. To intervene means to enter into an ongoing set of relationships for the purpose of changing them (Argyris and Schon, 1978).

The idea of intervention draws on a theory of action. Recent systems development approaches mainly rely on theories of systems and system change. On one hand this emphasis has led to more appropriate frames and methods for the dynamic regulation of projects, but on the other it has put aside aspects concerning how human action yields organisational change. We think that system development methods could be healthily rejuvenated by a merging of theories of systems' change and theories of action.

Our frame for intervention assumes that there are no reasons to think that work activities performed in developing a system should be of a different nature to the actual work currently being performed in organisations. It is the same kind of work, and this idea of intervention applies both to the activity of developing a system, and to current every-day work in organisations. Either involves some sort of intervention into situations that are never totally defined or clear. To work - be it a secretary's or a manager's work - is to intervene into situations, and to intervene is to make oneself part of the situation in order to change it. Thus the work performed by an analyst who analyses a project is basically of the same kind as the work performed in the project, and it is also the same work performed by the prospective user of the project's final product, the system.

That is why a practical theory of intervention applies to multiple domains, namely to the project evaluation domain (research work), to the project-proper domain (design), and to the products and work processes resulting from the project (computer-based work). Map-making initiates intervention in each domain: it contemplates the same kind of practice.

A major consequence of the intervention perspective is that it helps to break, or at least to reduce, the sharp distinction between development and use of technology that most systems development methods take for granted. Analysts tend to see system development as a process running from one established state of the organisation to another established state, where the products designed are finally plugged into the organisation and put into use by the users. That often creates situations in which it is difficult to implement the system and get the users to behave according to the system's specifications and prescriptions. Naturally designers and users blame each other: the users are accused of being incompetent or resistant to change, or even of being irrational; the designers on the other hand are accused of being unconcerned with the user's needs and all wrapped up in their formal models.

The recent interest in designing and testing systems prototypes can be seen as an attempt to reverse the patterns "from development to use", and to let practical applications and behaviours deeply shape the design process itself. By prototyping the designer tentatively creates simplified but typical work situations in order to test them and subsequently to transpose them into real situations of practice. That would hopefully help prevent undesired consequences and ease the merging of the new system into the organization (Budde et al., 1984). Prototyping and versioning are, in other words, conscious attempts to bring the learning dimension into the design process by reducing the distance between the designed system and the system-in-use.

In many respects the logic of intervention differs from the logic of analysis. It highlights and focusses on the situations as they are experienced by the actors: systems, functions, procedures, and technical equipment are not just wiped out as irrelevant. On the contrary, they are necessary elements of the actors' situation contributing to shape it, but they lie - so to speak - in the background of the situation. People use them, apply them, perform with them, talk about them, sometimes even play with them or talk to them: they are used as tools and programs to do work, but the work itself is made of punctuated sequences of situations which actors experience as meaningful. Thus practical intervention is concerned less with analysing and choosing - though it does not deny their importance - and more with understanding situations by encasing practical experiments in a context of action, by revealing latent conflicts of interest and by shifting and reframing problems. Contrary to some previous views on intervention put forward by socio-technical theorists (Bostrom and Heinen, 1977), intervention is here to be understood as an inquiry in the cognitive and learning domain rather in the technical-instrumental domain (Argyris and Schon, 1978).

Here we come to another basic issue for system development. By intervening into a situation the interventionist - designer, analyst, manager, or user - contributes to the shaping of the situation as much as anybody else involved in it. But it is unreasonable to think that he can unilaterally control the situation. Regulation is in most cases a question of coordination of different instances and actors, none of which can exactly predict and control the behaviour of the others. In organisations there are no such things as established situations that can be fully controlled. Situations, in a way, are always *emergent*, i.e., they display properties and features which are changed by the very attempt at determining, predicting, and controlling them. The real challenge for an interventionist is not the question of how to control the system or the process, but the question of how one can modify a situation when being *inside* it, of how one can make the intended course of events come about when actions are part of those events. A "good" intervention cannot be entirely planned in advance, expecting that the outcome will be exactly as planned. An intervention is not only, or not so much, a way to achieve pre-fixed objectives, as rather a way to construct and discover them through a process of inquiry.

A traditional and well-known approach to the issue of control is functional specialisation of work and diffusion of labour. In organisations there are people who *do* things, many different things, and people who *think* about how things should be done. The latter also monitor the ways things are actually done. This is a typically managerial view of how work is organised in organisations: knowledge and cognitive equipment are supposed to be concentrated at the top level, whereas going down the hierarchical ladder one should find increasingly stupid and routine jobs. On the contrary, we claim that cognitive skills are perhaps the most diffuse resources among people in organisations, irrespective of where they sit in the hierarchical ladder. Furthermore, even people who do things with their minds often do not reflect on what they are doing: that happens to top managers as well as to secretaries. We should put the managerial spectacles aside for a moment and realise that human beings performing cognitively-based work cannot be very distant in their cognitive resources. As we said above, a practical theory of intervention points to a view of work as "intervention-into-situations" where there are no substantial differences in the cognitive skills needed to understand a situation. The difference is rather to be found in the domain of action addressed by the intervention.

To make a final point, the tools which have been developed and presented in this paper address the key issue of how relevant knowledge is constructed and used in practice in system development projects. We cannot help thinking that an interesting extension of the "mapping" approach could be in the broader domains of organisational design and organisational change. System development is, after all, an instance of organisational change. We have the feeling, as other authors do (Wildavsky, 1983), that information gathering and processing in organisational settings are often overestimated to the detriment of an inquiry into the knowledge base of competent action. And competent action is what is most needed in organisations to foster effective change. But we feel that a great deal of knowledge relevant for action is often lost in rigorous but irrelevant or unusable information. A necessary condition for competent action is then also lost. Not to speak of wisdom. But we shall leave that for some other time.

REFERENCES

Argyris, C. (1980). The Inner Contradiction of Rigorous Research. New York: Academic Press.

Argyris, C. and Schon, D.A. (1978). Organizational Learning: A Theory of Action Perspective. Reading, Massachusetts: Addison-Wesley.

Bostrom, R.P. and Heinen, J.S. (1977). MIS problems and failures: a socio-technical perspective. *MIS Quarterly*, September, pp. 17-32.

Briefs U., et al., (ed.) (1983). System design for, with, and by the users. Proceedings of the IFIP WG 9.1 Working Conference, Riva del Sole, Italy, 20-24 September, 1982. Amsterdam: North Holland.

Budde, R. et al., (ed.) (1984). Approaches to prototyping. *Proceedings of the Working Conference on Prototyping*, Namur, Belgium, October 1983. Berlin: Springer Verlag.

Ciborra, C. (1984). Management Information Systems: a contractual view. Beyond Productivity: Information Systems Development for Organizational Effectiveness. *Proceedings of the IFIP WG 8.2 Working Conference,* Minneapolis, USA, August 1983, Th. Bemelmans, (ed.). Amsterdam: North Holland.

DeMarco, T. (1979). Structured Analysis and System Specification. New York: Yourdon Press.

Enderud, H. and Borum, F. (1981). Conflicts in Organizations - illustrated by systems development examples. Copenhagen: Nyt Nordisck Forlag. (In Danish).

Flores, F. and Ludlow, J.J. (1981). Doing and speaking in the office. *In*: *DSS: Issues and Challenges*. G. Flick and R. Sprague (ed.). London: Pergamon Press.

Jackson, M. (1983). System Development. London: Prentice-Hall.

Hammer, M. and Ziesman, M. (1979). Design and implementation of office information systems. *In: Proceedings of the New York Conference on Automated Office Systems*, New York.

Hice, G.F., et al. (1978). System Development Methodology. Amsterdam: North-Holland.

Lanzara, G.F. (1983). The design process: frames, metaphors and games. *In: System design for, with, and by the users*. U. Briefs et al., (ed.). Amsterdam: North-Holland.

Lanzara, G.F. (1983). Reframing System Design: An Intervention Perspective, Unpublished manuscript, University of Bari.

MARS (1984). MARS: a Research Project on Methods for Systems Development. *Reports* No. 1-5, University of Aarhus (nos 2-5 in Danish).

Matthiassen, L. (1981). Systems Development and Systems Development Method. *DAIMI*, PB-136, University of Aarhus.

McCaskey, P. (1981). Mapping: Creating, Maintaining, and Relinquishing Conceptual Frameworks. Harvard Business School.

Yourdon, E. (1982). Managing the System Life Cycle. New York: Yourdon Press.

Weinberg, G.M. and Freedman, D.P. (1982). Handbook of Walkthroughs, Inspections and Technical Reviews. Little Brown and Company, Boston.

Wildavsky, A. (1983). Information as an Organizational Problem. *Journal of Management Studies*, 20 (1).

Wynn, E. (1979). Office Conversation as an Information Medium. Ph.D. Thesis, Dept. of Anthropology. Berkeley: University of California.

Wynn, E. (1983). The User as a Representation Issue in the USA. *In: System design for, with, and by the users*. U. Briefs (ed.). Amsterdam: North Holland.

TOWARDS EFFECTIVE COMPUTER AIDS TO PLANNING IN COMPUTER PROGRAMMING
Theoretical Concern and Empirical Evidence drawn from Assessment of a Prototype

Jean-Michel HOC

Université de Paris 8, UFR de Psychologie
Equipe "Psychologie Cognitive du Traitement de l'Information Symbolique"
France

The work presented in this paper has been supported by ADI (French National Agency for Informatics) and done with the collaboration of J. Guyard, J.P. Jacquot, and M. Quéré from CRIN (CNRS Informatics Research Center at the University of Nancy), who have implemented the software tools.

Abstract

For about fifteen years, a lot of research work has been published on the psychology of programming. In most cases diverse kinds of static characteristics of the programming environment have been emphasised, for example, language features or program lay-outs. In addition, attention has very often turned to novices and very seldom to professional programmers. The growth of software factories requires a shift of attention towards dynamic aids to expert programmers' activity. This paper is devoted to *planning*, which is a crucial feature of this expert activity. It briefly describes a framework for the study of planning, derived from psychology and artificial intelligence, and reports evidence drawn from an empirical assessment of computer aids to programming. It illustrates the relevance of a theoretical approach to designing experimental situations, the enrichment of the framework gained from empirical evidence, and the benefits of this procedure in designing effective computer aids. The results stress: (a) the crucial role of *problem type* in planning guidance needs, (b) the limitations of traditional programming languages when subject wants to express *schematic representations* at the onset of design, (c) the disturbances in working memory when *parallel presentation of information* is not available, and (d) the importance of *familiarisation effects* with new tools (even with experts) before getting relevant evidence from experimental assessment.

INTRODUCTION

Today, software ergonomics does not only concern the users of the programmers' software but the programmers themselves. In searching for software of better quality and lower cost, computer aided software engineering systems are rapidly growing at such a pitch that they may be called software factories. Considerable progress has been made towards the implementation of dynamic computer aids to programming. For example, program editors are becoming more and more powerful and are not only aids to the final steps of programming (program development) but also to the very first steps in designing programs (problem analysis).

Cognitive ergonomics has not yet directly attacked computer aided software engineering, whereas a lot of work has dealt with programming in general. Nevertheless, only a little empirical evidence is available on professional programmers and programming strategies or methodologies. Theoretical backgrounds for this kind of research may profit by being elaborated within the framework of the psychology of problem-solving. In other respects, from the psychological research point of view, the analysis of computer aided problem-solving is a good way to understand human problem-solving itself. In fact, this kind of situation leads the subject to manifest otherwise covert parts of his or her activity. Thus, the psychology of programming is not a routine application of cognitive theories, but a domain where elaboration of these theories is made easier and desirable, especially for designing effective computer aids to human problem-solving.

From the point of view of designing software factories, the assessment which will be presented is modest. It is concentrated on the program design step and follows several pieces of work on learning top-down programming methods (Hoc, 1983a) and on planning direction (Hoc, 1981), contrasting a *prospective* strategy (the statements of the program being elaborated by following the order of execution) and a *retrospective* one (in the reverse order). This work takes place in the larger perspective of the study of *planning* strategies in problem-solving (Hoc, 1987), from the double point of view of *anticipation* (delayed knowledge of results) and *schematisation* (use of schematic representations, graphic or not).

In fact, planning may lead the subject to remove execution details. This removal permits the subject to use schematic representations far from the details and elaborate the statements in orders sometimes very different from the execution order. Many computer aids lead the subject to follow a top-down strategy. In other respects, retrospective strategy is often recommended in mathematical problem-solving for it reduces the problem space and leads the subject to precisely justify each subgoal by the related goal. Beginners have a lot of difficulties in following these kinds of strategies and we want to know if that is also the case for professional programmers.

In beginners, the reasons for these difficulties have clearly emerged from the previous studies which have been cited. The beginners cannot follow a top-down strategy, since they do not know enough program plans or schemata and have few assessment criteria at their disposal for anticipating the efficiency of a particular plan. They very often follow a prospective strategy, since they elaborate the statements by mental execution of the program. They think more in terms of operations than of static relationships or properties.

With expert programmers, top-down and retrospective strategies are possible, but not necessarily implemented. A strategy may be available without being implemented in that the conditions of its implementation may be unfulfilled. These conditions concern the programming environment, especially computer aids when they exist, the type of problem to be solved, and the subject's characteristics. In the present empirical work an assessment of a prototype of computer aids to these top-down and retrospective strategies has been chosen in order to obtain a situation where the conditions of implementation of these strategies are approximated (the MAIDAY environment: Guyard and Jacquot, 1984). Thus, from the point of view of the programming environment, the situation was as suitable as possible to observe these strategies.

But, the purpose of the assessment of these computer aids has not been restricted to ergonomic suggestions of modifications or extra aids to these two kinds of strategies. The expert was expected to use a wider variety of strategies. If the programming environment is intended to be effective in most situations, it must not be restricted to these two kinds of strategies. Thus, this experiment had two aims: the assessment of the MAIDAY environment, and the test of hypotheses related to the conditions of implementation of planning strategies in this kind of environment. In this paper, stress will be put on general outcomes rather than specific suggestions for modifying of the tools.

In the first part of this paper, a theoretical framework derived from cognitive psychology and artificial intelligence is proposed for the study of planning in programming. The second part describes the prototype used in this study and assessed (the MAIDAY environment): a definitional language (MEDEE) and its syntactic and semantic editor (MEDEDIT). The third part is devoted to the method followed for the assessment: typology of programming problems, experimental design, and hypotheses. The main results are reported in the fourth part and discussed in the conclusion.

1 PLANNING IN PROBLEM-SOLVING: A Framework for the Study of Programming Activity

1.1 Programming as a Problem-Solving Activity

A problem is considered as a subject-built representation of a task for which he or she has no acceptable procedure at his or her disposal to reach the goal. Thus, the subject has to develop a procedure elaboration activity: a *strategy* which requires a higher control level than the straightforward execution of a well-known procedure. Hence, a task cannot be defined as a problem without reference to a cognitive system of a certain kind. With regards to programming in a procedural language, the goal is the expression of an operable procedure for a well-defined device: the formal machine underlying the language statements.

Three high-level types of problems can be contrasted in relation to the types of representations and strategies used by the subject at a given time during the course of problem-solving:

1. State transformation problems in which the task is represented as a path in a problem space of states, linked by transformation rules. The strategies may be diverse: trial-and-error, means-ends analysis (Newell and Simon, 1972), etc. Programming may trigger this kind of problem-solving when the subject develops a certain type of *procedural* strategy, by mentally executing the procedure he or she is writing. It is always possible to model a problem-solving situation, whatever its type, as a search in a problem space of states. But the subject does not always use this kind of model.

2. Structure induction problems implying a task representation in terms of discovering relations between elements. A well-known strategy is hypothesis testing (Simon and Lea, 1974). In programming the subject encounters this kind of problem when, for example, he or she infers data structures.

3. *Design problems* for which the goal is represented as a set of constraints not adequate enough to directly obtain a detailed representation of the goal. Strategies consist in resolving conflicts between constraints and introducing new constraints to refine the goal (Stefik, 1981). A programming problem may be of this kind when the subject develops a *declarative* strategy, especially in static or declarative languages which express properties and relations between objects rather than operations to be executed.

1.2 Planning: Schematising and Anticipating

Planning is usually defined as generating a series of operations, before executing them (i.e., without feedback from execution), in state transformation situations. From this restricted point of view, programming is obviously a planning activity. But, more generally, planning requires more than this single temporal anticipation and does not only concern state transformation problems. Its main feature is *schematising*.

In planning, when the problem is complex, the removal of implementation details leads the subject to use schematic representations, certainly because of working memory span limitations, but above all because of the availability of high-level knowledge. This is why beginners encounter many difficulties in planning (see for example Hoc, 1983a, Adelson et al., 1984). With such activity a *plan* has to be considered as a hierarchically structured representation of a procedure or a state (initial, intermediary or goal) which actually guides the subject's activity (Miller et al., 1960). Information processing models of human problem-solving and artificial intelligence systems have successively described several planning strategies. Maybe each of them can be an acceptable model of a particular subject in a specific situation.

The first of them was what Newell and Simon (1972) called the *"planning strategy"* in state transformation problems. It consists of elaborating a procedure at an abstract level: a planning space where certain details of the task are ignored. This abstract procedure guides the elaboration of a more detailed one at a lower abstraction level, and so on until taking all the details into consideration. This rigid *top-down* planning strategy may fail and all the work must be done anew, as can be seen in beginners who start with a plan incompatible with the operation of the computer (Hoc, 1983a).

The concept of abstraction space can be extended to all types of problem, but a single dimension is not enough. Rasmussen (1984), for example, proposes two dimensions in the context of industrial process control: the relationship between two objects belonging to two spaces may be of a whole-part kind, or of a specification-implementation kind. This latter dimension hierarchically organises functional descriptions of objects and operational implementation of these descriptions. For instance, a heating component in a plant can be analysed in terms of thermodynamic laws (specification level) before being instantiated in an electric device, leading to the necessity to take electricity laws into consideration (implementation level). In programming, this dimension is important to cover the whole software life cycle, from specification to software development. For example, a sorting problem can be analysed in terms of general mathematical properties before being implemented by a specific procedure which will imply new and specific properties.

Crucial property of computer aids to planning is the possibility of dealing with schematic representations. Languages which are defined at a single abstraction level, the detailed one, may prevent the subject from developing planning strategies. For example, in despatch translation by journalists, Pavard (1985) has shown that using a text editor produced results of worse quality than using a typewriter. Feeling that interesting aids were available for manipulating the surface of the text induced very different strategies with which the subjects directly translated the main proposition and tried to insert subordinate ones. But these strategies led the subjects into language conflicts and complex surface modifications. With a typewriter, the cost of the modifications was high and led the subjects to plan, before typing the whole sentence. The moral of the story is not to reintroduce typewriters but to design 'idea editors' which can aid in organising ideas before writing correct sentences.

With STRIPS and ABSTRIPS, Sacerdoti (1974) tried to improve the top-down strategy by using specific knowledge on the relative importance of details in the abstraction process. Later he proposed a *non-linear* model (NOAH: see Sacerdoti, 1977) which introduces execution order only when the abstraction space gives decision criteria. The strategy basically remains a *top-down* kind, even if it is more flexible. Traditional programming languages induce a too early introduction of execution order in writing the program. This idea of differing tactical choices is good. But very often expert subjects develop several plans in parallel before choosing amongst them when decision criteria are available for evaluation, as has been shown in chess (de Groot, 1965) or in programming (Adelsor et al., 1984). In order to help working memory management, computer aids must include parallel presentation of information.

More recently, Hayes-Roth and Hayes-Roth (1979) proposed a psychological model, using the *blackboard* technique, which included *top-down* and *bottom-up* components in planning. For example, plans are possibly elaborated from detailed representations and revised after evaluation at lower levels. This model is more general and can include the preceding ones, taking into consideration individual differences and specificities of situations. Following Piaget's theory of equilibration between assimilation and accommodation, the articulation between top-down and bottom-up components is certainly a general characteristic of human planning. Computer aids have to make this articulation easy.

But these models remain specific to state transformation problems. With MOLGEN (Stefik, 1981) the way is opened to account for planning strategies in design situations where *constraint management* is of central concern. Traditional procedural programming languages induce *prospective* strategies which generate instructions by following the execution order. More generally in planning, and especially in programming temporal anticipation may be made easier by implementing *retrospective* strategies, generating the program in the reverse order. Necessarily, these strategies are declarative and lead to a static representation of the program, defining relationships between objects instead of instructions to a machine.

Following this principle, the programming problem is no longer a state transformation problem but a design problem. Our experiment was performed in an environment where this kind of strategy was assisted.

These general considerations about planning, and about computer aids for it, will now be illustrated and detailed in the presentation of the results of an experiment stressing the users' actual needs.

2 THE MAIDAY ENVIRONMENT: Tools to Guide Retrospective Planning in Programming

2.1 Main Principles

The tools have been especially designed to help users of a structured and top-down programming method (without imposing it) - the 'deductive method' defined by Pair (1979) - which presents the following features:

1. It is *definitional*, in that it leads to definition of objects in relation to others, as is the case for algebraic variables, versus assignments of values to computer variables. An object is defined only once: hence, it can only get one value during a particular execution of the program, as opposed to a computer variable (memory cell). For this reason, the present concept of *object* is static - its value can be directly determined by its definition (and those of objects used in its definition) - whereas the concept of computer variable is dynamic, in that an evaluation of this kind of variable is relative to a particular point in the execution of the program.

2. The method is *retrospective*, in that it consists, at first, in defining the results in relation to intermediary results, towards the data (the definitions are introduced in the reverse order, in contrast with the execution order). This feature implies that the user has a clear representation of the goal at his disposal and that he can use a knowledge base organised in the form of a set of algebraic definitions, as described in physical problem-solving, for example (Larkin and Reif, 1979).

3. The method is of a *top-down, modular and structured programming* kind. When an object cannot be defined by a simple algebraic or logical definition, its complex definition (structured definition) is iterative (recurrent object: e.g., a running total) or conditional (conditional object: e.g., a differential premium) and refers to modules which are considered as subproblems and to be defined later.

2.2 The MEDEE Language

In relation to these properties, the basic unit of the language is the *definition of objects*, as can be seen in the left column of Figure 1, presenting a MEDEE algorithm for calculating a test group mean, standard deviation, and size.

PRINCIPLE		
Definitions	Types	Comments
1 result = print(mean, stdev, size)	result(edit)	11 INI: 'initialises'
5 mean = total/size	2 mean(real)	
7 stdev = sqrt((sqrs-(total pow 2)/size)/size)	3 stdev(real): 'standard deviation'	12 OBSERVATION: 'processes an observation'
9 total, sqrs, size: INI for x in data repeat OBSERVATION	4 size(integer)	
	6 total(real): 'sum of observations'	
	8 sqrs(real): 'raw sum of squares'	
	10 x(real): 'observation'	

OBSERVATION		
13 total = @total + x 14 sqrs = @sqrs + x pow 2 15 size = @size + 1		

INI		
16 total, sqrs, size = 0		

Figure 1.   *MEDEE algorithm for calculating a test group mean, standard-deviation, and size.* (In each column, the numbers on the top of the lines indicate the order of writings, in following a retrospective strategy)

There are three types of definition (not all of them are shown in the figure):

-   simple definition (logical and algebraic formula, reading, and printout).

  e.g.: mean = total/size; result = print(mean,stdev,size).

-   conditional definition (a kind of case structure).

  e.g.: a: if cond1 then a =.. if cond2 then a =.. if.. else a =..

-   iterative definitions.

  e.g.: total: total = 0; for x in data repeat total = @total + x.

Each object must be defined only once but a single definition may define several objects. Consequently, in a recursive formula, each element of a series is a distinct object: the symbol '@' is used in order to differentiate the previous element (i-1) from the current one (i), as in line 13 of Figure 1. Obviously, an iterative definition defines the last elements of series. Array cells or record fields cannot be directly defined: that must be done by a definition of the whole array or record, using special operators.

Several objects may be defined conditionally or iteratively. In this case, everything on the right of "then" and "repeat" is expressed separately in the form of labelled modules. Then, the algorithm can be seen as a tree of modules, the first of them being called "root", the others "structured" (iterative or conditional). So we will use analogical terms from genealogy, such as "parent" or "child" module.

Initialisation modules take place in the left part of structured definitions. They are only employed to define the first elements of series. Objects which are used by structured modules and are constant (along series or between conditional modules) must be defined in the 'parent' module, out of the initialisation module.

In each module, there are three columns:

-   a left one for formal definitions of objects,

-   a central one for lexical definitions of objects (types and comments),

-   and a right one for lexical definitions of modules (comments only)

2.3 The MEDEDIT Editor

The editor is stratified into four levels, in relation to hierarchical access to entities: the environment level opens access to algorithms, the algorithm level to modules, the module level to definitions, and the definition level to components of definitions. In the current version of the editor, the first two levels are very poor. In the future, at the environment level, tools should permit the subject to use old algorithmic wholly or partly in designing a new one. In the same way, at the algorithmic level, tools should be designed in order to shift modules within the algorithm. In the current version, a module is entirely dependent on the structured definition which uses it: it cannot be introduced or moved independently of this definition. But this restriction is not definitive. At present, the tools mainly deal with the last two levels: "module" and "definition".

A multi-window display is used, with dedicated keys. The central part of the display is a vertical scrolling zone (98 lines, of which 24 lines are visible through the window), where the accepted definitions of the current module are listed, with the format of Figure 1. Around this part, five other zones are respectively devoted to: display of current level, messages from the system, current definition being validated (temporary storage), list of objects to be defined for the current module, entry being composed from the keyboard. At any time, a listing of the current state of the algorithm may be obtained by a specific command.

In each module, the editor updates a list of objects to be defined. In this list, two kinds of objects may be differentiated: the objects occuring in the right part of the structured definition using the module (to be defined in the module) and objects used in some definition of the module. Among these latter objects, some must be defined in the ancestry of the module, namely those which are constant for iterations or conditionals.

Three types of functions are available:
- editing functions (e.g., parsing a definition),
- control functions (e.g., checking contextual consistencies, as type consistency or accessibility of an object: an object cannot be used in a module if it is defined in a collateral module without appearing in common ancestry),
- "clever" functions (e.g., updating lists of objects to be defined, aids in initializing recurrent objects: when a recurrent definition is introduced, as $x=f(@x)$, the object (x) is added to the list of objects to be defined in the corresponding initialisation module).

The user is guided by explicit scripts of a question answering kind, with automatic execution of the editing functions. In Figure 1, the numbers indicate the order of the entries, in following a retrospective strategy. But the scripts do not impose this kind of strategy: in a module, the definitions may be introduced in an arbitrary order. Nevertheless, in the current implementation, the user cannot define a "child" module before entering the definition which uses it in the "parent" module. When the user enters into a module (by an appropriate command), he or she has access to the updated list of objects to define.

The main script is the definition creating script, initiated by the command ".crdef":

- the user enters the definition;

- if the definition is syntactically correct, it appears in a temporary storage zone devoted to a definition being validated;

- for each unknown object (not yet known in the module or its ancestry), the system asks for a comment and the object type;

- if the definition uses modules, the system asks for a comment for each one;

- if there is no contextual inconsistency, the definition is accepted and appears, with all other information, in the module.

The only way to modify a definition is by adding or deleting objects in the left part of the definition. Deleting the last object implies deleting the definition and, if the definition is structured, deleting all the modules used by it. When an object used in a definition of a module appears to be constant for this module, but not yet defined in the module, a command permits the user to carry its lexical definition (central column) up to a module in the ancestry. Later, we will see that these restrictions put difficulties in subjects' way.

3 METHOD AND HYPOTHESES

The method followed in this study is half-way between experimentation and observation. This study is an experiment in that factors are manipulated (problem type and familiarity with the tools); it is an observation in that clinical analysis of individual protocols plays a large part. The small size of the sample (ten subjects) does not permit us to state statistical inferential conclusions: the study is mainly exploratory.

3.1 Subjects

Ten subjects as a favour consented to take part in this experiment which took about 15 hours for each of them. These subjects were professional programmers, trained at Nancy IUT (a kind of Polytechnic) where "deductive method" and MEDEE language are taught (without using any editor).

Before the experiment, the subjects received one half day's training in using the language and the editor. Then, each subject had to solve two problems on the terminal. Two subjects were excluded from the analysis, since they left the experiment before completing the first problem. Consequently, the results include only eight subjects. Moreover, some subjects had fully solved only one problem.

3.2 Typology of Problems and Hypotheses

3.2.1 Preliminary study

A preliminary study on a typology of programming problems was done with the same subjects (Hoc, 1983b). We inferred the typology from subjects' classifications of a corpus of 27 problem statements used for the examinations at Nancy IUT. The subjects received the instructions to classify the statements in relation to the strategies which they would expect to follow for solving them, without doing it at all (as in the experiment of Chi et al., 1981, for physics problems). After classifying them, the subjects had to name the classes and characterise each problem (presented in a random order) in relation to several dimensions of classification of strategies. For example, they had to reply to questions such as: "are you expecting to try to execute a solution on specific examples before writing the program?"

At the same time, Weiser and Shertz (1983) used a similar method, but without this kind of instruction and from a corpus strongly structured by data, algorithms, and problem domain structures. They found the same classification as their a priori classification. Nevertheless their experiment used very simple problems, in comparison with ours, hence their results are less relevant to strategic features than to recognition of structures which are easy to extract from such simple problems.

From the classification derived from our own experiment, we have excluded problems requiring very unfamiliar algorithms. As a matter of fact, solving these problems requires the implementation of a programming strategy by mental execution of the program (Hoc, 1981), clearly incompatible with the examined tools. Conversely, we also excluded problems for which the structures of the programs were too obvious. We retained two dimensions, relevant to planning, from our classification: planning direction and planning guidance type.

3.2.2 Typology of problems

Planning direction may be prospective or retrospective. In following a prospective strategy, the program structure and the operations are generated in the order of execution: from the data to the results. Conversely, a retrospective strategy proceeds from the results to the data.

Planning guidance type refers to the way by which the subject obtains the structure of the algorithm (program plan) and may be declarative or procedural. It is declarative if the plan is explicit in the structure of the data or the results: this is the case for business problems, where the physical organisation of the data or of the results introduces strong constraints on the program structure. It is procedural if the plan is not explicit but must be constructed from the procedure itself (e.g., the tower of Hanoi puzzle). This typology is presented in reference to strategies. But it is based on classifications of problem statements which we will now specify. These classes must be conceived as extremes on more continuous dimensions. The experimental problems have been designed in order to strengthen the oppositions.

a. Prospective declarative problems (*PD*)
The program structure is strongly suggested by the data structure and very weakly by the structure of the results. The selected problem (air club accounts) was to match two lists of data and go through a list of data (a kind of updating schema).

b. Retrospective declarative problems (*RD*)
Conversely, the program structure is mainly implied by the structure of the results rather than the data structure. We have chosen a problem (newspaper ecological competition) where two lists to be edited respectively represented the subgoal and the goal of the problem.

c. Prospective procedural problems (PP)

In these problems, neither the structure of data nor of the results is very useful, but a procedure, executable by hand, is easily triggered. But the program plan is not obvious for all that. A documentation problem, with logical relations between key-words, was presented. The data structure and the structure of the results were weak.

d. Retrospective procedural problems (RP)

Once more the structures of the data and the results are not very useful in these problems, but the procedure is not obvious. Nevertheless, the program structure is mainly related to the goal-subgoal structure which will be constructed. The procedure is elaborated from a list of definitions of variables, in the subject's knowledge base. At first, the definition of the result is searched for in the list, then the definitions of intermediary results, and so on until reaching data. When the problem implies the joint obtention of several results, this retrospective strategy permits the subject to optimize the program, by searching for a maximum number of common subgoals useful in achieving each goal. A statistical problem of this kind was selected (quality control). In this typology, *prospective direction* or *procedural guidance* does not necessarily imply the implementation of a mental execution strategy. Nevertheless, the combination, *prospective-procedural*, does.

The surface complexities of the four optimal algorithms of the selected problems were equated and the algorithms constructed by the subjects were of the same complexity:

- — depths of the tree of modules: 3 or 4,
- — frequencies of modules: 9 or 10,
- — frequencies of objects: between 18 and 25,
- — frequencies of definitions: between 23 and 29.

3.2.3 Hypotheses

In the language, with this editor, conditional or iterative structures must be expressed in a definitional form: the expression of the control structure ('if then else' or 'for') is not sufficient, the expression of the objects to be defined by the structure is necessary. This form constrains the subject to anticipate the goals (objects to be defined) of a possibly complex part of the algorithm. Thus, the tools were expected to induce retrospective strategies and to lead to many difficulties with the prospective problems, and to few difficulties with the retrospective ones.

Among the prospective problems, the procedural one was expected to be the most difficult, in relation to the definitional nature of the language (expressing static definitions versus dynamic operations). Among the retrospective problems, the procedural one was also expected to be the most difficult, but not for the same reason. Processing with a knowledge base of definitions, from the results to the data, is clearly compatible with a retrospective and definitional strategy. But working with a program structure made explicit in the structure of the results (declarative problem) is easier.

Due to the constraints of expressing precise conditional or iterative definitions before accessing low-level modules, and of going through the algorithm by means of a limited window, the editor was expected to create a lot of planning difficulties, especially in parallel information processing and articulation between top-down and bottom-up components of planning.

3.3 Experimental Design

The subjects had four 3 hour periods at their disposal to solve two problems. They were randomly distributed in two independent groups, defined by the factor "planning guidance type". Within each group, a latin square design was chosen, in relation to the order of assignment of the modalities of the factor "planning direction". Nevertheless diverse breakdowns did not wholly permit us to satisfy this design, as can be seen in Table 1. The term "session" refers to the union of all the periods used for one problem. The subjects had instructions not to work on a problem between working periods.

Table 1.   Experimental design (the subject numbers are written in parentheses)

	Session 1	Session 2
Declarative problems	PD (1,5,9)	RD (1,9)
	RD (2,6)	PD (2,6)
Procedural problems	PP (3)	
	RP (4,8)	PP (5,8)

At the beginning of each session, the subject received a problem statement. He worked alone, without an observer, directly at the terminal. Inspection of draft sheets has shown that they were used very little. Nevertheless an instructor was available in case of system breakdown or for answering questions on the language or the editor.

3.4 Method of Analysis

Each subject's basic protocol contains all the entries (editor commands and expressions in the language) and their times of occurrence. Each protocol has been hierarchically divided into two types of unit. The basic unit is the *definition version* (a final definition may have been preceded by one or more versions). The definition versions are gathered in higher level units - the *module versions*: a new version of a module occurs when the definitions of the module are completed or modified after quitting the module.

Each definition version has been characterised from the following points of view :

— the current hierarchy of goals and subgoals leading to the entry of the version,

— the choice of means to achieve the most detailed subgoal in the hierarchy,

— and the feed-back provided by formulating expressions in the language and by the editor.

By a clinical analysis of individual protocols, behavior has been characterised in relation to four main categories of determinants: the strategy followed by the subject, the language structure, the editor structure, and the more minor disturbances (such as clerical errors). This analysis permits us to describe strategies and difficulties at a general level, and to identify the effects of problem type. More global variables have been evaluated in order to identify the same effects at a higher level. The main results of these analyses will now be presented.

4 MAIN RESULTS

4.1 Clinical Analysis of Protocols

First, we will describe the subjects' strategic features and their relation to some difficulties with the editor and the language: (4.1.1) common to all types of problems and (4.1.2) type specific. Next, we will sum up the main difficulties.

4.1.1 Strategic features common to all problems

a. Retrospective strategies
The most frequent strategy was retrospective, as predicted by our hypothesis: in most cases an object is used in a definition before being defined itself. Accordingly, the difficulties encountered on prospective problems will be related to the implementation of a retrospective strategy for this type of problem. Within the framework of this strategy, the list of objects to be defined, updated by the editor, in each module is well used. Nevertheless, there are two restrictions in this utilisation:

— In general, the list is composed of several sublists, the last one containing the sublist of objects used by the last written definition and the preceding ones containing objects used by earlier definitions. For all subjects and problems, among 40 possibilities of choice between these sublists, in deciding to define a new object, 29 concerned the last one. Consequently the retrospective strategies were of a depth-first kind.

— After choosing the sublist, when it included several objects (159 cases for all subjects and problems), the order of the objects in the list was followed in 114 cases (72%). Very often, when the order is not followed, the subjects were skipping objects which are difficult to define.

Although the editor was designed to help retrospective strategies, these strategies caused difficulties with the editor. As a matter of fact, in iterative modules the subjects were led to introduce objects which were constant within the iteration, when they used them in some definitions. Thus these objects had to be carried up to the 'parent' module. But the carrying up procedure was tedious with the editor.

b. Prospective strategies

Prospective strategies were rare and appear more difficult to assist, at this problem conceptualisation level, in as much the subjects' goals are difficult to infer. Nevertheless, structure-based editors are intended to aid these strategies: a comparative assessment, in relation to the present study, would be desirable to test this hypothesis. Very often, in this study, when these strategies were linked to mental execution of the program in writing it, they led to distortions in using the language: the definitional contents were lost for the benefit of procedural contents which led to misleading analogies with the syntax of traditional procedural languages, as will be detailed later.

c. Planning strategies

Clearly, planning strategies articulated two components: a *top-down* and a *bottom-up* one. The editor forces subjects to initiate planning by the top-down component. The top-down component was depth-first rather than breadth-first. When a "parent" module possesses several "children", the user may introduce all the structured definitions before going down to the next level (breadth-first strategy) or as soon as a structured definition is written (depth-first strategy). For all subjects and problems, among 29 possibilities of choice, 13 (almost 50%) gave preference to breadth. Within a breadth-first strategy, the subject may go on with this type of strategy, by defining all the same level modules before going down or ending a subtree. Among 24 possibilities of choice (again for all subjects and problems), only 7 (less than one third) continued with a breadth-first strategy.

Accordingly, in relation to the definition of either objects or modules, the strategies were depth-first rather than breadth-first, although our subjects were professional programmers. Two research works have shown that, in a familiar environment, expert programmers follow breadth-first strategies as opposed to novices who follow depth-first ones (Jeffries et al., 1981; Adelson et al., 1984). This kind of strategy makes processing of interactions between collaterals easier. An interpretation of our subjects' behavior may be given in relation to working memory management. The tools force subjects to introduce very precise expressions right away. Hence, information in working memory was very detailed, even at high levels in the planning tree, and only a very narrow part of the algorithm was able to take place in this memory. Thus, the subjects were only able to take very local relations into consideration, which induced depth-first strategies.

The lack of presentation of the current overall structure of the program led to diverse perturbations in working memory, especially to forgetting of the current level in the program tree.

The bottom-up components of planning strategies encountered important difficulties, as we will see later: in carrying up objects (constants of iteration or conditional objects defined in collaterals to be used in the current module), in modifying control structures of structured definition. In general, the higher the module where a structured definition is being introduced, the more fuzzy the representation is. Sometimes the subject must wait to reach a very detailed level before getting necessary information to choose the appropriate form for a control structure, very high in the hierarchy. Some errors remained in the algorithms, since the subjects were reluctant to enter into too fastidious corrections of parent modules. Some other errors in parent modules are sometimes rescued by awkward modifications in child modules.

d. Generalisation strategies

Generalisation strategies were also encountered. In following this kind of strategy, the subject restricts the problem at first to a simpler one, with a simpler tree, before introducing the complexity. The complexity of the procedures of modification with this editor made this strategy difficult to follow.

4.1.2. Problem specific strategic features

Here, we will present the strategic features per type of problem, but common to all the corresponding protocols, in order to show the effect of this factor. The following features concern both the first and the second session, although the difficulties were better overcome during the second one.

a. Prospective declarative problem (PD)

Following a retrospective strategy led the subjects to take the data structure into consideration too late. However, in this problem, the program structure is strongly constrained by the data structure and it was distorted by according too much consideration to the structure of the results. It is a wonder that three subjects in four were not able to represent the matching of the two lists in the language, though this kind of updating schema is very familiar to professional programmers.

Some difficulties in using the language show that this kind of distortion is not irremediable. In this updating problem, using a permanent file (list of all air club members) and a temporary one (list of members having flown) to calculate the invoices, the temporary file is important in the conceptualisation of the problem. But the MEDEE language did not permit the subjects to express this object directly as a whole in the program. That would be the case for most traditional procedural programming languages. But in these languages, the subject may be guided by mental execution in designing the program. In this definitional language and especially when following a retrospective strategy, that is not possible. The central concept is the definition of objects and object structure plays an important role in structuring the program. Hence, the structures of all the objects, fundamental in the program structure, must be directly expressible.

b. Retrospective declarative problem (RD)
Even for a problem compatible with a retrospective strategy, the subjects encountered difficulties with the language and the editor. These difficulties, very manifest on this problem, have been described earlier:

— With the obligation to introduce the structured definition using a module before defining this module, the editor forces subjects to begin by following a top-down strategy. But in writing the 'parent' module the subject does not have a precise representation of all the objects to be defined in the 'child' and used in collaterals, or to be used in the 'child' and defined elsewhere. This latter case appears very often in the course of a retrospective strategy. These necessities may be detected when writing the 'child' and then several objects must be carried up to the 'parent'. But carrying-up procedures are very tedious with this editor.

— In the same way, when the subject is high in the tree, he has no assessment criteria at his disposal for the choice of a precise control structure. But the tools demand the same precision at whatever level in the tree and a modification of a structured definition is costly: the subject must delete the definition (and, consequently, all the descendants of the definition).

c. Prospective procedural problem (PP)
Attempts to follow prospective strategies are observed, but they neglect the structure of the results. In other respects, generalisation strategies are very often inferred. Retrospective strategies led to the same difficulties as in the retrospective declarative problem.

d. Retrospective procedural problem (RP)
In this problem, the result broke down into several joint results, for which common intermediary results had to be defined. The retrospective strategy which the subjects followed was not efficient at finding these intermediary results. We did not anticipate this outcome since we expected the contrary. But in all problems and especially in this one, the subjects' strategies were of a depth-first kind rather than breadth-first. So they did not wait for the

introduction of all the definitions of a module before going down in the tree. They went down to a module as soon as they wrote the definition using it. Consequently, they were not able to examine the diverse results in parallel, in order to discover the common intermediary results. Very often, it was only when they arrived at very detailed level modules that they detected inaccurate overall plans and the editor required them to make very tiresome modifications.

4.1.3 Main difficulties with the editor and the language

a. As we have seen, three kinds of limitations in the current state of the *editor* were very important constraints for subjects to implement their planning strategies:

- The procedures for carrying up objects are too laborious, in view of their frequent utilisation in bottom-up components of strategies.

- The near impossibility of modifying a definition without deleting it is also a bottleneck in using the editor for the same reason.

- Finally the only access to the algorithm (by a window opened on fully detailed parts) does not permit the subjects to be aided in maintaining a representation of the overall structure of the program in working memory, for locating the current position in the tree or displaying relations between collaterals.

b. Without entering into the details of the difficulties encountered by the subjects in using the *language*, most of them are of a semantic kind. We can sum them up in three main points:

- A lot of errors reveal that sometimes the subjects tried to express dynamic contents of traditional procedural languages in this definitional language. That led to distortions in some expressions: for example, the special sign @ designed to express the preceding element of a series in an iteration, was sometimes used in order to give several successive definitions of the same object outside of any iteration.

- Other errors show that the subjects had difficulties with the actual elements contained in the language or with the relations defined between elements and expressions. First, we have seen that some elements were lacking: e.g., certain object types to directly express very important objects in the definitional conceptualisation of the problem. Second, a lot of content units were new for the subjects and led to diverse confusions: e.g., between the "edit" type (printing of an object) and "string" type. Third, the subjects were put off by the lack of homology within certain relations between content and expression. In semiotics, the general meaning of homology is the reproduction at the expression level of the same kind of structure as at the content level. For example, in MEDEE, when several elements of an array must be changed, the use of the 'tchg' operator (defining an array) introduces a hierarchy between these elements whereas they are not in any hierarchical relation at all:

> Considering the necessity to define an object only once, if an array 'a' must be defined as an array 'b', except two elements to be changed, the best way of writing it is:
> a = tchg (c,i,x)   where i and j are the indexes of the elements
> c = tchg (b,j,y)   and x and y the new elements.

— Finally the subjects very often omitted contextual information in their expressions. Here, we call contextual information that which can be deduced from the context. For example, a field of a record may be expressed without reference to the name of the record, since this relation is expressed in the type declaration, and the record name inferable from the module context. These omissions may be seen as forms of reduction of the representation space in solving a subproblem, excluding information which is constant within this subproblem. In most cases, an editor could fill in the gaps, so long as the user can validate this kind of operation.

4.2 Quantitative Results

After this relatively fine grain analysis of protocols, we will now turn to a more global evaluation of performance, in order to sum up the main effects of the types of problems on the overall performance. Nevertheless, this analysis will also be descriptive in view of the exploratory nature of this experiment. It suggests hypotheses to be tested on a larger sample, with the help of an automatic computation of the variables which will be presented here: solution time, strategies implemented, and difficulties encountered by the subjects.

4.2.1 Solution time (Figure 2)

All the graphs will be presented with the same format:
— rank order of session along the abscissa,
— prospective problems correspond to the thicker lines (PD declarative: continuous line; PP procedural: interrupted line),

—   restrospective problems correpond to thinner lines (RD declarative: dotted line; RP: one point since it was solved only in first session),

—   the points correspond to means: near each point the standard deviation is written in parentheses (in order to avoid taking differences between means into consideration when the standard deviations are too large), except when one value is available.

—   two points linked by a line (2 sessions for the same problem) were not obtained with the same subjects, because a latin square design was used (see Table 1).

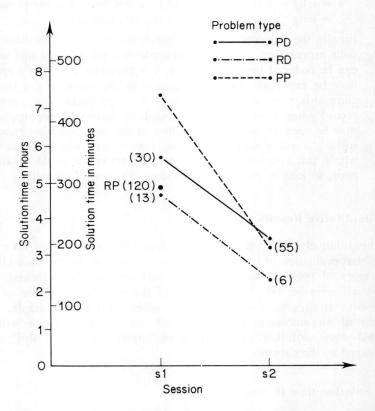

Figure 2.   Combined effects of session and problem type on solution time. In brackets: standard deviations (except when only one value is available)

The average solution times are between 5 and 8 hours in the first session and between 2 and 4 hours in the second. Solution times decrease by half from the first to the second session, for all problems. Even with experts, familiar with the problem domains and the language, the tools cannot be assessed in one session, because of this large familiarisation effect.

On average, the times for prospective problems are greater than for retrospective problems by one third. This is the global manifestation of the fact that the tools were less appropriate for solving prospective problems than retrospective ones.

4.2.2 Strategies

a. Planning direction (prospective vs retrospective)
The variable is the ratio of "retrospective" objects (i.e., used before being defined), when the language permits the user to choose an order. From the subjects' choices, between 55% and 70% of the objects were "retrospective". No familiarisation effect is observed, neither is any clear problem type effect. The tools appear to have clearly induced retrospective strategies. A control group would have been certainly useful in order to reinforce this interpretation, but we guess that the strategies would not have been as retrospective in a traditional environment as they were in this one.

b. Relative importance of top-down component in planning (Figure 3)
The variable is the ratio of definition versions introduced in the first versions of the module: the other definition versions were considered as related to bottom-up component. A large familiarisation effect is noted which increases the importance of the top-down component by a half (except for the prospective declarative problem for which the difficulties remain). Whatever the session, the problem expected to be the most compatible with the tools (retrospective declarative) is solved with a more important top-down component than the problem the least compatible with them (prospective procedural).

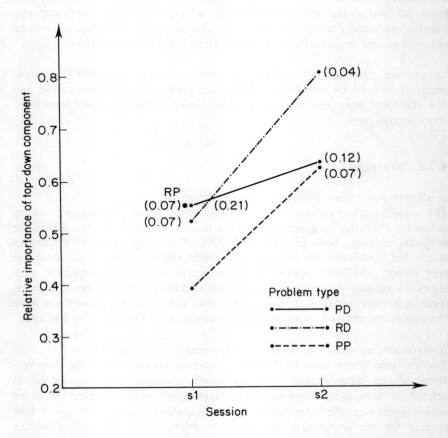

Figure 3.   Combined effects of session and problem type on relative
                 importance of top-down component. (Ratio of definition
                 versions introduced in the first versions of the module).
                 In brackets: standard deviations (except when only one
                 value is available)

4.2.3 Difficulties

We have separated difficulties directly related to the utilisation of the
language from difficulties more linked to the problem-solving strategies.

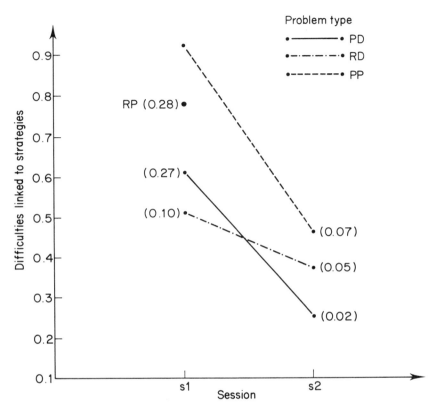

Figure 4.   Combined effects of session and problem type on difficulties linked to strategies. (Ratio between extra versions of definitions correctly expressed in the language and final versions) In brackets: standard deviations (except when only one value is available)

a. Difficulties linked to strategies (Figure 4)
These difficulties are evaluated by the ratio between extra versions of definitions which are correctly expressed in the language and final versions. The familiarisation effect is again important: this kind of difficulty decreases by 30% to 60% between the two sessions. But they remain relatively high in the second session where one extra version is observed for two to three final versions. In the first session the problems which are most contrasted, according to compatibility with the tools, are also the most different (in the

expected direction): these difficulties are twice as high for the prospective procedural problem than for the retrospective declarative one. In the second session the difficulties are again highest for the prospective procedural problem, least for the prospective declarative problem. There, the difference seems to be related to planning guidance: declarative problems leading to less difficulties.

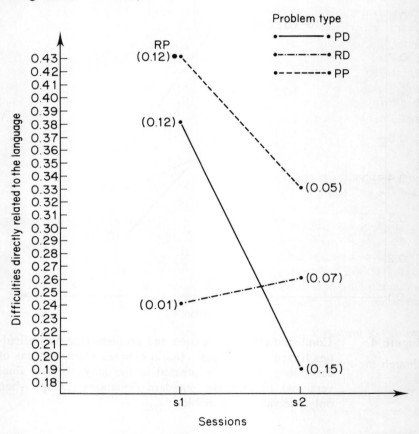

Figure 5.   Combined effects of session and problem type on difficulties directly related to the language. (Frequency of elementary errors per versions of definition correctly expressed in the language) In brackets: standard deviations (except when only one value is available)

The frequencies of error generation are not presented here. In the second session, they are relatively low (2 generated errors for 10 final definitions) and constant for all types of problems. In the first session, they have the same magnitude for retrospective problems, but they are much higher for prospective problems (5 to 7 for 10 final definitions).

b. Difficulties directly related to the language (Figure 5)

Here, we examine profound difficulties in the utilisation of the language: clerical errors and slips are excluded. The variable is the frequency of elementary errors per versions of definition correctly expressed in the language. The familiarisation effect is important, except for the retrospective declarative problem where error rate is low and constant. In spite of large standard deviations, two facts are clear: the retrospective declarative problem (the most compatible with the tools) leads to the least frequent errors in the first session and the prospective procedural problem (the least compatible) to the most frequent errors in the second session.

DISCUSSION AND CONCLUSIONS

This study has led to precise suggestions for modification of the tools. In this discussion we will not enter into the details of these suggestions. Rather we will emphasise elements for a more general discussion about this category of tools. Nevertheless, since the sample was small and the perspective exploratory, the conclusions must be treated with due caution, as hypotheses that are reasonable but require further test.

Typology of problems

Although the typology of problems, elaborated for this assessment, remains relatively global, it has appeared relevant. The hypotheses which we have set concerning a priori incompatibilities between certain types of problems and the tools have shown themselves to be justified.

From the point of view of planning direction, the tools had the clear effect of inducing retrospective strategies, whatever the type of problem was. Even when the problem invited the strategy of prospective planning by the data structure or triggering procedures executable by hand, the strategies observed were retrospective rather than prospective. This phenomenon shows that strategies are determined by a global situation which is defined by the interaction between a subject, a task, and an environment (here corresponding to the tools which are used).

But trying to use retrospective strategies on prospective problems led to more difficulties: by comparison with retrospective problems solution time was longer and logical errors were more frequent (first session). Very often, the problem that was least compatible with the tools (prospective procedural) was solved with greater difficulty than the most compatible (retrospective declarative): strategies were less top-down, difficulties in defining objects greater (first session), difficulties in using the language more important.

The planning guidance factor taken alone had a slighter effect: the prospective declarative problem led to less difficulties in defining objects than the prospective procedural one (second session). But there is a lack of data for the retrospective procedural problem in the second session. Nevertheless, the relative poverty of data structures (and structures of results) in the language cannot permit the subject to derive benefit from declarative guidance. Moreover, an enrichment of the language on this point could aid the implementation of retrospective strategies on a prospective declarative problem, as shown by the clinical analysis of protocols.

Familiarisation with the tools

The noticeable familiarisation effects show that, even with expert users trained in this language, extra learning is necessary: not only learning of the editor, but also extra learning of the language. In the past, when the subjects wrote a program in MEDEE, they had no feed-back from any editor and they had to translate the program into another programming language before the execution. So, they might write incorrect expressions without detecting the errors. In this experiment, the subjects had difficulties with the semantics of the language. Maybe, the syntactical similarity between MEDEE and traditional procedural languages such as PASCAL is the reason why acquisition of the MEDEE definitional (or static) semantics is hard. As a matter of fact, in some contexts, MEDEE can be used with a procedural semantics without syntactical distortion, but in general the acquisition of the specific semantics is necessary to avoid these syntactical distortions. For example, the expression 'c = @c + 1' can be understood as "add 1 to the previous value of c" in an iterative module, but this content does not take into account that this expression must not be used outside of an iterative module, due to the fact that the expression '@c' also codes the fact that 'c' is a recurrent object. So the expression 'c = 0; if condition then c = @c else c = @ + 1' is not correct if 'c' is not recurrent. Maybe MEDEE semantics was not sufficiently taught in the subjects curriculum.

Planning strategies

Further research must be developed on the design of aids to planning strategies. In this study, we have clearly seen that the level of precision required by the language was not compatible with certain representations used during planning in designing the program. These representations are at first abbreviated or schematic: a too strong constraint of precision in writing highest level modules may lead to important difficulties in later revisions. It may even be asked whether this constraint was not the reason why subjects had followed depth-first strategies.

In designing computer aids for programming directly on the terminal, the language must be not only a programming language, expressing precise algorithms, but also a program designing language, expressing preliminary skeletons to be detailed later. Consequently, it would be useful to search for more schematic expressions to be accepted in the language and used as transitory formulations during program design before the user can decide in favour of a possible precise alternative. In this perspective, a research project in the field, developed in traditional professional environments, would be very useful.

A planning strategy develops in a hierarchy of abstraction spaces which must be sometimes used in parallel. Thus, diverse levels of representation of the algorithm must be available at the same time unless shifts from one level to another disturb working memory, as has been shown. Furthermore, plan revisions must be easy: this editor made these revisions very time-consuming, disturbing for working memory. Certain kinds of revisions were linked to generalisation strategies which led to an incremental enrichment of the problem representation. Aids to this type of strategy would also be aids to program modification.

The precision requirements in using the tools are joined to consistency requirements. Consistency is obviously necessary, but it leads to the need for an explicit statement of contextual relations, which produces important working memory load. It would be convenient if an editor took such tasks in hand and, at the same time, interrupted the design strategy as little as possible. In other words, an editor should be able to introduce certain subordinate details, in order to permit the user to concentrate on major aspects of the design. Nevertheless, it is necessary that these editor actions could be validated by the user.

Finally, retrospective strategies appear to be more easy to aid than prospective strategies. The data collected show that the difficulties encountered in developing retrospective strategies were linked to insufficient editing aids and language constructs rather than to actual impossibilities of implementation of retrospective strategies. The most important restriction of this language and its editor was related to aids to articulate top-down and bottom-up components of planning.

REFERENCES

Adelson, B., Littman, D., Ehrlich, K., Black, J. and Soloway, E. (1984). Novice-Expert Differences in Software Design. In: INTERACT '84. B. Schackel (ed.), Vol. 2. Amsterdam: Elsevier, pp. 187-192.

Chi, M.T.H., Feltovitch, P.J. and Glaser, R. (1981). Categorization and representation of physics problems by experts and novices. Cognitive Science, 5, pp. 121-152.

de Groot, A.D. (1965). Thought and choice in chess. Den Haag: Mouton.

Guyard, J. and Jacquot, J.P. (1984). MAIDAY: an Environment for Guided Programming with a Definitional Language. 7th International Conference on Software Engineering. Orlando, Fl.

Hayes-Roth, B. and Hayes-Roth, F. (1979). A Cognitive Model of Planning. Cognitive Science, 3, pp. 275-310.

Hoc, J.M. (1981). Planning and Direction of Problem-Solving in Structured Programming: an Empirical Comparison between two Methods. International Journal of Man-Machine Studies, 15, pp. 363-383.

Hoc, J.M. (1983a). Analysis of Beginners' Problem-Solving Strategies in Programming. In: The Psychology of Computer Use. T.R.G. Green, S.J. Payne, G.C. van der Veer (eds.). London, Academic Press, pp. 143-158.

Hoc, J.M. (1983b). Une méthode de classification préalable des problèmes d'un domaine pour l'analyse des stratégies de résolution. Le Travail Humain, 46(3), pp. 205-217.

Hoc, J.M. (1987). Psychologie cognitive de la planification. Grenoble: Presses Universitaires de Grenoble.

Jeffries, R., Turner, A.A., Polson, P.G. and Atwood, M.E. (1981). The Processes Involved in Designing Software. *In: Cognitive Skills and their Acquisition.* J.R. Anderson (ed.). Hillsdale, N.J.: Erlbaum, pp. 255-283.

Larkin, J.H. and Reif, F. (1979). Understanding and Teaching Problem-Solving in Physics. *European Journal of Science Education*, 1, pp. 191-203.

Miller, G.A., Galanter, E. and Pribram, K.H. (1960). Plans and the Structure of Behavior. London: Holt, Rinehart and Winston.

Newell, A. and Simon, H.A. (1972). Human Problem-Solving. Englewood Cliffs, N.J.: Prentice Hall.

Pair, C. (1979). La construction des programmes. *RAIRO Informatique*, 13, pp. 113-137.

Pavard, B. (1985). The Conception of Word Processing Systems. Paris: CNAM, Laboratoire de Physiologie du Travail, Research Report.

Rasmussen, J. (1984). Strategies for State Identification and Diagnosis in Supervisory Control Tasks, and Design of Computer-Based Support Systems. *Advances in Man-Machine Systems Research*, 1, pp. 139-193.

Sacerdoti, E.D. (1974). Planning in a hierarchy of abstraction spaces. *Artificial Intelligence*, 5, pp. 115-135.

Sacerdoti, E.D. (1975). A structure for plans and behavior. New-York: Elsevier,

Simon, H.A. and Lea, G. (1974). Problem-solving and rule induction: a unified view. *In: Knowledge and Cognition.* L.W. Gregg (ed.). Potomac, Mar.: Erlbaum.

Stefik, M. (1981). Planning with Constraints (MOLGEN: Part 1). *Artificial Intelligence*, 16, pp. 111-140.

Weiser, M., Shertz, J. (1983). Programming problem representation in novice and expert programmer. *Int. J. of Man-Machine Studies*, 19, pp. 391-393.

SECTION 3

COMPUTERS AND THE INDIVIDUAL

This section is concerned with the application of the theory-based and systems orientated approaches of previous sections and deals with three very specific situations: those of computer-assisted learning (chapter 8), programmer productivity (chapter 9), and the introduction of new technology (chapter 10). All aspects which can affect the individual, either through employment or education and training, are shown to require the application of human-centered (or in CAL, adaptive) principles from cognitive ergonomics. This requirement relates the abstractions of theoretical models of HCI through the medium of the systems design process to the implementation of real applications. Indeed, Davies sees opportunities for more collaborative involvement in order to cross-fertilise and to inform the design of technology itself, making it really '*future-proof*'. This, surely is the major aim of cognitive ergonomics for the computer systems we work with.

In the realm of Computer Based Training (for the most part in school situations), van der Veer and Beishuizen present a rationale for the provision of adaptive teaching capacity under certain circumstances. This can compensate for the range of personality characteristics, intelligence levels, problem-solving abilities and cognitive styles which exist along a dimension of changeability. They summarise a number of years of research findings and describe numerous experimental tests with actual systems to teach arithmetic, reading, simple programming and to adapt to differences in both student preferences and learning styles. The rationale behind this work is to provide a 'responsive environment' to deal with the diversity of cognitive development and to build systems and a 'study machine' based upon sound cognitive ergonomic principles.

At a time of increased attention to advanced programming methodologies and environments, Curtis usefully focuses on the available evidence related to variations in individual programmer's performance, and, in particular, on methods of predicting and reducing individual differences. This work relates to the programming environments discussed in section 2, but shows that these must take account of current cognitive ergonomic findings. Note must be taken of individual differences before any benefits in productivity can be reaped, and attention should be focused on a cognitive science of programming which links new theories and emerging methodologies to form the basis of a new body of knowledge.

Davies' chapter provides an overview of the area of job automation and the introduction of new technology into process control environments and into factories. He presents current research on the effect of technological change upon individual workers and the work environment in terms of skill change, technological determinism, job design and labour process traditions. The importance of a cognitive ergonomic viewpoint in job design, as determined by system and management factors, is brought out and the critical factor of avoiding design by default highlighted with a contrast between traditional and new job-design principles. A final part specifically presents a number of case studies to explore and illustrate the relationship between the theories and shop-floor practice.

COMPUTERS AND EDUCATION
Adaptation to Individual Differences

Gerrit C. van der VEER, Jos J. BEISHUIZEN

Free University, Amsterdam
Netherlands

INTRODUCTION

In this contribution a review will be presented of a long-term project on computers in education, for the greater part concentrated on the primary school. This research went on at the Free University of Amsterdam for 15 years. During that time a lot of changes took place: theoretical notions developed, hardware possibilities were realised as new generations of computer systems became available, and application in the classroom was facilitated both by these facts and by the changing appreciation in society, of which teachers are part.

In this large scale project (comprising 95 man years of the research team, not to mention teachers and pupils) it was unthinkable that goals did not change. New hypotheses replaced former ones, and research in other centres influenced the directions of thought. But the central topics of research remained the same:

- The role of computers in education, and their effect on the traditional learning and thinking in the school. In this respect concentration was on individualisation, that is adaptation of the teaching strategy to individual differences between students.

- The new teaching strategies that may be derived from the introduction of computers in the classroom and the extent to which the existing tool-box of the teacher is enriched and provided with new elements in the learning environment.

- New components that may be inserted in the curriculum, as a result of the availability of computers (cognitive skills that are not part of the traditional subject matter in primary schools).

These questions were investigated from the point of view of cognitive psychology. Adaptation to individual differences in cognitive functions was the main interest in this project, guiding the experiments and observations over the years.

Section 1 will present a historic overview of the project. In the second section a dimension of changeability will be introduced, that will be a guideline for developing goals for adaptation to individual differences. Section 3 contains a systematic overview of empirical data on the relation between the changeability of variables, and the possibilities to adapt in teaching with the help of computers. Observations from real life classroom situations are illustrated in section 4, after which the contribution ends with some remarks on the role of the teacher and the impact of computer applications for the curriculum.

1 HISTORIC OVERVIEW

The project started in a laboratory environment, with a single-user computer system. Theoretical questions were considered, regarding the interaction between teaching strategies (the external conditions, realised by the computer system) and the aptitudes of the pupil (the interval conditions). Teaching strategies included the use of simple student models for decision of optimal allocation of units of learning material, and amount of tutor (computer) or student control of the sequence of units. Aptitudes considered were problem-solving strategies, personality factors and a priori knowledge.

The learning material in this first stage was designed for experimental purposes, aimed at the evaluation of theoretical psychological hypotheses, although there was a structural resemblance to "normal" school material in most cases. The content of experiments was often a "complete" course (a circumscribed domain of artificial learning material), tutorial in nature. In these cases there was no direct involvement of a human teacher. The introduction of the subject-matter was delegated to the computer program.

After some years the development of hardware enabled the continuation of investigations in the "real" world. At this point different fields of interest presented themselves. On the one hand there was occasion to observe the different ways of application of computers that arose as a function of teacher strategies, classroom organisation and pupil attributes. Twelve primary schools in Amsterdam took part in this field study, in which the computer characteristics may be described as a "responsive environment", that is a situation that facilitates a diversity in cognitive development.

On the other hand experiments continued to take place, albeit of a different nature. Within the rich situation of the real classroom, studies were conducted of the possibilities of the new medium for stimulating problem-solving behaviour and metacognitive skills like "learning to learn". These experiments compromised between a certain amount of experimental control and a fair amount of real life influences, including individual differences that could to a certain extent be statistically controlled, and teacher and group variability that for the greater part could not even be measured, since the investigators were not fully aware of all relevant variables.

2 ADAPTATION AND THE CHANGEABILITY OF COGNITIVE FACTORS

2.1 Adaptation in Education

Adaptation in education means attention to individual differences. Whether optimal learning results may be expected is to a large extent dependent on the close matching of the learning situation (including teaching style, level of difficulty, speed of presentation) to the characteristics of the pupil. Matching means tuning of "tutor" and pupil to each other. This process may take two different directions:

— Adaptation make take the form of educating the pupil in the direction of an "average" student, to which the learning conditions are optimally fitted, or to a "good" student, who has mastered the necessary basic skills and obtained sufficient a priori knowledge for participating in the learning discourse.

— The learning situation may be adjusted to the individual pupil, accepting the fact that the end product of learning effort will not be of a uniform nature for different students. Both the resulting general level and the quality of knowledge and skills will divert.

Often the optimal strategy combines elements of both directions. The most successful method of adaption is determined by the possibilities of changing the pupils' characteristics.

2.2 Changeability

Research on the use of computers in learning situations has shown a variety of results, with seemingly casual cases of success and failure. At least part of these phenomena seem to be due to the fact that some of the chacteristics by which individual students may differ are easy to affect, while in the case of other attributes, an educator has to invest a lot of effort to produce a fair change. Some traits even seem to resist any influence from the outside world. In order to structure these observations, Van Muylwijk, Van der Veer and Waern (1983) introduced a model of changeability of cognitive functions that is illustrated in Figure 1.

Stable, resistant   Mainly defined by
to change   influences from outside

◄───►

personality factors:	cognitive styles:	strategies:	knowledge structure:
Intelligence	Field	Heuristic/	Episodic
Extraversion/	(in)dependence	systematic	memory
introversion	Visual/verbal		Semantic
Fear of failure	Operation/	Serialist/	representation
Creativity(?)	comprehension	holist	Rules
	learning		Skills

Figure 1.   Dimension of changeability

The dimension of changeability represents an indication of the ease with which cognitive functions may be changed. On the extreme left, personality factors like intelligence, introversion/extraversion and negative fear of failure are located. These are generally considered to be stable features. It seems impossible or at least very difficult to change them in a reasonable amount of time. As far as such stable personality traits define the learning process, adaptation of the learning environment is obvious. In the traditional educational situation, organised by levels of ability, only intelligence has been treated in this way.

At the extreme right hand side, knowledge and skills are positioned. The content of episodic memory, the details of actual knowledge represented, rules, and skills are the result of influences of the environment (external conditions) in combination with more stable personality characteristics (internal conditions). In this model any cognitive faculty that is to the left of another is a determinant of qualities that are more to the right, in combination with outside influences. The development and adaptation of knowledge structure and stategies are feasible goals for education, provided individual differences are taken into account.

In the middle of the dimension of changeability is the domain of cognitive styles such as field-dependence, problem solving styles like the concepts elaborated by Pask (1976), and the domain of strategies such as a heuristic or algorithmic approach (De Leeuw, 1983), serialism or holism. Strategies are conceived as domain-specific and adjustable, cognitive styles as rather stable products of talent and education.

2.3 Adaptation in Computer Aided Learning

This study is an application of notions, taken from cognitive psychology, to phenomena in computer assisted learning. To this end an overview will be presented of the results of experiments that show the relevance of internal and external conditions of learning for the effects of the use of computers in the learning situation. These experiences will be integrated with observations on the employment of computers in the daily life of the classroom.

Although a lot of information has been collected, it is not yet opportune to draw final conclusions. There is still no end to technical development. Nowadays there is an explosion in the introduction of micro computers in schools, and even in the home. At the same time, tremendous effort is invested in developing a fifth generation of computer systems with new architectural concepts and new "intelligent" ways of interacting with human partners. This might restrict the validity of our conclusions to a limited period of time.

For the near future it has to be emphasised that the teacher is irreplaceable in the unique human competence for dealing with a wide variety of educational problems in interaction with considerable individual differences. In this respect the computer is only a tool, with special possibilities to adjust to individual learning behaviour. In the future both this tool in itself, and expertise on its application will certainly improve, but only a teacher who is able to realise the possibilities can use it to its full extent.

3 ADAPTATION IN LEARNING WITH COMPUTERS, INTERNAL AND EXTERNAL CONDITIONS

Whilst illustrating the interaction between internal conditions (individual differences in cognitive functions) and external conditions (facilities incorporated in computer systems and strategies of computer use) in learning, the dimension of changeability will act as a guideline. The relations between internal and external conditions that will be described in this section are partly studied in the form of field observations. Some effects have been investigated in experimental situations, either in strictly controlled laboratory settings, or in classroom situations (in which case we tried to control for relevant variables as much as possible). Field studies in classroom situations were, however, preferable in most cases where teaching of a realistic nature was involved, because of the time span and time schedules involved, and because of the influence a totally new situation might have on our subjects. Mainly in the case our experimental subjects were primary school students, it was in fact impossible to locate the experiment in a laboratory environment. In most cases intelligence factors were measured and "evened out" in calculating statistics. The analysis will start with the most readily changeable aspects of cognition.

3.1 Knowledge and Skills

Observations in primary school revealed that the practice of elementary skills was a very important contribution of the computer, once the teachers (and the pupils) were allowed to choose for themselves (cf. Suppes, 1979). This emphasis on exercises is in agreement with the increasing attention on individual differences: skill training and exercises aiming at extending or reinforcing the personal knowledge structure were chosen by teachers both for remedial purposes, and for individual (self-paced) practice after the introduction of new material to the group. This form of computer use replaced group-wide exercises (which teachers more and more consider old-fashioned) and is more practical than individual coaching by the teacher of his many pupils.

3.1.1 Arithmetic - an example of successful adaptation

Teachers asked for a lot of training programs in the domains of spelling, arithmetic and some language aspects. Arithmetic turned out to be the subject that profited most: considerable gain in learning was found when a computer program was applied that adapted the amount of detail of feedback and helped the actual behaviour of individual students. This effect surpassed the effect of written exercises with the same material, and the difference remained stable even when tested after four months (Kok, 1984). The success seems to be due to the structure of the feedback: the hints provided by the programs decreased in generality if more and more help was needed. The student was always encouraged to solve at least part of the problem by himself. However, if attempts were unsuccessful, the problem was split. After solving the subproblems the original question could again be tackled. Those students who needed no help at all, or could solve the problems after general hints only, were encouraged to find a solution in their own way. In fact they were never confronted with strategies of splitting up problems and solving subproblems. Students who did need this kind of help, however, were able to work without it more and more as the course progressed. In order to apply this method, it is a condition that the problem can be divided in a logical way (as seen from the point of view of the problem solver), and that the splitting up of problems can be applied adaptively, depending on the actual problem-solving behaviour of individual students.

3.1.2 Reading - some negative results

In understanding text a different result was found. A structure of feedback and help comparable to that for arithmetic did not improve learning beyond what could be gained with the seemingly inadequate feedback of written comments, handed out one day after the exercise was finished. Apparently, the kind of problems (identifying the central topic in a piece of text, finding the main actor in the story etc.) and the quality of the material (natural language with its rich semantics) are not optimally dealt with in multiple choice questions, as the students were asked by our program. The processing of natural language and the analysis of the semantics of a response are beyond the possibilities of the kind of systems we use. This asks for an amount of artificial intelligence that is, as far as we know, not yet operational in actual educational situations. On the other hand, our observations are in accord with Perfetti (1983), who makes a clear distinction between two components of the process of understanding written language, supported by empirical evidence:

—   decoding, or pattern recognition, leading to the identification of the written units (words, phrases);

—   understanding, or integration of this verbal input with available knowledge.

There is, however, an interaction between these components. Understanding will only be possible as far as the decoding process has been successful, whereas decoding might be improved by "guesswork", derived from understanding the environment of the fragment to be encoded.

Both for younger children and for bad readers in general, the first aspect of reading behaviour requires a fair amount of attention, at the expense of the second component, as both have to be effectuated within the limited capacity of working memory. The kind of help and feedback that was available in our programs concerned the combination of semantic units from the text and the integration of these with available schemata, clearly aiming at the second component. Perfetti reports positive effects of computer application in the domain of the first aspect only.

Practice of skills in interaction with a computer makes sense if the kind of interaction is directed at identifying or decomposing the real problem. Training higher level skills (understanding coherent text) in a situation where conditional lower ones (coding written material) are only partly mastered, requires more than just a plain effort in changing the pupil's aptitudes. It will be necessary to account for differences in the availability of the basic skills, asking for a flexibility of adaptation that in some cases is difficult to effect in a computer program.

3.1.3 Optimal adaptation - teacher or computer?

Bernaert (1978) reports a field study in which the the students were allowed to choose freely the order of units of student-tutor interaction. The units were distinguished in exercises, examples and introduction. It was observed that the student asked for more introduction and examples if the experimenter acted as a teacher, whereas if the computer was the teacher, exercises were preferred from the start. The group that learned at the computer produced about twice as many errors as their fellow students with the human teacher, although this teacher in fact gave literally the same standard instruction text and examples as the program did.

From these observations may be concluded that the preferable allocation of tasks is to leave the introduction of new material to the teacher. Aspects of inter-human interaction, too delicate to analyse, let alone to provide in a computer program, are essential to the pupil. After the introduction is presented the computer may be allocated the task of presenting exercises and allowing pupils to practise at their own pace. If however there exists a situation in which the computer should be used for introduction of new material, one should not allow primary school children to select the order of the units, but let the program guide them in a tutorial way. Only after they have received sufficient instruction and examples, they should be allowed to take over control, choosing the way they wish to proceed.

3.2 Strategies of Learning

Strategies are readily changeable, although this takes some time and effort. There are cases in which a teacher or a teaching computer program is best adapted to the pupil. The first two examples will show just that. In the other, situations are illustrated in which it might be better to have the student change his strategy.

3.2.1 Adaptation to differences in student preferences for strategies

a. *Serialism/holism*

These strategies are derived from the work by Pask (1976). They turn out to depend on the kind of task, as Pask suggested (Beishuizen, Van der Veer, 1985). Serialism in an experimental transformation task (translating one set of geometrical screen images into another one) is not related (or even slightly negatively related) to serialism in a teach back task (having the student reproduce the content of an essay that had just been read).

Van der Veer and Beishuizen (1986) give an overview of the possibilities of application of these notions to computerised learning situations, in this case for adult students. If one measures serialism/holism in a verbal domain (comprehension of a text on biology), students profit considerably if the teaching strategy of a computer program presenting verbal material (syllogistic reasoning) matches the strategy of the pupil. A holist teaching strategy in this case is defined as presenting the elements of an algorithm separately before integrating them. A serialist teaching strategy consists of adding the elements of the algorithm one after the other. Figure 2 presents the resulting mean solution time for four criterion problems.

With this learning material none of the two teaching strategies is to be preferred, nor is any of the two learning strategies. In accordance with Pask's theory, the results suggest possibilities for matching computer teaching style to learning style. This applies to learning material or skills that consist of several parts to be mastered individually and then integrated. A necessary condition for the application is to start with an indication of the preferred strategy of each student (testing procedures are described by Van der Veer and Beishuizen) or, alternatively, to have the students choose for themselves, from options that show them clearly what kinds of teaching sequence are available, and what the reasons for choosing any of them could be.

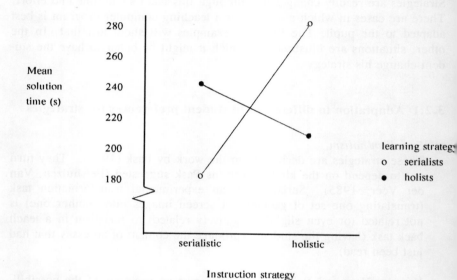

Figure 2.   Average solution time as a result of student learning strategy and teaching strategy

b.   *Search strategies*
In tasks concerning the search for information from large databases using keywords and combining sets, two strategies may be distinguished. One is characterised by the immediate combination of subsets once they are found, the other by an approach in phases, first constructing a number of subsets before actually combining (part of) the collected information into the resulting set.

We found that the process of search (in domains unknown to the student, with an apparently vague structure) can be facilitated by a computer coach that advises the searcher to be consistent in the preferred method, although generally speaking the two approaches are equally successful (Beishuizen, 1984; Beishuizen and Van der Veer, 1985). Adaptation to the individual student by a computer coach (a kind of metacommunication, initiated by the computer program) again requires either the diagnosis of the preferred strategy or the presentation to the student of a reasonable opportunity to decide the manner of guidance.

3.2.2 Education towards optimal strategies

a. *Coding strategies*
In learning to write computer programs, a distinction can be made between learning to structure one's problem solution (programming) and learning to code the solution into a computer language. Van der Veer (1983) found that the coding behaviour of novices showed striking individual differences. It proved to be systematically related to the amount of experience in mathematics. University students with no mathematical background used abbreviations and one-letter identifiers whenever possible, deteriorating the readability of their programs, and giving themselves the impression that they had only learned tricks. Students with some years of mathematical education wrote programs which were understandable and mentioned having learned a useful way of attacking problems from the programming course.

In another experiment on learning a simple coding language, the time needed for mastering the language turned out to be positively related to the amount of mathematical background (varying between 75 and 104, minutes for "extreme" groups), although students with or without a considerable amount of mathematical experience did not differ in performance on additional programming exercises after the language was mastered.

The conclusion from these experiments is that it might be useful to prevent the use of one-letter commands and object names (which means *not* to adapt to individual preferences), and on the other hand, not to worry too much about the variability in prior experience with abstract notation. Experience with a simple computer language designed in the light of these results showed that even primary school children are able to master the skill of coding. They use names which are workable to them and which help them to remember the meaning of identifiers and procedures, provided their creativity does not bring them to choosing names with which the associated semantics are incompatible with the meaning in the program (this section is not intended to deal with real "programming" in the sense of creating algorithmic solutions to problems - that will be treated in 4.2.).

b. *Risk taking behaviour*

The introduction of the computer in the learning situation may induce new learning strategies. When given a choice in a learning domain of mechanics, between doing exercises, examples or instruction, students showed a tendency to take more risks by switching to exercises earlier than they would have done in the normal situation. Because of this more time has to be spent practising each unit. The less-talented pupils especially showed this behaviour. Their results and scores on transfer tests are lower than in a setting in which the computer program prevents them from making their own choices, using an educational decision model instead (Bernaert, 1978).

From this experiment may be concluded that it might even be worse to adapt to the wish of individual students. Below a certain level of aptitude it is better to prevent pupils from arranging their own strategy, and decide on rigidity on the part of the computer.

c. *Heuristics and algorithms*

In the field of problem solving, tutorial programs either emphasise a more heuristic approach, or teach an algorithmic approach to certain problems. This last strategy always leads to correct solutions within the problem domain, but this gain is of restricted value. Transfer to problems of a related type, or to a related domain, may not, or not always, be solved with the same algorithm, and on all occasions this method loses its optimality as soon as transfer to a more remote domain is involved, whereas a heuristic strategy may be applied even in these cases.

De Leeuw (1983) experimented with problem domains of arithmetic and logic. He found transfer to be facilitated by computer programs that were based on a heuristic approach (which was inferior regarding the learning results on the original domain, as might be expected) and in fact this method showed better results even on the original problem domain after a time lag (some days or a few months). For this type of material, the presentation according to a heuristic strategy induces a kind of problem solving behaviour that has long term positive effects.

3.3 Cognitive Styles - Adaptation to Individual Differences

These kinds of individual differences are the result of a long term interaction between stable personality characteristics and educational and cultural influences. In human-computer interaction one should not expect to be able to influence them, so adapting the teaching strategy seems to be the only way to take differences into account.

3.3.1 Learning styles from conversation theory

Pask (1976) developed, in his Conversation Theory, several dimensions of cognitive style which describe relatively permanent ways of integrating new information in pupil-teacher or human-computer situations. After considerable psychometric research on the tests that Pask invented for that purpose, we developed measurement scales and scoring methods resulting in three dimensions:

a. *Tendency to learn*
   This factor does not indicate a capacity, but the amount of effort invested in collecting information and memorising. The respondent is totally free, the instructions do not necessarily suggest that he should memorise, but some do so spontaneously and consistently.

b. *Operation learning*
   This style indicates a tendency or possibility to attend to details, resulting in the deduction of specific rules and procedural details, and the availability of tools to construct procedures when needed. This style also leads to consistency with regard to related details of the knowledge domain.

c. *Comprehension learning*
   This style directs the learning effort to global relations, to induction of general rules and descriptions, to trace relations between different, even remote, parts of the domain, and to the construction of an overall view. One tends to reconstruct forgotten details on the basis of general structure and analogies.

When somebody has the capacity to choose between these last two style dimensions in accord with demands of the actual situation, Pask speaks of versatility.

The aforementioned strategies serialism and holism are situation dependent derivatives from these styles. Versatiles may show a tendency to holism, operation learning might lead to serialism, although the relation is probably not too strong. General intelligence tends to correlate positively with all three style dimensions, (for groups of university students typically in the order of .40 to .65) so the best method for the interpretation of effects of these styles is to refer to significant partial correlation coefficients or analyses of covariance, "evening out" intelligence.

We applied these styles only to students of high schools and universities so far. In a course on COBOL we found positive relations between tendency to learn and performance tests during the course (van der Veer and van de Wolde, 1984).

In another study (Van der Veer and van de Wolde, 1982), students who were above median on versatility showed an average learning time for an experimental computer language of 75 minutes, while the other half needed 105 minutes on average. Once a computer language is mastered, these individual differences seem to be less important, but when problems of an obscure abstract nature have to be solved, non-versatiles turn out to be disabled. This disability disappears as soon as an identical problem is stated in meaningful terms (see Figure 3, in fact the meaningful problem was presented before the abstract version, but none of the students detected this).

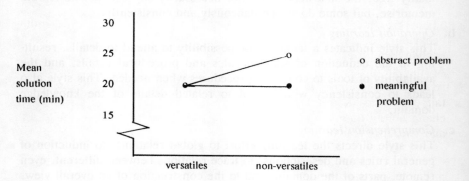

Figure 3.   Solution time as a function of versatility and problem semantics

The addition of meaning to a programming exercise is apparently sufficient to remove the handicap of non-versatiles. The flexibility of choice that is needed for the solution of abstract problems is no longer needed. In constructing exercises for programming courses, this should be taken into account.

3.3.2 Field dependence

The tendency to actively structure the situation (field independence) in contrast to being affected by irrelevant aspects in the environment (field dependence) is an important determinant of problem solving behaviour. Field independent pupils are able to apply a method or strategy (be it heuristic or algorithmic) learned in solving problems of syllogistic reasoning in new, related domains (correlation .48 after partialing out pretest scores and verbal intelligence). They perceive analogies and differences between old and new problem types, and they are more accurate in drawing schemes as an aid in problem solving (De Leeuw, 1983). Field dependent pupils on the other hand, need more assistance during the problem solving process, with levels of feedback varying from very general remarks to problem specific hints. Facilities like this are difficult to provide in traditional school environments, but they can be provided in computer assisted situations. Adaptation to individual differences in this respect may be characterised as providing additional structure in the environment in which the students work.

3.4 Personality Factors

These group of factors are the most stable characteristics of cognitive behaviour. It does not make sense to invest effort in changing them by applying sophisticated tools, as long as there is no theoretical base for this. Adaptation of the content and structure of the learning material to the personality or the ability level of the pupil is the only possible way to give a fair chance to disadvantaged students. At this extreme of the dimension of changeability observations were made of two aspects, general ability level and "negative fear of failure".

3.4.1 General ability level

Field studies in primary school revealed that children with low scores on verbal and technical ability tests and on tests for educational achievement were not capable of choosing an optimal sequence of tasks within a learning environment (Bernaert, 1978). In an experiment on learning mechanics half of the students were given the possibility to choose any order of learning tasks (instruction, examples, and problems) within a unit of learning material, and to decide independently when to proceed to the next unit (the order of which was fixed). For the other half the learning material was presented in an individually adapted order, defined by a decision model derived from strategies teachers preferred when working with individual students (which they can only rarely afford to do in the normal classroom situation). This order was defined by the following rule, for each unit of learning material:

1. First present a general introduction on the topic.
2. Present a complete instruction on the topic.
3. Present a new example.
4. Present a new problem, deliver feedback on the student's solution, offer the possibility of correcting any error.
5. After three solutions that were correct at the first attempt, proceed to the next unit.
6. After three errors, go back to 2.
7. If the solution was not correct at the first attempt, go to 3 otherwise go to 4.

In this second condition the low ability group spent more time for study (on the average 280 minutes against 210 without guidance, see Figure 4), but they scored higher on a criterion test and they scored even better on transfer tests for related new learning domains, compared with students of the same ability category, who decided for themselves. When working without the computer's "guidance", these risked too much by trying to do exercises at once, bypassing the possibility of receiving instruction and examples. But even when coached adequately, the weaker pupils need more practice than do the gifted (who studied for 180 and 170 minutes in the two conditions).

There are more computer assisted learning situations in which the effects of low intelligence could be nullified (Kok, 1984). In learning the position value of numbers with the help of computer exercises, there turned out to be no relation between Raven-scores and learning effects (difference between pre and post test), although this relation was present with paper and pencil exercises. The weaker pupils showed considerable gain from practice with the computer, but hardly any gain from written material.

The two cases above are examples of situations in which the application of adequate computer assisted teaching strategies compensated to a certain extent for the lack of ability of the pupils. For other types of student-computer interaction intelligence is an important source of variation (Beishuizen and Brazier, 1984). In learning a programming language constructed especially for primary school children, there is a significant correlation (.78) between a criterion test score on coding, and the Raven intelligence test, consistent with reports on the Brookline LOGO project (Watt, 1979). Both in our project and the LOGO project, however, even the weak students were capable of showing a certain level of creative behaviour in using a programming language, showing hidden talents that remained unexploited in traditional classroom situations.

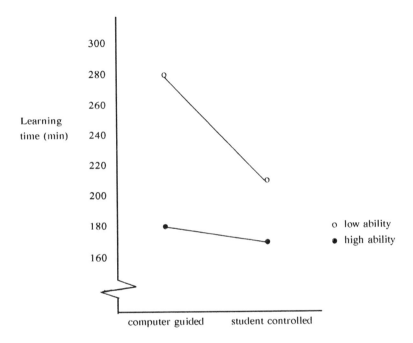

Figure 4.   learning time on a computer assisted learning program on mechanics

3.4.2 Negative fear of failure

Negative fear of failure may be characterised by a paralysing effect on achievement in situations in which the performance is observed by others, or is perceived as highly important for inter-human relations (examinations, public performances, competition). A lot of attention has been given to this handicap, that in every day school life is responsible for much disappoint-ment, frustration and failure.

De Leeuw (1983) investigated to what extent fear of failure might be compensated. Extensively structuring the situation is one form of compensation. When teaching to solve mathematical problems on number series, an algorithmic approach (a method in which the solution is found step by step, with the security of a valid solution), helped to overcome negative fear of failure. This resulted in both a better score on the criterion test and a better one on a transfer test on problems that were of a higher level of difficulty (these results were only recorded if the original problem domain was not too narrow, i.e., contained several distinct types of series instead of only a few). In the broad problem domain the quantity of help asked from the computer program was positively related to the amount of negative fear of failure score. Partialing out mathematical ability, the partial correlation coefficients between number of help requests and negative fear of failure remained considerable and statistically significant at 3 of 4 levels of help: .65, .61 and .53. Only the most specific help level was rarely used at all. Generally speaking the students with negative fear of failure asked for more help, ranging from general remarks about the problem being considered to more specific information levels, in decreasing order of frequency. Students without this handicap profit more from a heuristic approach. After a considerable time delay, in fact, a heuristic method gives the most stable results for all pupils, as has already been shown in section 3.2.1., paragraph c. This leads to the disappointing conclusion that compensation for negative fear of failure is only feasible if one aims at a circumscribed problem domain, for a short period of time.

There is, however, a positive effect of learning with computers: answers to questionnaires showed that the computer is perceived as a non-human object, and pupils experience this as a safe situation, even when they are in fact keeping pace with others. The students in the project spontaneously mentioned a lack of the kind of competition that is so often perceptible in normal classroom situations.

4 ADAPTATION IN THE CLASSROOM, THE COMPUTER AS A RESPONSIVE ENVIRONMENT

This section deals with observations made in the classroom without applying experimental methods. Therefore the results are dependent on unknown influences and on specific situations in the different schools. The effect of computers in the school was explored in the highest grades of 12 Dutch primary schools. The pupils were about 10 to 12 years old. In this environment the educational goals are changing – more differentiation within the class is being strived for and more attention is being paid to individual differences. These differences should be observed to their full extent at primary school level, because children are sent to different secondary schools depending on their capabilities. Experience in primary schools shows first of all that the introduction of new material is preferred to be done by the teacher. The computer is used for independent practise in a variety of problem-solving domains. It does not replace the teacher, but it is a device with special qualities, a possibility to enrich the learning environment. In evaluating its application possibilities the research team refrained from intervention in the teaching method, apart from the introduction of special features such as a pupils' programming language and a couple of field experiments (these were mentioned in section 3).

4.1 The Study Machine

"The Study Machine" was the name of a prototype integrated educational system that was made available to teachers and pupils. Incorporated in this system were a number of different features:

a. *tutorial* lessons, most of them created at the request of the teachers, some of whom structured the content or volunteered as coach for the programmers;

b. *drill and practice* lessons in large quantities, the content of which was provided by the teachers, who inserted this material into template lessons of a simple and rather rigid nature;

c. *games*, most of them chosen because of their problem-solving nature;

d. possibilities for *self testing* of aptitudes, in the format of multiple choice tests with indications of certainty;

e. a tool for *database retreival* with the help of a coach, the strategy of which might be chosen by the teacher or the student;

f. a simple *programming language*, mainly for string handling, enabling a sophisticated programmer to insert standard preludes to special domains of programming exercises.

The integrated system enabled teachers to independently decide when, for which pupils and for which task the computer was used. The "computer" consisted of one terminal for each school, connected via a dial-up telephone line to a system that was very easy to use (e.g. the Unix system was masked). The time the study machine was in operation in the classroom turned out to vary between 1.5 and 16 hours a week, a student-session taking between 10 and 30 minutes. The best place for the terminal turned out to be in the classroom.

The teachers generated a lot of ideas for new lessons, helped to define didactic aims and created exercises themselves, especially in the domains of arithmetic, language and geography. In this way the study machine developed into an expanding environment within which simple exercises, structured learning units, problems in the form of games and a programming language are the elements that were considered most important.

Some teachers used the study machine for group-education, others for individuals who needed special attention, or for remedial aims. In nearly all cases that were observed the general aim was to enhance knowledge and skills, at the same time taking into account the actual level of the individual pupil. Teachers, when left to their own intuitive ideas, stick to the right hand side of the dimension of changeability when employing a computer. The domains in which the study machine was used most will be illustrated in the next sections.

4.1.1 Arithmetic

In this domain the teachers asked for problem-oriented exercises. The computer programs were written according to their specifications, as far as the structure of the intended solutions was concerned. It turned out that their analysis was sometimes considered rather old fashioned by colleagues who favoured more recent theories about arithmetic problem-solving.

The exercises are grouped into levels of uniform difficulty and after every 10 items an overview of the results is given. After an error the problem is gradually divided into smaller units. In some programs a recommendation is built in about the best level for further practice.

The domain includes topics on simple operations like addition, subtraction and division, exercises that were regularly used as complementary to group-wise treatment and practice of these skills. For multiplication, proportions and percentages, remedial use was observed to be very successful. Exercises on linear measures were often combined with a computer lesson about their application.

4.1.2 Language

In this domain teachers preferred to make much use of the different template lessons that were available. This offered them rather rigid structures, but that was hardly ever felt a real problem. The teacher can insert new material in a very easy way.

Spelling exercises have been especially popular, mostly for remedial goals but sometimes in group instruction. A considerable gain in learning has been observed. Together the teachers created a total of about 150 different spelling lessons, but some teachers only used the exercises their colleagues constructed. Other teachers even constructed new lessons which can only be used by a few pupils with special spelling problems.

A second template lesson provides the opportunity to create lessons in which a pupil has to fill in the appropriate words, which can be chosen from a set of words provided along with the exercise. In this way another 150 lessons were written by teachers, about grammar and proverbs, Turkish-Dutch translation of phrases, and also lessons outside the language domain for which these templates were originally constructed, about arithmetic problems, geography and history.

These types of template lessons were used quite frequently. In fact more time was spent using these two template facilities (with their many available exercises) than on any other part of the study machine.

Reading comprehension is the subject of the third template, which however did not show better results than written exercises (in 3.1.2. an experiment on this material is described) and is hardly ever used.

4.1.3 Games

The games in the study machine are included because of specific problem solving behaviour required to win - systematic search within well-known domains such as numbers, restricted by properties like primes, squares or divisibility. A number of game lessons are constructed in levels that may be chosen according to the problem-solving behaviour of the student, sometimes done automatically by the program, sometimes only as advice to choose another game. Some of the games are aimed at abilities that are part of the normal curriculum (most of them mathematics). These are used by some of the teachers in combination with classroom introduction of the subject matter. Remedial teachers were observed to apply some of the games in cases of specific learning problems, probably in order to enhance motivation. But, most of the time, games are considered by the teachers as just a pastime, although they all allow their pupils to spend some time on them.

4.2 A Programming Language in the Primary School

The availability of programmable machines is a new element in the school situation, not comparable with problem-solving situations that might be found in schools before the computer age. Based on previous experiments with programming language constructs and their relation to individual differences, a programming language was defined that combined neat control structures, readable naming, interactive editing and automatic syntax checking. A problem-domain dependent standard prelude releases users from administrative details and provides the solution to detailed problems that are not relevant to the pupil or the problem-solving process. The language was learned with the help of a written guide which presented for each element of the language: explanations, examples to be copied, exercises in coding and questions to induce expectation about reactions of the computer. The learning was self-paced, and, on average, took 6th grade pupils 30 hours. Case studies showed that students are capable of creative manipulations with problems, just like Watt (1979) found in the Brookline project. Coding is readily mastered at this age. In a few cases they even show progressive refinement in constructing the algorithm (Beishuizen and Van der Veer, 1985), although this is an exception. Figure 5 gives an example of a procedure constructed spontaneously by a 12 year old student before he expanded procedures "Arithmetic" and "Grammar".

```
--pro studymachine
--make answer := ''
--ask 'What do you want to do?' $ answer
--if answer = 'grammar' then do grammar
---butif answer = 'arithmetic' then do arithmetic
---else write 'you may choose grammar or arithmetic' , newline
--do studymachine
--end studymachine
```

Figure 5.   Example of a program by Marco

Pupils are able to produce examples and applications of syntactic concepts. The creation of an original program of any volume however may be found with only a few gifted children. The development of a new skill or a systematic change in problem-solving strategies could not be detected in children of this age group. Weizenbaum seems to have been right, when he states (Foppema, 1983): "A certain amount of maturity is a condition to create a real program. You will not expect a 14 year old to do the job of an engineer".

4.3 Motivation

In order to study the opinions and attitudes of the users of the study machine, separate questionnaires were constructed for pupils and teachers. For several years running these were filled in at the end of the school term.

Responses collected from the pupils showed a positive evaluation of the computer as such. If it was left to the students, they would spend between 2 hours a week to 2 hours a day (which they are in fact never allowed by their teachers) working with the computer. The students' positive attitude remains stable even once they are accustomed to the situation having worked with the computer for up to 3 years. The most important arguments they mentioned were: when making an error one is not laughed at; feedback is provided immediately and errors can be corrected right away; one can keep to one's own pace; typing is preferred to handwriting (writing difficulties are the cause of problems in a variety of domains at school). During the years of data collection the arguments given to justify the preference for computer exercises shifted from arguments based on the learning gain expected, to such arguments as "the computer is pleasant AND instructive", and "one learns more in a pleasant situation".

5 CONCLUSIONS

5.1 The Role of the Teacher

The creation of a tutorial program is a specialist's job. Experience with an author language or with a high level programming language is a prerequisite, as is either knowledge of the learning material or the co-operation of an expert. The ratio of 100 hours of development to one hour of tutorial program often stated is quite probable. In the primary schools there does not seem to be much need for this type of C.A.I. (computer aided instruction). Teachers do not need to be replaced. Venezky (1983) mentions the "teacher directed classroom", in which the computer is only an instructional tool, which facilitates individualisation. Our observations confirm this idea: practice of skills, problem-solving exercises and the coaching of strategy development are tasks for which the use of a computer is an improvement, acknowledged by teachers and pupils. Some tutorial aspects are recognisable in these programs, aspects which are relatively easily implemented (e.g., in arithmetic). The interaction in the case of language education asks for more advanced design techniques. "Simple" solutions like multiple choice are not effective.

Template lessons that may be filled in by the teacher are naturally simple in structure and uniform in feedback. This appears to have been accepted: the pupils themselves stated that the direct feedback and the possibility of correcting mistakes was the most important characteristic of these programs. We observed that the increase in learning confirms these statements.

Arguments that are mentioned by the teachers in favour of the use of a computer concentrate, on one hand, on individualisation, an approach which focuses on the pupil's weak points, and on the other hand, on difficult parts of the learning material. The actual results will never be fully credited to the computer. A computer is a tool, that may be useful in combination with other tools. Topics such as: improvement of spelling and reading, variations in the approach to learning material, the practice of standard algorithms and the enhancement of motivation, are mentioned as positive effects. Teachers observed that children are not afraid to make errors and that they sustain the search for solutions longer than in other situations.

5.2 Applications

The most frequent task for which computers are employed in the primary school is practising cognitive skills that are located at the right hand side of the dimension of changeability, although some kinds of computer application is directed at learning strategies. Teachers seem to have the intuitive feeling that these are the tasks that are optimally delegated to (or shared with) the computer. Alternation with traditional means provokes motivation, as does the direct feedback and the possibility to determine one's own pace.

There are some types of use that are directed at more stable student characteristics: the possibility to refine "help" in phases is efficient for less skillful pupils, (e.g., in arithmetic, and for pupils handicapped by negative fear of failure). This "help" should not be thrust upon a student. They themselves perceive its usefulness "for certain mistakes". The best method is to give a pupil a second opportunity to recover from the error before the help is offered, and if that fails, to try to solve at least part of the problem.

The arrangement of the exercises in levels enables the student to transfer to a level of difficulty based on a diagnosis of ability. Often the student will decide what to do next depending on feedback about previous results. In other cases the teacher determines the next level after evaluating the progress. A third possibility is to leave the decision to the program. Although this seems to be very adaptive (to the level of the student), it is not very transparent. The student might develop the idea the computer is more "intelligent", or might get irritated, because a fixed decision rule dominates human reason.

5.3 Enrichment of the Learning Environment

In the traditional classroom situation only restricted possibilities are available for the adaptation of the teaching strategy to individual differences. The assistance of a computer enables us to apply methods based on cognitive psychological theories:

Learning processes with problem-solving aspects are best conducted with heuristic strategies. Systematic assistance at the stage in which that strategy is to be discovered leads to long-term gain and positive transfer to new problem domains. An algorithmic method is only momentarily efficient but does not help a general approach.

Individual differences between serialist and holist strategies, a task dependent variable, may be compensated for by adapting the teaching strategy of the program to the student. When searching for information in a database, for instance, the program may determine the personal strategy of the pupil and coach him, if his behaviour deviates, by advising what step should be taken next, thus improving results.

Negative fear of failure may be compensated for by providing help facilities that are structured from general to specific. Gradually the pupil will develop independence in the task domain. Field dependent pupils also profit from being given the opportunity to structure the situation.

Independence in applying for help and in determining the order of exercises is a useful aspect in the learning environment. But less talented children lack the ability to know when and how much information they need. In that case a computer program structured according to didactic principles is more successful in guiding the learning process. The the more gifted children profit from freedom.

The availability of a computer is the cause for the development of new elements in the curriculum. Programming languages are often expected to stimulate the development of cognitive styles and problem-solving strategies. In the primary school this could not be confirmed though, unintended, creativity seemed to be facilitated. For older students, programming languages are useful tools, and in that case, several aspects of cognitive styles and of prior knowledge are relevant, both for the time that should be allowed to master the language, and for the choice of programming exercises. Information retreival (searching databases) is another new element, where individual strategies indeed may be taken into account.

REFERENCES

Beishuizen, J.J. (1984). Informatie verzamelen in een bibliotheek: coaching en zoekstrategieën. *In: Leren met computers in het onderwijs.* A. Dirkzwager, S.D. Fokkema, G.C. van der Veer, J.J. Beishuizen, (eds.). Den Haag: S.V.O.

Beishuizen, J.J., Brazier, F.M.T. (1984). Leren programmeren op de basisschool. *In: Leren met computers in het onderwijs.* A. Dirkzwager, S.D. Fokkema, G.C. van der Veer, J.J. Beishuizen, (eds.). Den Haag: S.V.O.

Beishuizen, J.J., Veer, G.C. van der. (1985). Een responsieve leeromgeving voor hoogbegaafde kinderen. *In: Hoogbegaafden in onze samenleving.* F.J. Mönks, P. Span, (eds.). Nijmegen: Dekker en Van de Vegt.

Bernaert, G.F. (1978). Sturing in het onderwijsleerproces, cognitieve capaciteit en leersituatie. Den Haag: S.V.O.

Dirkzwager, A. (1975). Computer-based testing with automatic scoring based on subjective probabilities. *In: Computers in Education.* O. Lecarme, R. Lewis, (eds.). Amsterdam: North-Holland.

Foppema, R. (1983). Huiscomputers zijn niet nuttig. Trouw, 28 December 1983, pp. 12.

Haylock, D. (1983). Computers and Children in the Primary School. *Journal of curriculum studies*, 15, pp. 230-231.

Kok, E.J. (1984). Effectiviteit van computeronderwijs - getalstructuur. *In: Leren met computers in het onderwijs.* A. Dirkzwager, S.D. Fokkema, G.C. van der Veer, J.J. Beishuizen, (eds.). Den Haag: S.V.O.

Leeuw, L. de (1983). Teaching problem solving: an ATI study of the effects of teaching algorithmic and heuristic solution methods. *Instructional science,* 12, pp. 1-48.

Muylwijk, B. van, Veer, G.C. van der, Waern, Y. (1983). On the implications of user variability in open systems. An overview of the little we know and of the lot we have to find out. *Behaviour and information technology,* 2, pp. 313-326.

Pask, G. (1976). Styles and strategies of learning. *British Journal of Educational Psychology,* 46, pp. 128-148.

Perfetti, C.A. (1983). Reading, vocabulary, and writing: implementations for computer-based instruction. *In: Classroom computers and cognitive science.* A.C. Wilkinson, (ed.). London: Academic Press.

Suppes, P. (1979). Current trends in Computer-Assisted Instruction. *In: Advances in Computers.* M. Rubinoff, M.C. Yovits, (eds.). New York: Academic Press.

Veer, G.C. van der (1983). Individual differences in cognitive style and educational background and their effect upon the learning of a programming language. *In: Psychologie des Programmierens.* H. Schauer, M. Tauber, (eds.). Wien: Oldenbourg.

Veer, G.C. van der, Beishuizen, J.J. (1986). Learning styles in conversation - a practical application of Pask's learning theory to human-computer interaction. *In: Man-Computer Interaction Research - MACINTER I.* F. Klix and H. Wandke (eds.). Amsterdam: North Holland Elsevier Science Publishers.

Veer, G.C. van der, Wolde, J. van de (1982). Psychological aspects of problem solving with the help of computer languages. *In: Computers and Education,* 6, pp. 229-234.

Veer, G.C. van der, Wolde, J. van de (1984). Leerstijlen bij mens-machine interactie - een bewerking van de smokkelaarstest van Gordon Pask. *In: Leren met computers in het onderwijs.* A. Dirkzwager, S.D. Fokkema, G.C. van der Veer, J.J. Beishuizen, (eds.). Den Haag: S.V.O.

Venezky, R.L. (1983). Evaluating Computer-Assisted Instruction on its Own Terms. *In: Classroom Computers and Cognitive Science.* A.C. Wilkinson, (ed.). London: Academic Press.

Watt, D. (1979). Final report of the Brookline LOGO project, part III: Profiles of individual student's work. M.I.T.: Cambridge, Massachusetts.

THE IMPACT OF INDIVIDUAL DIFFERENCES IN PROGRAMMERS

Bill CURTIS

Microelectronics and Computer Technology Corporation (MCC)
Austin, Texas 78759, USA

Abstract

Managers readily admit the sizeable individual differences they have observed in skill and performance among programmers. Although these differences are part of the popular lore in software engineering, the seriousness of their impact is usually overlooked in identifying the points of greatest leverage for improving programming productivity and quality. This paper organises and reviews data bearing on individual differences among professional programmers collected by the author and others in laboratory experiments and on actual projects. The paper argues that individual differences are still the largest source of leverage available for improving productivity and quality. Unfortunately, they receive miniscule research attention in relation to their impact on software development performance and costs. Finally, the productivity improvements promised by many advances in software technology will be masked by the continued impact of individual differences on productivity data.

1 THE RANGE IN PERFORMANCE AMONG PROGRAMMERS

In 1967, Harold Sackman and his colleagues (Grant and Sackman, 1967; Sachman, Erickson, and Grant, 1968) reported 28:1 differences in performance among professional programmers. Their data were criticised at the time of publication by Lampson (1967) and more recently by Dickey (1981). Both critics argued that the 28:1 differences were not reliable because the data were contaminated by differences caused by other factors. Dickey cites differences between time-shared and batch systems, the languages used for implementation, and the fleeting experience some of the participants had with the system and programming language they were using.

Dickey reassessed Grant and Sackman's (1967) data and suggested that the range ratio comparing the best and worst performance be scaled down to a more modest 5:1. Nevertheless, as Dickey lamented, the size of individual differences claimed by Sackman et al. became part of the popular lore in software engineering. This ratio was accepted partly because it coincided with the subjective impressions of most managers.

In response to Dickey's critique, I looked back at some data my colleagues at Genaral Electric and I had collected a few years earlier (Sheppard, Curtis, Milliman and Love, 1979). We had used a pretest for our debugging experiment both to screen out professional programmers who could not perform the experimental task and to accustom the participants to the tasks they would subsequently perform. We started by inserting a one-line bug in a program that found the greatest common divisor of two numbers (problem 1). After we had run half of the participants in the study, we decided that this pretest was too hard and we switched to an accounting problem (problem 2). The 27 programmers debugging each program were presented with the same bug and identical conditions for finding it. Thus, differences in scores more closely reflected differences between the skills of individual programmers than had been true in Sackman et al.'s study. After reassembling these data, I reported the results presented in Figure 1 (Curtis, 1981).

On what was ostensibly the harder program (program 1), the range ratio of best to worst performance was about 8:1. As is evident from the distribution scores in Figure 1, the bug inserted in program 2 was easier to find. However, the range ratio obtained was roughly 22:1. One poor programmer took 67 minutes, and when he stopped he had identified only the instruction the bug was in, but not its exact cause. If we delete this individual's data, we still have a range ratio of 13:1, since two programmers required 39 minutes to diagnose the bug correctly. Thus, we had replicated the dreaded <20:1 performance differences that could not be argued cleanly from Sackman et al.'s data. Even with the worst score removed, the range ratio was still greater than an order of magnitude. Worse yet, these ratios may have been conservative, since we had to dismiss six professional Fortran programmers from the experiment because they could not perform the task.

Data which exhibit the greater than 20:1 range ratios are usually collected in laboratory experiments. Such experiments are frequently criticised for their lack of generality to real world programming environments (Lampson, 1967; Brooks, 1980; Sheil, 1981). In the context of individual differences, we must question whether there is something about laboratory experiments that promotes a wider distribution of performance scores than would be characteristic of real programming environments.

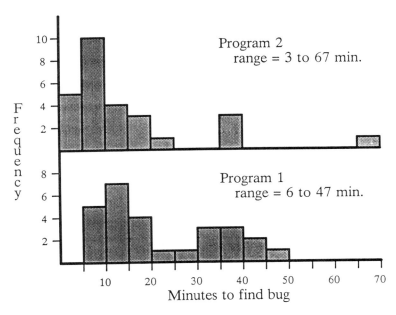

Figure 1.   Distribution of minutes to find one bug on two pretest
              programs (from Curtis, 1981)

McGarry (1982) reported data obtained in the Software Engineering Laboratory, a joint effort between NASA, the University of Maryland, and Computer Sciences Corporation to collect rigorous data on actual Fortran development projects that ranged from 2,000 to 110,000 source lines of code. The productivity data in terms of average source lines of code per hour are summarised for differences among projects and among individual programmers in Figure 2.

For individuals on small projects (< 20,000 lines), the range ratio was about 22:1. For larger projects (> 20,000 lines), the ratio is about 8:1. Although these data confound individual differences with differences in the modules assigned to different programmers (and possibly with other environmental factors), they are suspiciously similar to those we obtained in the laboratory. McGarry explained the greater individual differences variation observed on small projects by reporting that newer programmers, among whom greater variability in performance was characteristic, were typically assigned to these projects (personal communication).

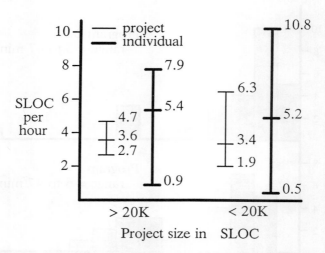

Figure 2.   Productivity means and ranges from NASA/SEL (from McGarry, 1982)

2 VARIABILITY AND EXPERIENCE

This greater variability among less experienced programmers was observed in the experiment (Sheppard, Curtis, Milliman and Love, 1979) from which the data in Figure 1 were obtained. While the data in Figure 1 came from the pretest, the data in Figure 3 came from the experimental tasks. Each participant searched for a one line bug in each of three programs. These programs differed in application area, control flow structure, type of bug, and length. These factors were counterbalanced for the purposes of the experiment, and all programmers worked with each level of each factor once in their three tasks. Nevertheless, with 81 different experimental programs (the permutations of 3 different levels for each of four different factors), the 27 programmers in each of the two experimental blocks saw different sets of programs.

Each data point in Figure 3 represents the average of the three debugging times obtained on each participant's three experimental tasks. Thus, in these data individual differences are also contaminated with other factors. Nevertheless, we see the same characteristic variability among less experienced programmers reported by McGarry. In particular, the range ratio for programmers with 3 years of experience was still an order of magnitude, even with an individual programmer's best and worst performances averaged together. We found that for programmers with three or fewer years of experience, the breadth of different programming experiences was the best predictor of performance.

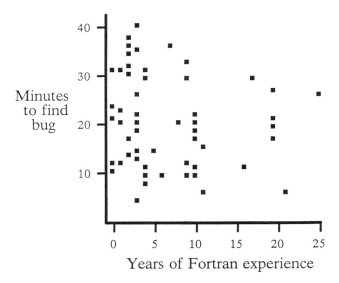

Figure 3.   Distribution of debugging time by experience (from Sheppard et al., 1979)

An important observation to draw from these data is that the strength of individual differences among programmers continues to emerge above the confounding factors in performance data. For instance, Basili and Hutchens (1983) found characteristic profiles for individual programmers in their ability to handle increases in the complexity of the programs they developed. Similarly, even with factors confounding the data we reported in Figure 3, we nevertheless found that other measures of individual differences were still significantly associated with performance differences. This result suggests that the percentage of variation in performance scores

accounted for by individual differences may be much greater than that
accounted for by other factors.

3 THE IMPACT OF INDIVIDUAL DIFFERENCES ON LABORATORY EXPERIMENTS

If individual differences in programming skill are as important a factor in
overall programming performance as the range ratio suggests, then they
should account for a larger proportion of the variation in performance on
programming tasks than should other factors. Indeed, Brooks (1980), Sheil
(1981), and Moher and Schneider (1981) have attributed the frequent
failure to find significant effects for experimental factors in empirical
research on programming to the overwhelming impact of individual differences among the participants. That is, so much of the variation in performance is associated with individual differences among participants that it
masked the performance variation accounted for by the factors under study
in the experiment.

Table 1.　　Impact of Individual Differences on the Prediction of Program Comprehension by Software Metrics

	Percent of variance		
	E	v(G)	lines
Data aggregated by program (n = 27)	1.7	12.3	28.1
Exceptional group removed (n = 24)	14.0	30.3	37.2

A particularly nasty example of how these individual differences can affect
the data obtained from an experiment occurred in Curtis, Sheppard, Milliman, Borst, and Love (1979). In this experiment, we were comparing the
ability of three software metrics (lines of code, McCabe's v(G), and
Halstead's E) to predict comprehension performance. Each of the 27 different programs used in this study was seen by three different professional
programmers. One particularly cruel manifestation of Murphy's Law is
that one possible random assignment of participants to conditions will place

three of the four best programmers (as measured by common pretest scores) in the same group. Naturally, this unfortunate random gathering of stars affected some otherwise promising trends in the data. With the data for the three programs seen by this group removed, the percent of variance in comprehension scores predicted by the three metrics improved dramatically (Table 1).

In 1979, Sylvia Sheppard, Betsy Kruesi, and I initiated a research program on the human factors aspects of how information was represented in software documentation. We looked at three forms of symbology (natural language, pseudocode, and ideograms), three types of spatial arrangements (sequential, branching, and hierarchical), and three different types of programs. Wiser from our previous experiences with individual differences variation, we meticulously crafted our repeated measures (within subjects) experimental design to allow us to statistically account for variation among participants.

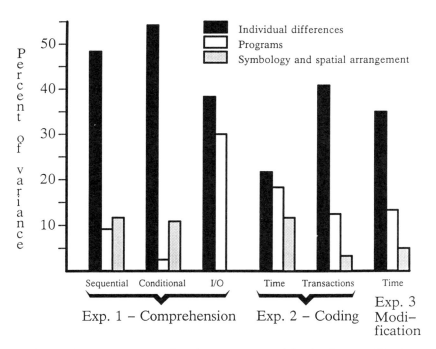

Figure 4.   Per cents of variance accounted for in the specification studies reported by Sheppard et al. in 1981

The percentage of variance in performance accounted for by different factors in the experiments on comprehension, coding, and modification are presented in Figure 4 (summarised from results reported in Sheppard, Kruesi and Curtis, 1981; Sheppard and Kruesi, 1981; Sheppard, Bailey and Kruesi, 1981). The variation related to individual differences typically accounted for one third to one half of the variation in performance. The percentage of variance accounted for by differences among the experimental programs varied widely from 2% to 30%. When the experimental factors (symbology and spatial arrangement) had a significant effect on performance, they accounted for 5 to 13 percent of the variance. The residual error which could not be accounted for by any of the factors measured in the experiment typically accounted for one quarter of the variation in performance. Because of their small size, percentage of variance for interactions among factors and replications are not presented.

Consistently across these experiments, individual differences among participants accounted for the largest percentage of the variance in performance. This percentage was substantially larger than the variation accounted for by the experimental factors. Had we not used an experimental design which allowed us to separate this individual difference variation from the residual (unaccounted for) variance, we would not have obtained some of the statistically significant results we reported for symbology and spatial arrangement.

4 THE IMPACT OF INDIVIDUAL DIFFERENCES ON ACTUAL PROJECTS

Although individual differences account for substantial performance variation in laboratory studies, they could have less impact on large software development projects where many other factors affect performance. On the cover of his landmark book Software Engineering Economics (1981), Barry Boehm presented the data summarised in Figure 5. These data represent the relation impact on productivity of numerous factors measured on 63 software development projects in his COCOMO project database. These factors are used to determine the anticipated productivity of a project for use in estimating its cost.

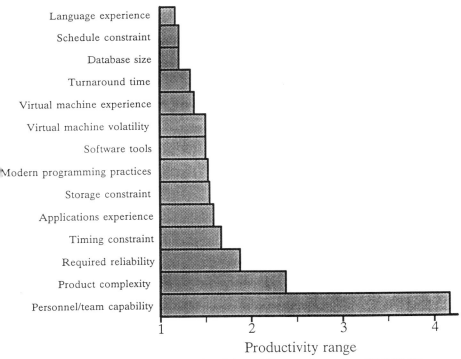

Figure 5.   Impact on productivity of factors from the COCOMO
database (from Boehm, 1981)

The single greatest impact on productivity of any factor in Boehm's data
was for the capability of the personnel composing the team assigned to the
project. Boehm's chart indicated that, all other things held equal, a 90th
percentile team was about four times more productive than a 15th percentile team. The next most important factor, product complexity, had only
about half the impact of team capability. Factors such as modern programming practices and software tools had just over a third as much impact.
These data led Boehm to conclude, "Personnel attributes and human relations activities have by far the largest source of opportunity for improving
software productivity" (1981, p. 666).

Walston and Felix (1977) found similar data from their database of 60 projects completed by IBM's Federal Systems Division. The largest factors
dealt with the complexity of the customer interface and the involvement of
the ultimate users with the development of requirements. The next most

important factors all dealt with programmer experience and qualifications. The range of productivity differences between the upper and lower groups was 3 to 1.

Neither Boehm's nor Walston and Felix's data will show the extreme range of individual differences presented in section 1, because of the way in which their data were collected. Personnel capability on actual projects is usually rated on a team basis, thus averaging the effects of individual differences. Further, the ratings are usually obtained on subjective questionnaires and reflect a manager's particular bias toward what is important in team capability and his personal baseline for evaluating them. However, questions which potentially elicit less subjective opinions, such as the amount of experience the team has had with similar applications or with the programming language, exhibit similar results. Thus, while these project data under-assess the size of individual differences, they nevertheless indicate the dramatic effect these differences have on project performance, as expected from the experimental data.

Similar problems in data collection resulted in an even more modest impact for individual differences on project performance in data collected by my Programming Measurements group in ITT (Vosburgh, Curtis, Wolverton, Alvert, Malec, Hoben and Liu, 1984). Only 4% of the variance in productivity was accounted for by such differences. However, these data came from 44 projects in 17 locations spread over 9 countries. There was no common baseline for comparing programming skills across these projects, and thus the ratings of personnel talent by the managers that provided the data are not adequate for comparing capability and performance.

Confounding factors make the data from actual projects on individual differences hard to interpret. Where data were collected in a single division of a company (e.g. Boehm and Walston and Felix), there is more likely to be a common set of experiences that allow managers to rate the capability of project personnel. Under such circumstances skill differences account for a larger percentage of the variance in productivity data, and often are the most significant factor. Nevertheless, no study has employed sufficient measurement controls to assess the actual skill differences of project personnel and their real impact on actual projects. Data such as those of McGarry suggest that a better controlled study might lead to even more dramatic results.

One of the important components of individual differences variation captured by Boehm and by Walston and Felix was the amount of previous experience with the programming language, development environment, and application domain. These data indicated that some aspects of individual differences that contributed to performance were developed through experience. Note that it is not the years of professional experience that contribute to performance, but the amount of relevant experience. Sheppard, Curtis, Milliman and Love (1979) observed a similar result.

This observation on the impact of relevant experience in the project data concurs with our experience in the laboratory. Sheppard et al. (1979) reported that it was the breadth of experience rather than the length that consistently correlated with performance. In fact, we could not find significant correlations between years of professional experience and performance in any of the three experiments. However, the number of programming languages known usually correlated modestly with performance. There was some evidence in our data that the relationship between breadth of experience and performance was primarily true of less experienced programmers.

5 WHERE IS THE LEVERAGE ON PROGRAMMING PRODUCTIVITY ?

The thesis of this paper has been that individual differences among programmers exert a dramatic impact on software development performance. Although measurement problems often make interpretation difficult, the data presented from both laboratory experiments and actual software development projects frequently support the thesis (and sometimes dramatically so).

Therefore, I feel much more confident in stating a conclusion similar to that already reached by Boehm (1981):

The single greatest point of leverage for improving programming productivity and quality is in reducing the impact of individuals at the lower end of the performance distribution.

There are numerous methods for reducing the impact of poor programming performance. Some of them are:

1. improved selection techniques;
2. job placement strategies and continuing education;
3. better programming tools and environments;
4. automation of many functions previously performed by programmers.

Over time, item 4 may have the greatest impact on productivity improvement. However, a perusal of the literature on automatic programming suggests that we are quite far away from realising the promise of this technology. Most of the research money in software engineering is being placed on item 3. Tens to hundreds of millions of dollars have been spent on new programming languages, techniques, methodologies, and tools. The data presented by Boehm and others suggest that these targets exert much smaller leverage on improving productivity than the continued presence of large individual differences among programmers. Thus, the first corollary to the main conclusion is that:

Corollary 1:
The productivity improvements expected from advanced programming methodologies and environments will be elusive, because they will be masked by the effects of individual differences in performance.

I do not intend by the arguments I have made to suggest that we should reduce the level of research on programming methodologies and environments. This research is crucial to the long term solution of major problems in software productivity. Nevertheless, the benefits to be derived from these advances will not be realised if programmers at the lower end of the distribution are as poor at using them as they have been at using current programming technology. The effect of modern programming practices on productivity was much smaller than the impact of programmer capability in both the Boehm and Walston and Felix data. In the experimental research reported in Sheppard et al. (1979), we frequently found ourselves dismissing as many as 1 in 6 professional programmers, because they simply could not perform the task. Once the impact of individual differences variation on actual projects has been reduced, the true benefits of advanced software engineering technology will play a more pronounced role in the productivity results.

6 THE RESEARCH AGENDA

Corollary 2:
Research money spent on eliminating the lower tail of the individual differences distribution will result in a greater near (and perhaps mid-) term return on investment in terms of productivity, quality, and costs than will money spent on many other research issues in software engineering.

In relation to its impact on programming productivity and quality, research on individual differences has received miniscule research funding. The single greatest point of leverage managers currently exercise in controlling their productivity and quality is in selecting and placing the personnel who will perform their projects. Although promising techniques are available, they are generally (almost cavalierly) overlooked by most programming managers.

Although the promise of many initial attempts to create selection procedures exceeded the results (Mayer and Stalnaker, 1968), more recent attempts seem to have recaptured some of the original promise (Bloom, 1980). Many of the early tests of programming aptitude were developed from existing tests of cognitive skills. Most of the evaluation literature on these tests showed that they provided modest prediction of performance in software training programs (i.e., correlations typically ranging between .3 and .5). General tests of verbal and mathematical skills have both been shown to correlate with training performance, as have personality measures that assess the extent to which individuals choose to work in an orderly way (Whipkey and Stephens, 1984). Among more basic cognitive capacities, Love (1977) has shown a relationship between digit span (a short term memory performance test) and programming performance.

Programmer selection tests tend to focus on skills that will help novices learn to program. They are less valuable for predicting the skilled performance of experienced programmers, since factors other than native cognitive abilities or educational aptitude become important. Thus, the value of the tests is in selecting novices for training, but not for selecting experienced programmers in an industrial setting.

Recent advances in the cognitive science of programming (Curtis, 1984) should result in newer and more effective techniques for predicting and reducing individual differences. Many of these advances involve the dynamics of human information processing that underlie how people learn to program (Hoc, 1977; Du Boulay, O'Shea and Monk, 1981; Anderson, Farrell and Sauers, 1984; Bonar and Soloway, 1985). Principles drawn from this research can be used to design better instructional methods. Other advances involve designing programming languages and specification techniques that are better matched to human information processing (Green, 1980). Rigorous research on the psychological aspects of programming has been difficult, especially because of the weak methodologies characteristic of early studies (Brooks, 1980; Sheil, 1981). Nevertheless, better methodologies are emerging (cf. Sheppard, Kruesi and Curtis, 1981; Anderson,

Farrell and Sauers, 1985; Soloway and Ehrlich, 1984), and the results are beginning to form a useful body of knowledge (Curtis, 1985).

The software engineering community has focused too narrowly on advanced technology for productivity solutions. As a result, large opportunities for improvements are missed, because they do not fit predisposed notions of how to attack the problem. These predispositions are understandable when the solution requires research in an area that has been plagued with difficulties and is not well understood by the general community. Yet in so doing, we search for our lost wallet only under the streetlamp, because the light is better there.

REFERENCES

Anderson, J.R., Farrell, R. and Sauers, R. (1984). Learning to program in LISP. *Cognitive Science*, 8(2), pp. 87-129.

Basili, V.R. and Hutchens, D.H. (1983). An empirical study of a syntactic complexity family. *IEEE Transactions on Software Engineering*, 9(6), pp. 664-672.

Bloom, A.M. (1980). Advances in the use of programmer aptitude tests. *In: Advances in Computer Programming Management.* T.A. Rullo, (ed.). Philadelphia, Hayden, Vol 1, pp. 31-60.

Boehm, B. (1981). Software Engineering Economics. Englewood Cliffs, NJ: Prentice-Hall.

Bonar, J. and Soloway, E. (1985). Preprogramming knowledge: A major source of misconceptions in novice programmers. *Human-Computer Interaction*, 1(2), pp. 133-161.

Brooks, R. (1980). Studying programmer behaviour experimentally: The problem of proper methodology. *Communications of the ACM*, 23(4), pp. 207-213.

Curtis, B. (1981). Substantiating programmer variability. *Proceedings of the IEEE*, 69(7), pp. 846.

Curtis, B. (1984). Fifteen years of psychology in software engineering. *Proceedings of the 7th International Conference on Software Engineering.* Washington, DC: IEEE Computer Society, pp. 97-106.

Curtis, B. (1985). Human Factors in Software Development - 2nd Edition. Washington, DC: IEEE Computer Society.

Curtis, B., Sheppard, S.B., Milliman, P., Borst, M.A. and Love, T. (1979). Measuring the psychological complexity of software maintenance tasks with the Halstead and McCabe metrics. *IEEE Transactions on Software Engineering*, 5(2), pp. 96-104.

Dickey, T.E. (1981). Programmer variability. *Proceedings of the IEEE*, 69(7), pp. 844-845.

Du Boulay, B., O'Shea, T. and Monk, J. (1981). The black box inside the glass box: presenting computing concepts to novices. *International Journal of Man-Machine Studies*, 14, pp. 237-249.

Grant, E.E. and Sackman, H. (1967). An exploratory investigation of programmer performance under on-line and off-line conditions. *IEEE Transactions on Human Factors in Electronics*, 8(1), pp. 33-48.

Green, T.R.G. (1980). Programming as a cognitive activity. *In: Human Interaction with Computers*. H.T. Smith and T.R.G. Green, (eds). London: Academic Press, pp. 271-320.

Hoc, J.-M. (1977). Role of representation in learning a computer language. *International Journal of Man-Machine Studies*, 9, pp. 87-105.

Lampson, B.W. (1967). A critique of "An exploratory investigation of programmer performance under on-line and off-line conditions". *IEEE Transactions on Human Factors in Electronics*, 8(1), pp. 48-51.

Love, L.T. (1977). Relating individual differences in computer programming performance to human information processing abilities. *Dissertation Abstracts International*, 38. Doctoral dissertation, University of Washington.

Mayer, D.B. and Stalnaker, A.W. (1968). Selection and evaluation of computer personnel - the research history of SIG/CPR. *In: Proceedings ACM National Conference*. New York: ACM, pp. 657-670.

McGarry, F.E. (1982). What have we learned in the last six years: Measuring software development technology. *In: Proceedings of the Seventh Annual Software Engineering Workshop*. Greenbelt, MD: NASA Goddard.

Moher, T. and Schneider, G.M. (1981). Methods for improving controlled experimentation in software engineering. *In: Proceedings of the Fifth International Conference on Software Engineering*. Washington, DC: IEEE Computer Society, pp. 224-233.

Sackman, H., Erickson, W.J. and Grant, E.E. (1968). Exploratory experimental studies comparing online and offline programming performance. *Communications of the ACM*, 11(1), pp. 3-11.

Sheil, B.A. (1981). The psychological study of programming. *ACM Computing Surveys*, 13(1), pp. 101-120.

Sheppard, S.B., Bailey, J.W. and Kruesi, E. (1981). The Effects of Symbology and Spatial Arrangement of Software Specifications in a Debugging Task (TR-81-388200-4). Alexandria, VA: General Electric.

Sheppard, S.B., Curtis, B., Milliman, P. and Love, T. (1979). Modern coding practices and programmer performance. *Computer*, 12(12), pp. 41-49.

Sheppard, S.B. and Kruesi, E. (1981). The effect of symbology and spatial arrangement of software specifications in a coding task. *In: Trends and Applications 1981: Advances in Software Technology.* Washington, DC: IEEE Computer Society, pp. 7-13.

Sheppard, S.B., Kruesi, E. and Curtis, B. (1981). The effects of symbology and spatial arrangement on the comprehension of software specifications. *In: Proceedings of the Fifth International Conference on Software Engineering.* Washington, DC: IEEE Computer Society, pp. 207-214.

Soloway, E. and Ehrlich, K. (1984). Empirical studies of programming knowledge. *IEEE Transactions on software Engineering*, 10(5), pp. 595-609.

Vosburgh, J., Curtis, B., Wolverton, R., Albert, B., Malec, H., Hoben, S. and Liu, Y. (1984). Productivity factors and programming environments. *Proceedings of the 7th International Conference on Software Engineering.* Washington, DC: IEEE Computer Society, pp. 143-152.

Walston, C.E. and Felix, C.P. (1977). A method of programming measurement and estimation. *In: IBM Systems-Journal.* 16(1), pp. 54-73.

Whipkey, K.L. and Stephens, J.T. (1984). Identifying predictors of programming skill. *SIGCSE Bulletin*, 16(4), pp. 36-42.

THE INDIVIDUAL AND ORGANISATIONAL IMPACT OF NEW TECHNOLOGY

Robert DAVIES

MRC/ESRC Social and Applied Psychology Unit
University of Sheffield, U.K.

1 INTRODUCTION

The aim of this chapter is to argue that, to a large extent, the nature of the impacts of new technology at both the individual and organisational levels, depend upon the implementation strategies of those with the responsibility for designing the system. The chapter begins with an overview of the major themes in psychological research relating to the implementation of computer-based new technologies in work settings. For the sake of simplicity, I will concentrate mainly on the area of computer aided manufacturing (CAM). Also, I will use the term "new technology" to refer particularly to the various information technologies involved in advanced manufacturing methods. Another distinction which is crucial to some parts of this argument is that between mechanisation and automation. Basically, automation is here conceived of as a process rather than an end state. Mechanisation is a transition phase through which most examples of automation pass. The essential difference between the two resides in the form of the tasks which are carried out by the two types of system. Mechanisation is seen essentially as a process whereby certain of the physical tasks previously carried out by individuals come to be performed by machines. Automation, on the other hand, also involves the performance by machines of certain of the judgemental and control procedures necessary in production.

One of the problems with the body of literature relating to the job content effects of new technology is the scarcity of relevant empirical studies. No doubt this is in part attributable to the speed of technological development and the rapidity of technological change, but also to the methodological difficulties posed by the diverse nature of the technologies in use in different applications. In addition, another salient feature of this literature is that a relatively small number of themes and concepts have tended to dominate what research has been done in the area. These include what is often called the "job design/redesign tradition", the "deskilling debate", which is usually held to be the major contribution of labour process theorists to the area, and the various arguments for and against the idea that economic, technological and political factors determine the outcomes of changes in work organisation and technologies. Without wishing to devalue these issues, this chapter attempts to demonstrate the importance of some other issues which can prove instrumental to the successful implementation of new technologies in the industrial setting. For example, there are questions relating to centralisation and decision-making and their relationship to flexibility; there are the more purely psycho-physical issues relating to the specific types of job demands posed by working with new technology, such as vigilance and other forms of cognitive demand; and further, there is the question of what constitutes a "good design" for a job in an advanced technological system.

In Section 6, the chapter addresses some of these theoretical issues by drawing upon case study material reported in the literature, the aim being to give some concrete examples of theoretical principles and outcomes. Finally, there is a summary, and a brief overview of the state of current psychological knowledge in the area, with some suggestions of likely or desirable future trends in research and applications.

2 A SELECTION FROM THE PSYCHOLOGICAL RESEARCH RELATING TO THE IMPACT OF NEW TECHNOLOGY ON JOBS AND ORGANISATIONS

As mentioned in the introduction, the literature has been largely dominated by themes emerging from the job design and labour process traditions. One of the major concerns of the job design tradition has been to argue the need to offer people meaningful and challenging work in order to promote psychological well-being and to encourage positive work attitudes. The labour process tradition, on the other hand, has focussed upon issues such as authority and control in the work place. Brief examples of work deriving from both these traditions will help to demonstrate their different approaches.

2.1 The Job Design Tradition

2.1.1 What is the job design tradition?

The job design tradition can be traced back to the beginning of the work humanisation movement in the 1960s, a movement which emerged as a reaction against the trend in managerial strategies towards work simplification and routinisation. Such strategies have a long and distinguished pedigree, stretching back to the "economic approach" advocated by Charles Babbage in the 1830s and to Adam Smith's demonstration of the economic values of division of labour in the late 1700s. More recently, these ideas found a dedicated exponent in Frederick Taylor, the instigator of the "Scientific Theory of Management" (1911).

2.1.2 Scientific management

Taylor's "theory" of Scientific Management was not a theory as such. Rather, it consisted of a series of techniques and approaches based upon an extreme rationalist managerial philosophy. Rationalisation is the term used to describe work organisation based on the subdivision and specialisation of work tasks, the standardisation of skills, and managerial emphasis on prediction and control. Taylor advocated not only the radical subdivision of work into small discrete tasks, but also the progressive concentration of the thinking, controlling and managing aspects of work in the hands and minds of managerial and supervisory workers, leaving the "operator" with fractions of tasks which demand minimal skill and involvement, and which can be controlled in pace to prevent deliberate variation in performance by the operator. It is not possible to accurately determine the extent to which Taylor's ideas influenced managerial practice during the first half of the twentieth century, but the pervasiveness of assembly line work and the relative expansion of managerial and supervisory functions compared to production functions during this time can be seen to bear witness to the ubiquity of Taylor's influence.

2.1.3 The job characteristics model

The work humanisation movement, then, developed as a result of concern about the effects of boring, highly repetitive and paced work on the psychological state of the worker. In addition, it began to be suggested that the nature of the work might have a direct effect on the person's attitude towards doing the job, and that this attitude in turn might have direct influence on motivation, commitment, and cooperation. One of the most influential job design theories to emerge out of the research of the 1960s and early 70s is the Job Characteristics Model described by Hackman and Oldham (1976). The model is based around the notion that there are a small number of fundamental dimensions on which jobs may be characterised, and which can be seen to be instrumental in the determination of attitudes and job behaviours. These Core Job Dimensions were described as:

— skill variety
   the number of different activities the job requires
— task identity
   the degree to which a "whole" or complete piece of work is involved
— task significance
   the job's impact on the lives of others
— autonomy
   the degree of freedom, independence and discretion which the job allows the individual
— task feedback
   the extent to which the job provides clear and direct information for the individual to assess his or her own performance

The extent to which each of these is present in a job influences the "felt meaningfulness" of the job, the amount of responsibility the individual attaches to their behaviour, and the extent to which the individual is aware of the consequences and outcomes of their behaviour. These in turn have a direct effect on motivation, performance and job satisfaction, and influence absenteeism and turnover. It is patently clear that the Scientific Management approach results in jobs which are inevitably impoverished with regard to all these characteristics.

2.1.4 Job redesign

The job redesign approach, then, argues for an enrichment of simplified jobs in terms of the core job dimensions and has suggested a number of strategies by which this might be accomplished. For example, job enlargement is a strategy which is aimed at increasing the variety of activities carried out by the individual, either by rotating between a number of equally fragmented tasks, or by expanding a job so that it incorporates a number of tasks requiring a similar level of skill (horizontal job enlargement). Another strategy (vertical job enlargement) aims to improve the amount of autonomy and responsibility experienced by the individual through the incorporation of an element of discretion regarding work methods, scheduling, and planning. The application of such approaches to a collection of individuals has resulted in the concept of the Autonomous Work Group, where the group makes decisions about allocation of tasks, organisation of work, self-monitoring of performance, etc. Various investigations as to the efficacy of these strategies in improving job satisfaction and motivation have suggested several different conclusions. Some studies have shown attitudinal effects as a result of job redesign, others have shown effects in terms of job performance. The occasional study has demonstrated both effects and attendant benefits in terms of productivity. However, it seems likely from the pattern of results which have emerged that, while the Job Characteristics Model undoubtedly identifies some important features of jobs which relate stongly to the way a person responds to a particular job, other factors such as organisational climate, supervisory style, and technology also influence satisfaction and work performance.

2.1.5 Does new technology diminish or enhance the content of jobs?

One of the more popular contexts for the study of the effects of changes in technology on job content has been industrial automation. As a result, much of the work has concentrated on process industries, for the simple reason that such industries are, by nature, the most conducive or susceptible to automatic control. Wild (1975) offers a particularly informative and practical analysis of many of the effects of mechanisation and automation, and describes in greater detail the findings of many of the studies cited below.

Mann (1962) reviewed studies in power plants and steel mills, and observed that automation tended to give rise to wide basic changes in content and structure of jobs, working conditions, career patterns, security, pay and the prestigiousness of the work performed. At higher levels of automation, jobs were found to be more demanding, varied, interesting and challenging for many workers. Technical understanding was found to be relatively more important. Hardin and Byars (1970) suggest that workers may expect increased job content as a result of automation, specifically increased demands on skills, knowledge and training. Davis (1962), Drucker (1955) and Emery and Marek (1962) all conclude that automation results in greater job complexity and more responsibility (intrinsic satisfactions), though often at the expense of (physical) inactivity.

Buchanan and Boddy (1983), in a case study of the effects of introduction of computerised control in a continuous process food factory, found that different applications of the technology had different effects on jobs. In one section the new technology replaced the skills of the operators, whilst, in another section, the same type of equipment was implemented in such a way that the skills of the operator were complemented, requiring the exercise of judgement and discretion in order to control the process. Buchanan and Boddy emphasise the importance of management objectives and the physical and organisational structures created by past decisions as strong influences on the style of implementation and the consequent effects on the nature of jobs. Davis and Taylor (1979) describe what they feel to be an inappropriate option as follows:

"When a sophisticated technical system is combined with a social system design suited for simpler deterministic technologies, inappropriately small and simple jobs result." (p. xii)

2.1.6 Summary

The job design tradition, then, set out to emphasise the importance of certain fundamental psychological variables in a person's reaction to their work, and to demonstrate that the fragmentation and simplification of work was likely to result in more problems than it solved. The Job Characteristics Model emphasised that jobs should provide variety, task completeness and autonomy for the people who are carrying them out. Several approaches for enhancing the quality or content of jobs have been suggested and tried with varying degrees of success, measured in terms of job satisfaction and productivity.

However, one might ask whether it is the case that the implementation of new technology in industrial and office production systems tends to result in such psychologically impoverished jobs? Looking at the evidence gleaned from studies of industrial automation it seems that jobs resulting from the introduction of computerised systems are often superior in terms of such important characteristics as demand, variety, interest and responsibility than those jobs which were replaced.

2.2 The Labour Process Debate

2.2.1 What is the labour process view of the impact of technology?

Within this tradition, the emphasis in research has been somewhat different. The labour process literature usually adopts a much more overtly political perspective. The argument here, as most eloquently described by Braverman (1974), has essentially rested upon the claim that the motive behind managerial innovation in terms of work organisation and technology stems largely from the desire to maximise control of the production process in the hands of management, to minimise the opportunity for worker disruption (as a political bargaining tool), and to reduce labour costs by minimising skill levels demanded of workers, and replacing workers wherever possible. This thesis has focussed to a large extent in recent years on the introduction of Numerically Controlled (NC) machine tools in various industries, and has centred on questions of the elimination of skill, control over the machine, etc. Numerically Controlled machines are those where the movements of a skilled operator are replaced by electronic servo-mechanisms. These in turn are determined by the program which runs the machine. This can take a number of forms, typically punched tape or magnetic tape/disk. In the typical engineering application, these programs determine such parameters as the number of cutting operations to be performed, the speed of the machine, the rate of cut, the depth of cut, etc. All these are the elements of the job which formerly made it a skilled occupation.

The advantages of such a system lie in accuracy and repeatability; the machine will carry on doing exactly the same machining job without being subject to fatigue or prone to random error. However, the programs for such machines are typically prepared by specialist programmers who do not necessarily need any experience of machining. Such tapes usually go through a process of validation before being utilised in production. Again, typically, this validation is seen as a task for the specialist programmer rather than the shop floor worker. If this is the typical style of implementation of this technology then the likely consequences are obvious. Shaiken (1979) describes the impact of Numerical Control machines as follows:

> "As a method of manufacturing, NC does more than remove decision-making from machinists and give it back to the programmers. It is the first rung of a vertical integration of the work place that seeks to locate all creative decisions as close to the design management hierarchy as possible. Along the way the skills of many workers are knocked off the ladder." (p. 9)

2.2.2 The effects of automation on skills

There has been a certain amount of dispute as to the overall effect of automation on the level of skill necessary; primarily there have been arguments suggesting that automation does away with the need for certain people by doing away with the need for the skills possessed by that type of worker. Other arguments have suggested that it is the nature of the necessary skill which will change, and so the traditional occupational structure and classifications will need to change accordingly. Davis (1971), commenting upon the upgrading/downgrading controversy, suggests that in automated systems, "... humans ... are ... required to respond to stochastic, not deterministic, conditions: i.e., they operate in an environment whose "important events" are randomly occuring and unpredictable. Sophisticated skills must be maintained, although they may be called into use only very occasionally. This technological shift disturbs long-established boundaries between jobs and skills". (p. 66)

Wild (1975) offered some examples of worker roles associated with different degrees of assembly automation as follows:

Level 1: the manual flow-line worker
Here, the worker's role is closely concerned with production per se. This type of job is typified by repetitiveness, short cycle times and mechanical pacing. There is generally a high sensori-motor component to the work, and there may be little functional interdependence between workers.

Level 2: in-line and ancillary work
Often occuring where mechanisation is not economically justified, this form of work organisation positions the worker either at a particular machine or work station. Thus, the in-line character of the work encourages the repetition, cycle time and pacing problems mentioned above. Additional problems of isolation, reduced physical involvement and lack of independence from the machine cycle can also occur.

Level 3: machine minding
The need for machine minding emerges whenever process and handling functions are mechanised but control functions remain under human influence. Machine minding can involve loading, performance monitoring, checking and minor remedial functions. Control of the system may demand wider skill or knowledge, though the job may also involve long periods of comparative inactivity.

Level 4: machine monitoring
The integration of control automation with process and handling mechanisation results in the need for close machine monitoring. In highly integrated systems, the job could be thought of as system monitoring. It is likely to provide fairly repetitive work interspersed with non-repetitive monitoring tasks. Thus, the job is likely to demand a relatively large attention span but a low level of physical activity, though it may also offer opportunities for close interaction with other members of a multi-skilled team. This interaction will be functional, and supervision may be low (see Wild, 1975, pp. 41-43).

Butera (in Butera and Thurman, 1984) has similar observations to make about the design of jobs at the four levels of automation to be observed in different forms of automated system. Type 1 systems involve isolated computer-assisted machines which require relatively high levels of operator intervention. Type 2 systems occur in circumstances where there are low levels of operating uncertainty, e.g. power plants and continuous processes. Type 3 systems occur where there is moderate to high uncertainty, but where little manual intervention is desired. Finally, Type 4 systems are similar to Type 3 systems, but here the high levels of uncertainty are deemed to require remaining high levels of manual work involving refitting, setting up, change overs, maintenance, etc.

In Type 1 systems which utilise isolated computer assisted machines, the application of the Taylorist requirement to minimise operator influence and time cycles often means that the task elements arise by accident more than design. This type of task is often referred to as "transitional"; that is to say, these are tasks which derive from intermediate levels of mechanisation and will be gradually eliminated by progression towards true automation. Butera suggests, however, that such tasks tend to be generated as rapidly as they are automated away.

In Type 2 systems where an automatic process provides low levels of operating uncertainty, 'passive' monitoring tasks tend to be somewhat anomalous since they combine a high level of monotony and a lack of purposefulness with often high levels of responsibility regarding damage or even danger. A second characteristic of this type of automation is that it usually represents the extreme case of job elimination and skill obsolescence.

In Type 3 systems where high operating uncertainty is coupled with low manual involvement, Butera is specific about the implications for the operator in terms of skills:

"... work consisting entirely of control tasks is radically different in terms of knowledge and skills required from earlier forms of industrial work. This results partly from the fact that automatic control systems eliminate the need for direct human observation and intervention at many stages of production processes. More important, the integration of control functions due to automation results in the need for decisions based on an entirely different kind of knowledge from non-automated systems. Once control systems begin to affect large, inter-related stages of the production process, human decisions need to be based on an understanding of the principles of the control system rather than on experience with a particular machine or job".

A further interesting comment by Butera on job design for this level of automation suggests that:

> "A negative possibility is when a job is designed in such a way that the worker may need neither manual skills nor experience concerning the specific industry or product. Thus the worker is not only physically remote from the product, but his mental work is based on abstract understanding of the control system rather than experience. Ultimately, it is more than skill which is lost: it is the entire concept of craft-based occupations and career patterns. Different consequences result from role designs encompassing a high degree of control over the computer and over the physical process: a good deal of communication and decision making, possibly within work groups, contribution to maintenance and innovation, and planned training and continuous career design."

For Type 4 systems where high operating uncertainty is coupled with a relatively high level of manual intervention, Butera states:

> "In type 4 automation, there are numerous opportunities to combine manual and control tasks during job design. Interdependent task relationships provide a certain amount of pressure for multi-skilling and group work. There is, however, nothing inevitable about the appropriate combination of tasks into jobs. It requires both technological choices and careful design."

2.2.3 Summary

This section has concentrated on one aspect of the labour process debate viz. that computer-based industrial technology leads to "deskilling" of jobs. My argument here has not been to suggest that new technology is not deskilling in any of its applications, but to suggest that the job content effects depend upon the way in which the technology is implemented. Much of the evidence reported here suggests that it is the nature of the skills which changes, due primarily to the distancing of the worker from the process or the product. The role of the worker in an automated system is generally broader than that of the worker in the non-automated system. Similarly, there seems to be a shift away from craft and manual skills towards more cognitive and perceptual skills and abilities. However, as Butera observed, job design options in automated systems are not inevitable; they need to be recognised, evaluated and made the subject of informed choice.

3 TECHNOLOGICAL DETERMINISM

Outside of the job design and labour process traditions, one or two other issues have occupied something of a central position in research into the effects of technological change on job content. One of these, emerging partly from the industrial sociology literature, is the controversy over "technological determinism". The notion of technological determinism suggests that the social organisation around a particular form of technology is primarily a function of (and therefore determined by), its technical specification. Thus, the determinist notion can be, and has been, used as an excuse for job simplification and the restriction of autonomy in many implementations of new technologies.

3.1 What is the Argument for Technological Determinism?

Two influential organisational researchers have argued in favour of this concept of determinism. Woodward (1965) carried out one of the formative studies of the influence of technology on organisational structure. One of her conclusions was to suggest that there is a "particular form of organisation most appropriate to each technical situation" (p. 72). Woodward had observed that, as the technology employed by an organisation became more complex, one could see attendant increases in such structural variables as span of managerial control, proportion of indirect to direct labour (e.g. increases in number of maintenance personnel, etc.), and proportion of managers to others in the workforce. Her argument was that the technology in use makes specific demands on the people who work with it, and where these demands result in changes in control and responsibility, these changes are likely to be reflected in the organisation structure.

Perrow's version of technological determinism was argued at a slightly more molecular level (1967). Perrow focussed upon the effect technology had on the degree of predictability of the work to be done. Work of a higher level of predictability allows for greater role specification and less discretion in task completion. Further, Perrow suggested that it is the level of role specification and discretion which influences organisational structure.

Now the relevance of this to the implementation of new technology is that the process of automation, where machines are used to carry out functions formerly comprising elements of peoples' jobs, can be seen as one which might result in constrained and simplified jobs, as predicted by Woodward and Perrow.

3.2 Jobs are Constrained, but not Determined, by the Nature of Technology

On the more basic level of mechanisation, machines are used primarily to replace physical movements of humans. True automation, however, can usually be seen additionally to be replacing human judgemental and cognitive functions by machinery. Bruyns (1970) suggested that the main effect of mechanisation is to restrict workers' actions, whilst automation takes over these actions. Many people would see such a process as inevitably resulting in simplified jobs. Looking at the historical development of automation, one can see that certain types of industry have proven more susceptible to the trend than others. Thus, the mass assembly and process industries have currently evolved a high level of automaticity, whilst the smaller batch assembly industries, which are more difficult to automate, are still in the transition period. The evidence on the impact of automation on jobs from both these sources is quite different. The history of automation in mass assembly has been typified by grossly simplified tasks, minute cycle times, and paced lines. The negative psychological outcomes have been documented (e.g. Walker and Guest 1952, Kornhauser 1965, etc.) and evidenced by the history of conflict and industrial battling which became the watchword of industries like motor assembly during the 60s and 70s. On the other hand, different trends have emerged from studies of automation in the process industries. As mentioned in Section 2, studies by Mann (1962), Hardin and Byars (1970), Emery and Marek (1962), Buchanan and Boddy (1983) and others have all suggested that automated systems can offer more challenging, meaningful, complex and responsible jobs.

It would be foolish to attempt to argue that the nature of a given form of technology is independent of the nature of the tasks which it entails. Rather, as Wild (1975) suggested:

"It seems reasonable to accept the position that tasks are 'embedded' in the technology and consequently technology or process factors are again seen as constraining influences on the nature of jobs and job designs. We cannot therefore take a deterministic view on the nature of the influence of technology on tasks, rather we must accept the position advanced by Wedderburn and Crompton (1972) who suggest that jobs are influenced by the constraints placed upon them, one of which is technology." (p. 33)

This view, rejecting technological determinism, has been adopted by a number of researchers, notably Bessant (1983), Clegg, Kemp and Wall (1984), Buchanan (1983) and Walton (1982); additionally, Child (1972) and Buchanan (1983) have described the strategic choices managers face when deciding upon and implementing a programme of automation. In Child's view, the design and development of organisational structure is "...a process in which constraints and opportunities are functions of the power exercised by decision makers in the light of ideological values". (1972, p. 2). Buchanan and Huczynski (1985) place the concept of technological determinism firmly into perspective with the following suggestion:

"To consider the impact of a particular technology is to consider the wrong question, or at best to consider only a part of the issue. Both technology and its effects are the result of a series of management decisions about the purpose of the organisation and the way in which people should be organised to fulfil that purpose. This implies that we should not be studying technology at all, but that we should instead be analysing managers' beliefs, assumptions and decision making processes." (p. 221)

3.3 Summary

In this secion I have attempted to show that, whilst technology can impose some limits to job content, the ultimate job design rests with management. Woodward and Perrow have both demonstrated something of a relationship between technology and structure: the argument which remains is concerned with the likelihood of a causal relationship between the two. Researchers like Child and Buchanan are more concerned with the influence of managerial motives underlying both the adoption of new forms of technology and the design of the associated social system. Such an approach is by no means necessarily less encouraging or constructive when it comes to making recommendations on organisational or job design; on the contrary, the emphasis is on management making effective reasoned choices, and the avoidance of design emerging by default.

4 AUTOMATION AND JOB DESIGN

Having examined both the job design and labour process debates, and particularly having placed the notion of technological determinism into perspective, one might then ask what conclusions might be drawn regarding the effects of the introduction of new technology on job content.

4.1 Automation Creates Distance

Much of the work on process automation shows increased distance between workers as a result of reduced interaction. However, there is an effect of scale here, inasmuch as a highly integrated automatic process will usually offer the opportunity for grouping of control machinery, allowing consequent grouping of individuals and more interaction, whilst a mechanised system is more likely to tie individuals down to particular separate locations. Automation can also affect relationships between workers and supervisors; the general view is that automation involves increased contact between the two groups, generally leading to improved relationships. Emery and Marek (1962) emphasise the fact that automation effectively distances the worker from the product or the process (or both). This has obvious implications for the nature of the increased skills which are expected from the worker in the automated system (see section 3); Davis and Taylor (1979) express this as follows: "In sophisticated technologies, people's roles shift from the tool and its use or guidance to the system and its maintenance, regulation and control" (p. xii). Davis and Taylor further define the change in role by referring to the man-product, man-machine and machine-product relationships:

"It follows that the more sophisticated the machine-product dimension is, the more limited the man-product relationship will be. Since the man-product relationship has been traditionally thought of as the job, what happens to the worker under conditions of sophisticated technology, i.e., minimal man-product relationship? One option, of course, is that the worker's role (defined as a set of rules and expectations from the employee as well as the organisation ...) diminishes and disappears with the job - that is the worker either is displaced, or continues working at the 'non-job' until a decision to retire or quit is made. Another option is that the worker's role enlarges as the job diminishes - that is, the role enlarges vertically as the worker, coming into contact with more members of the organisation to get things done, takes or is given responsibility for production supervision, quality control, and maintenance supervision. The role, then, becomes more complex, more demanding, as the job becomes simpler. This involvement via role enlargement is organically different from the kind of involvement included in horizontal job enlargement, in which the worker undertakes more, rather than fewer, of the man-product functions." (1979, p. xiii)

4.2 Automated Systems Need Managing

A further implication of such changes in the worker's role and function is that the emphasis on system management, with consequent vigilance and monitoring demands, consequences of breakdown, and comparative inactivity, all seem likely to be highly conducive to stress. Wild (1975) draws together much of the relevant evidence, and concludes:

"it seems generally accepted that in both mechanisation beyond a certain stage and automation the emphasis on inspection, monitoring, and control tasks increases while the amount of direct production activity decreases" (p. 38).

Faunce (1958) described the effects of mechanisation on transfer machining as involving greater responsibility, more alertness and perhaps greater fatigue. He further suggested that higher levels of mechanisation necessitate the use of greater skills, wider knowledge and the performance of supervisory duties, and thus may differ little from the effects of automation. However, he further pointed out that to achieve this situation involves passing through various levels of partial or intermediate mechanisation, which are characterised by the retention of some manual working, either processing or handling. This tallies with Bruyns' (1970) observation that the principal characteristic of the change from mechanisation to automation involves process control activities.

Primarily, this control is held to involve the supervision, servicing and maintenance of a self-activating production system, the elimination of disturbances, and ensuring operation within fixed limits. Bruyns suggests that the implication of such changes is that the worker eventually controls more of the process than they originally operated. This also involves a shift towards evaluation and working with abstract information, more time spent in communicating, and the previously mentioned distancing of the worker from the process. Such tasks require the worker to have a knowledge of the whole process, powers of imagination and combination, and the ability to bear stress caused by the intricacy of the process, the lack of direct control, sudden disturbances and the isolation of the job.

Crossman (1960) stated that, in continuous flow production, the skills of an operator are observational and interpretive rather than sensorimotor and manipulative. Further, the operator's interdependence with team members, supervisors and staff is based on the need for rapid information exchange rather than exchange of materials.

4.3 Job Design for Automated Systems

In Section 2, I described Butera's classification of four different forms of automated system. Type 1 systems involve isolated computer-assisted machines which require relatively high levels of operator intervention. Type 2 systems occur in circumstances where there are low levels of operating uncertainty, e.g. power plants and continuous processes. Type 3 systems occur where there is moderate to high uncertainty, but where little manual intervention is desired. Finally, Type 4 systems are similar to Type 3 systems, but here the high levels of uncertainty are deemed to require remaining high levels of manual work involving refitting, setting up, change overs, maintenance, etc.

Along with the four types of automation, Butera also identifies the principles which can and have been used in the design of jobs in instances of each type of system. Thus, jobs in cases of type 1 automation tend to be designed according to the principles of fragmentation, deskilling, simplification, etc. Attempts at improving such jobs have tended to concentrate on rotation and enrichment, and occasionally on more advanced methods such as autonomous group working: the problem with such attempts has been that the changes necessary in terms of layout, machinery, etc. are difficult to justify in comparison with the economic benefit accruing from the simplification of the job. With regard to types 2, 3 and 4 automation, Butera compares traditional design principles with those which are more likely to result in better designed jobs (see Butera and Thurman, 1984).

TRADITIONAL DESIGN PRINCIPLES

— job specifications prescribing a limited number of well-defined tasks
— use of all available work time in measurable activity
— clear-cut boundaries among jobs
— narrow, job-specific training
— segmentation of the workforce

—   information and co-ordination roles restricted to supervisors

Butera states:

"These old design principles assume that the bulk of the tasks which need to be carried out by workers are simple, manual, and repetitive. No roles exist which exceed the sum of elementary tasks formally specified. Control tasks and roles do not fit any of these assumptions."

NEW DESIGN PRINCIPLES

—   job specifications which combine manual, monitoring, computer control and direct control tasks

—   role specifications complementary to task specifications which give responsibility for functions, results, control of variances and co-ordination

—   use of multiple skills

—   work groups as internally managed units

—   career patterns which link manual and technical work and which overcome the boundaries between trades

—   training which combines both theoretical understanding and practical experience of large parts of the production process

Again, Butera comments:

"These design principles, while related to the merging nature of work under automation, do not occur inevitably. While there are costs of dysfunctional design, these costs are borne in part by workers and by society. Moreover, there is no guarantee that the enterprise will recognise the opportunities presented by better design or will choose appropriate approaches and techniques from the many competing schools of thought on the subject."

Whilst the nature of the technology itself may not necessarily determine the nature of the tasks associated with it,

"In types 2,3 and 4 ... the design of the control systems and other peripheral technologies can foreclose most of the real opportunities for improving Quality of Working Life."

4.4 Summary

This section has focussed on the changes in role associated with the transition to an automated production system, plus the broader issue of reconstructing the notion of what constitutes the job. The emphasis here has been on the distance which automatic systems introduce between the worker and the process or product. As Davis suggests, in such systems the worker is more concerned with system monitoring and control than with tools or materials. The implications in terms of skill are that people will be called upon to do much more monitoring and evaluating, to carry out more of the cognitive and reasoning tasks associated with system support. One of the less desirable possible outcomes of such changes is the increased incidence of stress.

Along with this shift away from sensory-motor skills to cognitive ones, Davis and Taylor emphasise that our very understanding of what constitutes the individual's job must also change. Thus, Butera's design principles emphasise the breakdown of several barriers, including those between traditional groupings of skills, between work conceived as manual and as technical, between traditional career paths, etc.

5 SUMMARY OF CONCLUSIONS DRAWN FROM THE LITERATURE

What conclusions can be drawn from this brief tour of the literature on automation and job design?

1. There are certain characteristics of jobs which can have psychological outcomes; for example, jobs or tasks which offer little variety, autonomy, meaningfulness etc. are likely in many instances to negatively influence attitude and even performance. In essence, psychological research has tended mainly to criticise job designs which subordinate people to the machinery with which they interact, and which offer the individual little or no opportunity for personal involvement or development.

2. Whilst the introduction of new forms of industrial technology and work organisation have often been used as a means or a rationale for job simplification and expansion of managerial control, many applications (particularly of advanced technologies and highly integrated systems) result in jobs which offer high levels of involvement and responsibility.

3. Certain forms of technology inevitably impose constraints on the nature of the jobs associated with them. However, there is no conclusive evidence that computer-based technologies lead necessarily to deskilled jobs. There is a widespread body of opinion which contends that automation using new technology is likely to demand different types of skills in different combinations to those traditionally expected.

4. Since the notion of technological determinism can be shown to have limited relevance in this context, it is important to be aware of the strategic choices posed by the implementation of new technology, and of the role of managerial objectives as well as ideology in the making of such choices.

5. Computer-based systems in the realm of industrial automation tend to put the worker in a different relationship to the production process; they become distanced from the product but more involved with the system itself. Observation, monitoring, and general "system facilitation" activities become fundamental.

6. A second effect in industrial automation has been observed which involves the breadth of the role of the operator. Many researchers have suggested that traditional boundaries tend to disappear, causing changes in communication requirements and patterns. Supervisory mechanisms often become less concrete. The operator is more likely to be multiskilled, to have to communicate with other people at different levels in the organisational hierarchy, and to bear a certain amount of responsibility for their own supervision.

However, some of the other factors which have had less attention in the research effort, but which are equally likely to be central to the effectiveness of implementation are as follows.

7. We are still in the early stages of understanding the actual patterns of cognitive demands associated with new technology. We know very little about the precise nature of attentional demand posed by, say, monitoring a group of automatic assembly machines. We are not in a position to talk authoritatively about such issues as the relationship between intellectual ability and the types of abstract reasoning necessary in system management. Similarly, there are numerous questions about the training implications of new technology, the need to minimise skill-loss in situations where certain skills will only be called upon infrequently, the effect of age on willingness and ability to work with these new machines, etc.

8. There has, in certain of the more technical disciplines, been a more or less implicit assumption that automation or computerisation of any kind offers advantages through its tendency to formalise and centralise operations and functions. From the socio-technical systems perspective, however, a reverse interpretation can be observed. Socio-technical researchers tend to point out the opportunities computerised systems provide for decentralisation of decision-making, increasing access to databases, improving communications by avoiding or doing away with artificial boundaries. These effects, they claim, not only offer many opportunities for improving job designs for individuals, but also for improving organisational performance. There is a shortage of objective, reliable evidence on the relative merits of centralised and decentralised systems, and on the tendencies of certain forms of technology and system design to increase rigidity, or "tight coupling" in the system.

9. One of the buzz-words in the realm of industrial automation is the term "flexibility". Although the term demonstrates tremendous face validity, and is commonly employed in concepts such as the "flexible manufacturing system", it is one of those concepts which has a nebulous and elusive character. A flexible manufacturing system is one which integrates automatic handling, processing and control of material. The flexibility stems from the computer control of the various functions, and the ability of the system to cope with a variety of products, changes in scheduling of work, minimal work in progress and inventory, etc. However, when one talks to managers of flexible manufacturing systems, it is by no means uncommon to hear them opine that, "the only problem with the FMS is that it isn't flexible". Often, such comments refer to the fact that the new type of system is simply not as subtle in its self-monitoring and adjustment as one which is based on human operators, that small changes can involve annoyingly complex planning strategies, that these systems do not have the intuitive "feel" for when things are going well or are about to get snarled up that is provided by people who can extrapolate from a wealth of subjective experience. Similarly, a lot is talked about increasing the flexibility of people. Can one select people who are more likely to be flexible in the work practices they are prepared to perform? Can one train people to be flexible? Is there an age effect, do historical demarcation principles obstruct the flexibility which could increase productivity? All of these are questions which managers want answered, yet in each of them it is difficult to establish precisely what they mean by flexibility.

6 CASE STUDIES INVOLVING NEW TECHNOLOGY IMPLEMENTATIONS

In this section I aim to describe some of the case studies which have been published in the area so as to explore the relationship between theory and outcome. I will try to demonstrate which of the theoretical propositions suggested above have been observed in these real-life applications. Each study yields evidence relating to a number of the propositions listed in section 5.

6.1 Case Study 1

Wall, Clegg, Davies, Kemp, and Mueller (1986) have been involved in an evaluation of the implementation of a Flexible Manufacturing System (FMS) in a large electronics assembly firm. As part of this study, they are attempting to provide some empirical support for some of the propositions relating to the impact of new technology on job and organisation design outlined above. In one questionnaire survey of 113 assembly workers, they assessed job content, perceived job characteristics and work attitudes in people who worked with computer-based equipment, and compared them with people who worked with more traditional manual assembly methods. They found no substantial deskilling effects as a result of the new technology. However, they did observe marked differences on these dimensions both between different forms of organisation for manual assembly (ordinary 'bench' assembly versus flowline working), and between different applications of technology. Two different types of application of computer-based technology were in use in the factory. One type involved computer assisted assembly aids which were designed to minimise human error in performance. The other type of application involved more advanced computer controlled automatic assembly machines. People working with the latter technology reported the highest levels of skill use and intrinsic job characteristics of all the groups involved in the survey. In addition, both groups involved in working with the new technology reported higher attentional and cognitive demands, lower manual dexterity demands and greater work role breadth (the latter being particularly noticeable for the people working with automatic assembly machines). Working with the computer assisted technology was reported as the most repetitive and the least amenable to personal variation of work; working with the automatic assembly machines was perceived as the least repetitive of all, and was deemed as equal to manual assembly in terms of the opportunity to vary one's work. In terms of work attitude, both groups involved with new technology reported greater enthusiasm and a less instrumental attitude towards work.

6.2 Case Study 2

Buchanan and Bessant (1985) describe a case study which looked at the effects of new technology on the role of process operators in a continuous process plant. The plant itself was involved in the manufacture of chemical pigments. Originally, the plant had been run on a batch production system which relied heavily on the craft skills of the operators. As a result of the introduction of computer-based information technology the plant was being transformed into a continuous process system, though because of the nature of the process a fairly high level of operator involvement was expected to persist (cf. Butera's Type 4, described in 2.2.2). The study itself involved an initial participant observation stage followed by a number of semi-structured interviews with plant operators.

Buchanan and Bessant's conclusions noted that, in the integrated system, process operators "... retained responsibilities that required skill, knowledge and experience to fulfil and their actions had a significant effect on the volume and quality of output". (p. 303). They also noted that one of the main goals of the operators was to try to eliminate failure and variations in production by the exercise of knowledge and anticipation. There was a shift away from some manual skills, but this was associated with increased demands on information processing and decision-making abilities. Social and communication skills became more important as a consequence of increased interaction with other groups such as technical and maintenance staff and management. The operators themselves reported that they found the work interesting and challenging, although the researchers cast some doubt on the generalisability of this finding, since the group of operators involved in the study were not necessarily representative. On the less positive side, increased distance and controlled pace of work were also noticed as a result of the automation.

6.3 Case Study 3

Kemp, Clegg and Wall (1984) describe a number of case studies which demonstrate that"... choices exist with regard to organising, managing and operating computer-based technologies. These choices are complex, inter-related and cross-functional and differentially impact on the patterns of psychological and organisational costs and benefits". (p.i). Their first case described the implementation of NC and CNC (Computer Numerically Controlled) machine tools in a small precision engineering firm. The management of this firm made certain strategic decisions about how the machinery was to be operated. Essentially they decided to tie in their capital investment with a further relative investment in the skills of their workforce. The machines were put under the operational control of skilled men, who, aside from tool setting and setting up of the machines, were also expected to prove out new tapes, perform simple programming duties and edit their own tapes where necessary. Specialist programmers and planners were thus cast into a supportive and facilitative role rather than embodying control functions. The perceived cost of paying extra for the skilled operators was felt to be acceptable in view of the value of the equipment. In fact, it was also pointed out that some savings were possible due to the avoidance of employing larger numbers of highly paid specialists. However, a further perceived cost lay in the relinquishing of a degree of control over production to the shop floor.

The second case illustrated a very different managerial rationale behind the implementation of the same type of machinery. In many ways (e.g. product, market, etc.), this company was similar to that in case 1, though it was bigger in size. The decision in this company was to minimise operator control, reducing their role to that of machine minding. Here, the company had chosen to invest in the "indirect functions", i.e., programmers and planners. The firm set up groups of specialists to deal with the various tasks associated with the control of the new machinery. Thus, this company incurred greater indirect costs, but made savings by offering a lower rate for the (now) downgraded job, and employing fewer skilled machinists. Managerial control of the production process was enhanced, but with an attendant cost in terms of a workforce which was less aware of production contingencies such as tool wear, scheduling, etc.

6.4 Case Study 4

While many examples of technological change resulting in deskilling have been reported (e.g. Braverman 1974, Wilkinson 1983, etc.), there is other evidence which refutes any causal link. Jones (1982) reports a study of five engineering firms which utilised NC equipment. He reports that two of these firms maintained a strict distinction between setters and operators, i.e., that the former were skilled craftsmen who set up individual machines for the next batch then moved on to another machine, while the latter were less skilled men whose primary task was to mind or monitor the machines. Both firms claimed that this strategy was due to the shortage of skilled workers. The other three firms used combinations of setter-operators and setters with operators. Jones points out further that "There were little or no supervisory duties here for setters and almost certainly fifty per cent of the operators were craftsmen". The main thrust of Jones' argument is the importance of factors as diverse as product and labour markets, organisational structures, and trade union positions as independent influences on forms of skill deployment. His conclusion is that

> "There is nothing inherent in the hardware of NC or its concept that would allow for the deskilling and control and surveillance assumed by both theorists of the labour process and publicists for NC installation. This is not to deny that such motivations exist among manufacturing management. It merely reasserts that management calculation cannot be concerned solely with labour costs and utilisation." (pp. 198-199).

6.5 Case Study 5

Blumberg and Gerwin (1984) studied the cases of five firms in various countries in order to explore adoption and implementation problems arising with new technology applications, and carried out a questionnaire survey in one of these firms to try to define the effects of Advanced Manufacturing Technology (AMT) on job content. They found some evidence of deleterious effects involving loss of control and reduced autonomy, little participation in work related decisions, low task identity (completing an identifiable piece of work), and reduced feelings of responsibility for results. Except for mechanics, workers reported dissatisfaction with certain aspects of their jobs and that they found their jobs stressful. This result was marked among loaders and operators who performed the most routine work. However, one difficulty with Blumberg and Gerwin's results is that they were forced to compare their results with a normative group of sixteen machine trades workers who took part in a wholly separate study by Oldham, Hackman and Septima (1978). Thus, they had results from a single firm which were compared with a normative group drawn from a completely different study. A different pattern of results emerged from the study by Wall, Clegg, Davies, Kemp and Mueller (1986) mentioned above (Case Study 1). Their investigations involved comparisons between groups of workers working with different types of technology within the same factory, so they avoided some of the methodological problems encountered by Blumberg and Gerwin. Wall, et al. found high levels of skill use and attentional and cognitive demand reported by people who worked with automatic assembly machinery. They also recorded lower dexterity demands and greater role breadth for the same group. Further, these findings were not held to be due to the nature of the technology itself, since they were not duplicated in the results for people who worked with computer aided machinery. The group concluded that "Clearly the AMT can either simplify or enhance jobs depending on the nature of the technology and how it is applied." (p. 29)

6.6 Case Study 6

Mueller (1985) offers one of the few case studies on the decentralisation/centralisation consequences of the introduction of new technology. In fact, this study also offers a chance to introduce an example drawn from the realm of computerised office systems. Although there are obvious distinguishing characteristics which differentiate such applications from the computer assisted manufacturing examples mentioned earlier, it is interesting to note some similarities in the two types of application also. In his paper, Mueller puts forward two arguments. Firstly, he emphasises that organisations have a choice when planning their computerised office systems, viz. whether to opt for a centralised or decentralised system. The middle and long term effects of the two types of system are very different. As Mueller puts it;

> "A centralised information system will fossilise a centralised organisation and inhibit any future attempts to decentralise. On the other hand, a decentralised system can support either a centralised or decentralised organisation. It therefore offers the more flexible and preferred choice." (p. 1)

The second argument proposes that a heavy investment in both participation and training is essential to the effective implementation of a decentralised system.

Mueller's study concerned the personnel department of a large UK electronics manufacturer. The organisation itself demonstrated the possibility for both centralised and decentralised structures to exist side by side, the personnel department operating a strongly decentralised system, while the production department was centralised. At the beginning of the study, personnel officers had no direct access to the computerised database, which existed on a main-frame computer at another of the company's sites. Requests for information passed through an administrative officer, and the database itself was only updated from the departmental mini-computer on a weekly basis. To avoid the problems resulting from the weekly updating delay, and the bottlenecks caused by limited access, on-line access to the local data-base (which was updated daily) was implemented for each personnel officer. The advantages of the new system lay in increased flexibility, accuracy and accountability for the personnel officer role. The study, Mueller argues, demonstrates the way in which a centralised information system can interfere with the objectives of a decentralised department. Also, that a decentralised system can enhance the autonomy of users, providing them with a more timely, flexible and credible database. Finally, that centralised and local systems may be designed so as to accommodate a mixture of centralised and decentralised structures within the organisation.

7 SUMMING UP

This contribution has looked at "Working With Computers" within the fairly narrow context of industrial automation and computer-aided manufacturing. However, there are undoubtedly conclusions to be drawn, generalisations to be made, and constructive principles to be derived which can be of benefit in a much wider context. I have attempted to show that working with computers poses as many potential problems as working with any other form of technology. However, I hope I have also managed to show some of the opportunities and possibilities which new technology offers in terms of job design and work organisation, and also in terms of organisational effectiveness.

Wherever people are to be purposely involved with systems based around new technology, there is nothing inherent in that technology which demands that the person need be subservient to the machine. There are undoubtedly personal motives and ideologies which can motivate the design of jobs which are boring, meaningless, unskilled and dissatisfying, but we have seen examples of researchers questioning the logic of designing work solely from the base-line of labour cost. Organisational objectives have to be the starting point in the development of any organisational system.

In my admittedly selective description of the psychological theory relating to new technology, I have tried to give a flavour of the types of qualities psychologists perceive as being conducive to healthy personal involvement and commitment to work.

In addition, I have tried to demonstrate that the responsiblity for ensuring that effective and humane use is made of this technology lies with those who make the strategic decisions about how it is to be implemented. Much of the work on system acceptibility (which I have not had space to discuss here) suggests that this responsibility can and should be effectively shared between all concerned parties, including the eventual users.

It is also undoubtedly true that the patterns of skills demanded in the near future of our society will change; this has been happening since the 1960s. This does not mean to say that there is any less of a place for skill in future work. The nature of the skills will change, but we will also come to recognise for what they are some of the human skills and abilities that up to now we have taken for granted. The great advantage that the human being demonstrates over any machine lies in the unique combination of planning, analysing, and the various other reasoning skills, coupled with the reflective and intuitive elements of thinking. The human worker is far more flexible and resourceful than the most advanced information processing machine presently conceivable. These are attributes which it will continue to be difficult to engineer out of our highly complex systems for some time yet. Within industrial psychology, engineering, systems design, and the various other involved disciplines, there needs to be an increasing awareness of the need to understand the importance of this human adaptability which we so often take for granted. All too often, the human being is seen as the source of error in system performance. It goes without saying that there is little virtue in demanding that people continue to perform tasks which, firstly they are not very good at, and secondly they would probably prefer to avoid anyway, given a better alternative. But that is not to say that a new conception of a person's role in a complex industrial system may not be developed, which emphasises and utilises the abilities and attributes which set them over and above the mere machine.

One of the fascinating aspects of research into new technology in the work place is the fact that there are opportunities for collaborative involvement from a large number of specialisms, including occupational psychologists, cognitive psychologists, software ergonomists, human factors specialists, engineers, system designers, trainers, personnel specialists, to name just a few. It seems likely that, as the use of information technology increases, we will observe a much greater cross-fertilisation of ideas and approaches between these various disciplines. Many psychologists are striving to get involved with and inform the design of technology itself. There is a tremendous need for more work on organisational issues such as decentralisation, on organisations as information processing environments, on supervision and control and on boundary issues. We need to see a lot more involvement on the level of psychophysical and cognitive demand associated with new technology. The 'conventional wisdom' of vigilance studies and signal detection theory is insufficient to answer the questions posed by Computer Aided Manufacturing in this area.

In short, the introduction of new technology into all our forms of organisation, not just those associated with work or production, issues a challenge to us all; we have the opportunities and the responsibilities to use these tools in ways which can enhance and enlighten the whole of our societies. If we get it wrong through lack of foresight, understanding or compassion, it is worth remembering that these are human, not technological, failings.

REFERENCES

Bessant, J. (1983). Management and manufacturing innovation:the case of information technology. *In: Information Technology in Manufacturing Processes*. G. Winch, (ed.). London: Rossendale.

Blumberg, M. and Gerwin, D. (1984). Coping with advanced manufacturing technology. *Journal Occupational Behaviour*, 5, pp. 113-130.

Braverman, H. (1974). Labour and Monopoly Capital: The Degradation of Work in the Twentieth Century. New York: Monthly Review Press.

Bruyns, R.A.C. (1970). Work and work motivation in an automated industrial production process. *Management International Review*, 19 (4-5), pp 49-64.

Buchanan, D.A. (1983). Using the new technology: management objectives and organisational choices. *European Management Journal*, 1 (2), pp. 70-79.

Buchanan, D.A. and Bessant, J. (1985). Failure, uncertainty and control: the role of operators in a computer integrated production system. *Journal Management Studies*, 22 (5), pp. 292-309.

Buchanan, D.A. and Boddy, D. (1983). Advanced technology and the quality of working life: the effects of computerised controls on biscuit-making operators. *Journal of Occupational Psychology*, 56, pp. 109-119.

Buchanan, D.A. and Huczynski, A.A. (1985). Organizational Behaviour: An Introductory Text. London: Prentice-Hall.

Butera, F. and Thurman, J.E. (1984). Automation and Work Design. Amsterdam: North-Holland.

Child, J. (1972). Organisation structure, environment and performance: the role of strategic choice. *Sociology*, 6, pp. 1-22.

Clegg, C.W., Kemp, N.J. and Wall, T.D. (1984). New technology: choice, control and skills. Paper presented to the *Second European Conference on Cognitive Ergonomics - Mind and Computers*, Gmunden, Austria, Sept. MRC/ESRC Memo 658, University of Sheffield, England, S10 2TN.

Crossman, E.R.F.W. (1960). Automation and Skill. London: HMSO.

Davis, L.E. (1962). The effects of automation on job design. *Industrial Relations*. 2 (1), pp. 53-73.

Davis, L.E. (1971). The coming crisis for production management: technology and organisation. *International Journal of Production Research* 9 (1), pp. 65-82.

Davis, L.E. and Taylor, J.C. (eds.) (1979). The Design of Jobs. 2nd. edition. New York: Goodyear.

Drucker, P.F. (1955). The Practice of Management. New York: Harper and Row.

Emery, F.E. and Marek, J. (1962). Some socio-technocal aspects of automation. *Human Relations*, 15.

Faunce, W.A. (1958). Automation and the automobile worker. *Social Problems*, 6, pp. 68-78.

Faunce, W.A. (1965). Automation and the division of labour. *Social Problems*, 13, pp. 149-160.

Hackman, J.R. and Oldham, G.R. (1976). Motivation through the design of work: Test of a theory. *Organiz. Behav. Hum. Perform.* 16, pp. 250-279.

Hardin, W.G. and Byars, L.L. (1970). Human relations and automation. *SAM Advanced Management Journal*, July, pp. 43-49.

Jones, B. (1982). Destruction or Redistribution of Engineering Skills?: The Case of Numerical Control. *In*: *The Degradation of Work?: Skill, Deskilling and the Labour Process*. S. Wood, (ed.). London: Hutchinson.

Kemp, N.J., Clegg, C.W. and Wall, T.D. (1984). Human aspects of Computer Aided Manufacturing. Paper presented to the *IEE International Conference on Computer Aided Engineering*, University of Warwick, Dec. 1984. MRC/ESRC SAPU Memo No. 661, University of Sheffield.

Kornhauser, A. (1965). Mental Health of the Industrial Worker: A Detroit Study. New York: John Wiley.

Mann, F.C. (1962). Psychological and Organisational Impacts in Automation and Technical Change. The American Assembly Spectrum Books.

Mueller, W.S. (1985). Computerized office systems - to centralize or decentralize? *Human Resource Management.*

Oldham G.R., Hackman, J.R. and Stepina, L.P. (1978). Norms for the Job Diagnostic Survey. School of Organization and Management Technical Bulletin, Yale University.

Perrow, C. (1967). A framework for the comparative analysis of organisations. *Am. Sociol. Review*, 32, pp. 194-208.

Shaiken, H. (1979). The Impact of New Technology on Employees and Their Organisations. Berlin: International Institute for Comparative Social Research.

Taylor, F.W. (1911). Principles of Scientific Management. New York: Harper and Row.

Walker, C.R. and Guest, R.H. (1952). The Man on The Assembly Line. Cambridge, Mass: Harvard University Press.

Wall, T.D., Clegg, C.W., Davies R.T., Kemp, N.J. and Mueller W.S. (1986). Advanced Manufacturing Technology and Work Simplification: An Empirical Study. MRC/ESRC SAPU Memo No. 764, University of Sheffield.

Walton, R.C. (1982). New perspectives on the world of work: social choice in the development of information technology. *Human Relations*, 25, pp. 1073-1083.

Wedderburn, D. and Crompton, R. (1972). Workers' Attitudes and Technology. London: Cambridge University Press.

Wild, R. (1975). Work Organisation: A Study of Manual Work and Mass Production. London: Wiley and Sons.

Wilkinson, B. (1983). The Shopfloor Politics of New Technology. London: Heinemann.

Woodward, J. (1965). Industrial Organization: Theory and Practice. London: Oxford University Press.

INDEX